REVOLUTION

REVOLUTION

THE RISE OF ARTETA'S ARSENAL

CHARLES WATTS

HarperCollins*Publishers*

HarperCollins*Publishers*
1 London Bridge Street
London SE1 9GF

www.harpercollins.co.uk

HarperCollins*Publishers*
Macken House, 39/40 Mayor Street Upper
Dublin 1, D01 C9W8, Ireland

First published by HarperCollins*Publishers* 2023
This updated paperback edition published 2024

1 3 5 7 9 10 8 6 4 2

A catalogue record of this book is
available from the British Library

ISBN 978-0-00-864651-6

Printed and bound in the UK using 100%
renewable electricity at CPI Group (UK) Ltd

Picture credits: p.1 (top) Imago/Shutterstock; p.1 (bottom) Laurence Griffiths –
The FA/The FA via Getty Images; p.2 (top) Tom Flathers/Manchester City FC
via Getty Images; p.2 (bottom), p.7 (top), p.8 (middle) David Price/Arsenal FC
via Getty Images; p.3 (top) Darren Walsh/Chelsea FC via Getty Images;
p.3 (bottom), p.4 (bottom), p.6 (bottom) Stuart MacFarlane/Arsenal FC via
Getty Images; p.4 (top) Alexandre Simoes/Borussia Dortmund via Getty Images;
p.5 (top) Nick Potts/Pool/AFP via Getty Images; p.5 (bottom) Shaun Botterill/
Getty Images; p.6 (top) Robbie Jay Barratt – AMA/Getty Images; p.7 (top) David
Price/Arsenal FC via Getty Images; p.7 (bottom) Eddie Keogh/Getty Images;
p.8 (top) Glyn Kirk/AFP via Getty Images; p.8 (bottom) Federico Guerra
Maranesi/MI News/NurPhoto via Getty Images.

MIX
Paper | Supporting
responsible forestry
FSC™ C007454

To Dad
Without you, none of this would have been possible.
Don't forget the KitKats …

CONTENTS

INTRODUCTION TO THE PAPERBACK EDITION

Mikel Arteta couldn't keep the smile off his face as he sat in the press room at Arsenal's London Colney training centre. Just a few days earlier Arsenal had claimed a vital 3–2 north London derby success at Spurs, a victory that saw Arteta become the first Gunners boss in 36 years to win successive league games at the home of their great rivals. And, with just three matches of the 2023–24 season remaining, his side sat one point clear of Manchester City at the top of the Premier League table, although City did still have a crucial game in hand.

It was as tight a title race as the English top flight had seen in years and the focus in that press conference was understandably on Arsenal's hunt for a first league title in 20 years. There were questions about trying to compete with City's winning machine, the relentlessness of a Pep Guardiola team during the run-in and about how Arsenal's young side were matching the reigning champions every step of the way. Arteta, as he always does, sat there and answered them all. But he was also very keen to point something out himself. 'Nobody asked me about qualifying for the Champions League,' he said. 'Not a single question.' And he was right. No one had. Because no one had really noticed.

Arsenal's win at Spurs the previous weekend had guaranteed a top-four spot for the second successive season. Whatever happened over the final three games, Arsenal would be playing in Europe's elite club competition once again in 2024–25. Just 12 months earlier that would have been a huge thing, a major story. But now the milestone just passed by without anyone giving it a second thought. 'This a good sign,' Arteta pointed out to us, as he broke into a laugh. 'Before you were all looking and saying, "How many points do Arsenal need to be in the Champions League? They've still seven to go and they only have three matches. Woah, they are in trouble." But now it is a different story. It's a great sign, by the way.' One journalist asked whether this was something that had been celebrated internally in the days following the win at Spurs. 'Celebrating? No,' Arteta replied. 'We know what the aim is now. Let's see if we can do it.'

Ultimately, they couldn't. Arsenal won those final three games of the season, making it 16 wins from their final 18 league games. Since the start of 2024, they had dropped just five points, amassing 49 from a possible 54. Yet still, for the fourth successive season, the title went to City, this time by just two points. It was a heartbreaking end to a record-breaking campaign, but it was another season under Arteta that saw Arsenal set new standards. They ended it with 89 points. Only the Invincibles of 2003–04 had ever amassed more during a 38-game season for the club. Arteta's team won 28 of 38 league games, a new club record in the Premier League era. And they scored 91 goals, again a Premier League record for the club. It was a season that clearly demonstrated the incredible transformation that has taken place at Arsenal since the Spaniard had been appointed. The fact that Champions League qualification was secured without any sort of fanfare highlighted how quickly the landscape has shifted.

Standards have changed at Arsenal under Arteta and so have the targets. It's no longer all about the top four. The title is what matters. Everything is now set up to try and finally bring the Premier League trophy back to north London. 'Don't be satisfied,' Arteta told the Arsenal fans as he stood in the centre of the Emirates Stadium pitch following the full-time whistle against Everton on the final day of the season. 'We want much more and we're going to get it.' A prediction as bold as that would have been laughed at when Arteta first walked back through the doors at the Emirates to replace Unai Emery in December 2019. But now it's incredibly difficult not to listen to those words and think he will be proven correct.

Arteta was devastated at missing out on the title in 2024, just as he had been 12 months earlier. But he was also proud of what had been achieved. He spent the evening after the Everton game with club staff, players and their families, and he spoke openly of the mixed emotions he was feeling. The crushing disappointment of getting so close was there for all to see, but there was also an immense sense of pride in the good work that had gone into pushing Manchester City all the way up to the final whistle of the final game of the campaign. Second place isn't good enough for Arteta, however. The desire to keep improving is what fuels him. He had that desire when he was first appointed in 2019 and he still has it now. 'You have to be more determined, you have to be more ambitious,' he said in the aftermath of the game, when asked how he and the club could take the next step and actually get past City. 'You need to have a lot of courage and push every limit. If we do what we have to do at the end, we will win it. When? I don't know. But if we keep knocking, it will happen.'

Arsenal is a club reborn under Arteta. There is a vibrancy and an ambition around the place that was nowhere to be seen just a matter of years ago. A connection with the fans that had been lost has been restored and revitalised. The Emirates feels alive again. The atmosphere over the last two seasons has been better than it ever has since the move from Highbury in 2006. Arteta spoke of the need to rebuild the relationship with the fans on the day of his appointment, and he has done that and more. 'We've always said just give us a team we can believe in,' Raymond Herlihy of the Arsenal supporters' group REDaction told me. 'This feels like the real deal and the fans are all the way in. We've got these players like Saka and White who we can really connect with, we've had Saliba coming in and then there's Mikel. You can see how energised Arteta is, how much he puts into it and how much he cares. We've got this absolute ball of energy on the touchline and we love it.'

When Arteta arrived he found a club that was on its knees, an institution that had lost its way and was in desperate need of a restart. It needed an identity again; it needed someone to come in and shake things up. In Arteta they found the right man at the right time. It hasn't all been smooth sailing and, as you will read in this book, there have been some very difficult moments along the way. But Arteta has never strayed from the plan he first laid out when he sat down with the Kroenkes and pitched to be the man to take the club forward. Despite the clear progress over the last couple of years, that plan is far from finished, which is something for every Arsenal fan to be excited about. The club has come a long way in a short space of time, but the journey is still only just beginning.

PART ONE

COMMITMENT

(PRE-2019)

Mikel Arteta could not hold back the tears any longer. It was 15 May and Arsenal had beaten Aston Villa 4–0 at a sun-drenched Emirates Stadium to bring the curtain down on the 2015–16 season. Arsène Wenger's side had just stolen a second-place finish from their rivals Tottenham and the mood was celebratory. Leicester City may have shocked the world and won the Premier League by ten points, but Arsenal, for the 21st successive season, had at least claimed the north London bragging rights once again.

But for Arteta the curtain wasn't just coming down on the season. It was coming down on his playing career. At 34 years of age and following a string of calf and ankle problems during his final two years at Arsenal, the Spaniard had had enough. With several coaching opportunities already being dangled in front of him, he knew the time had come to hang up his boots.

Wenger, the man who had brought Arteta to north London five years earlier, had given his captain the swan song he deserved, bringing him off the bench for the final couple of minutes so Arteta could receive the type of reception from the Arsenal fans that his five years of service warranted. It was a nice moment, one that was made even better when the Spaniard raced onto an Alexis Sánchez cutback to crash home Arsenal's fourth and final goal of the afternoon. His shot may have hit the bar and eventually gone in off the back of Villa keeper Mark Bunn, but for everyone inside the Emirates that day it was very much Arteta's goal.

Wenger rose from his seat with that proud fatherly smile of his to applaud his skipper, and Arteta leapt high into the north London sky and punched the air before being mobbed by his teammates. Then, just a few seconds later, it was all over. A professional career that started 17 years earlier had come to end. It was at that moment that the emotion got too much.

The final whistle was the catalyst for the tears. And when they arrived, they were very difficult to stop. Arteta is an emotional man and that was clear for everyone to see that sunny afternoon at the Emirates. Deep down, though, he knew the time was right. While his football brain was as sharp as ever, his body simply couldn't keep up with the demands of playing for a club like Arsenal anymore.

'To play at this club you have to be the best in your position,' he told Arsenal club media after the game. 'When you lose that, I think you should be away from this place. In the last few months, I probably didn't deserve to be here. The standards you need to play for this club, it cannot be eight out of ten, it has to be ten out of ten. When you cannot deliver that, it is not good enough.'

Arteta spent five years at Arsenal, having signed from Everton in 2011. He made 150 appearances for the club, lifting successive FA Cups in 2014 and 2015. He arrived amid a turbulent time. Arsène Wenger was into his third decade in charge and his future was a constant talking point. The club had left Highbury five years earlier. Leaving the stadium so many called home was gut-wrenching, but the board were adamant that the move to the Emirates was necessary if the club were going to remain competitive as foreign money flooded into the Premier League.

At the time of Arteta's arrival, however, Arsenal weren't competitive and the fans were growing ever more restless. He signed on a chaotic transfer deadline day, one that saw Wenger bring in four new faces during the aftermath of an embarrassing 8–2 defeat at Manchester United. The summer had seen Cesc Fàbregas leave for Barcelona and Samir Nasri join Manchester City. The mood was not good; it was rebellious, in fact. A growing number of Arsenal fans wanted change. They wanted Wenger gone. Arsenal were a club that had always prided itself on its stability, but in the summer of 2011 it felt anything but stable. In fact, the story of how Arteta was signed perfectly encapsulates the chaos that had descended around the Emirates at that time.

The calamitous defeat at Old Trafford a few days earlier was still fresh in everyone's minds, and the manner of the capitulation highlighted the obvious need for reinforcements, but time was running out. Arsenal needed to act quickly, and they did just that, with Arteta, Per Mertesacker, Yossi Benayoun, Park Chu-young and André Santos all signing amid a frantic final 48 hours of the summer window.

One man who was at the centre of it all was Dick Law, Arsenal's chief contract negotiator and Wenger's trusted ally.

'We did 25 separate transactions that summer, with either players going out or coming in,' Law explained. 'Certainly the one that was the most problematic on several levels was signing Mikel.'

At that time Arteta was Everton's star man. He had spent the previous six years at Goodison Park and had established himself as one of the Premier League's most consistent midfielders. So getting him out of Merseyside on the final day of the transfer window was always going to be difficult. For a few hours, in fact, it had looked impossible.

Ivan Gazidis, who was then Arsenal's chief executive, was the man leading the negotiations, and he had been told in no uncertain terms by Everton chairman Bill Kenwright that Arteta was going nowhere. By lunchtime, the deal was off.

'The pushback from Bill was unequivocal,' Law recalled. 'In situations like that you can either be bloody minded and just push on or, out of respect for Everton, you can take a step back. And we took a step back.'

It was at that point, however, that Arteta got involved. 'I don't know how and I don't know when, but somewhere between noon and 6 p.m., Mikel found out about it all,' Law explained. 'That's when the craziness started.'

Arteta, who had been at home, drove straight to Everton's training ground and marched into the office of manager David Moyes. He asked if Arsenal had been in contact, and when Moyes told him they had Arteta was adamant that he wanted to go. Kenwright went 'ballistic' when he found out, according to Law, but eventually agreed to do the deal. With just a few hours of the window remaining, however, there was still plenty of work to be done.

There simply wasn't time for a medical, so Arsenal had to rely on discussions with the Everton medical team. It was a gamble, considering Arteta had suffered a cruciate ligament injury two years earlier. But it was one Arsenal were willing to take.

'It's the only one I've ever done where the player was signed without a medical,' Colin Lewin, who was Arsenal's first-team physio at the time, told me. 'Two new signings on the same day could be murder, but four? You can imagine what it was like for me and the doctor running around, trying to fit people into scanners, get them back to the training ground to fill in forms, blood tests and everything else. All the time with media and commercial teams in our ears asking when they could have them.

'I remember Dick saying to me that there was the possibility of another one, and then later on it became apparent Mikel was going to happen. We said we'd maybe be able to use our contacts in Liverpool to get scans or an MRI done, but they were happy with the risk and went ahead with it. So between Gary O'Driscoll [Arsenal club doctor] and I, we spoke to the Everton staff. They were sending us all the recent images they had, all the rehab stuff Mikel had been doing. Obviously we knew that he had been playing 90 minutes week in, week out, which is a good sign that players are doing OK.'

The final stumbling block was Arteta's contract. Negotiations usually take some time, especially when it comes to agreeing on bonuses and clauses, but with the 11 p.m. deadline fast approaching, time was something neither Arsenal nor Arteta had.

'Mikel just cut right through all of that,' Law revealed. 'He said, "Forget the bonuses, this is the salary I want." The decision he made that day simplified the process completely. It was just, "This is what I want, we'll deal with the bonus schedules later." So in the end we got it all done in time, which was a miracle. It was Mikel's determination and his understanding of the process that ultimately made it happen.'

For those who know Arteta and have worked closely with him over the years, his actions on that deadline day in 2011 will not come as a surprise. His drive to be the best he can be has always been at the centre of his success.

'If any of this is revelatory about Mikel's character, it's his determination,' said Law. 'Most players would have said, "I gave it my best shot, but I'm going to be at Everton for another year." He wasn't going to do that.'

Those final 48 hours of the 2011 transfer window have always been viewed as a bit of a trolley dash by Arsenal, with the players who were brought in seen as panic buys following the disastrous start to the season the club had endured. That is something that Law argues against to this day, however. He accepts that signing Arteta was not planned, but he insists it was not a decision brought about by a sense of panic. 'It was opportunistic,' he said. 'A chance presented itself and we took that chance. The rest is history.'

Few would have predicted back then just how big an impact Arteta's arrival would have at Arsenal. He certainly didn't have it easy when he joined. While he may have proven himself as a quality Premier League player during his time with Everton, he was walking into an Arsenal changing room that had just lost Fàbregas and Nasri. Arteta was viewed by many as a replacement for the former and that immediately put a huge amount of pressure on his shoulders. Arteta could do a lot, but he was not a like for like swap for Fàbregas, who was five years younger and one of the finest creative talents in world football at the time.

So Arteta had to work hard to step out of the shadow left by his fellow countryman in north London, and do it at the end of a summer which Wenger himself had labelled as the 'most disturbed' in his first 15 years at Arsenal. And that's what he did from the moment he first walked through the doors at London Colney until the day he left in 2016. He was the man that captained the team on the day they finally ended their nine-year wait for a trophy, when they won the FA Cup at Wembley against Hull City in 2014. Arteta's name will not go down alongside some of the greats that have played for Arsenal over the club's long history, but that should not diminish his achievements as a player during his time at the Emirates. He was a well-respected figure, although not one that was always the easiest to get along with.

I remember sitting down with Jack Wilshere and a few other journalists in the summer of 2022. It was before Wilshere was given the under-18s coaching job at Arsenal. He had just come home from a stint in Denmark playing for AGF, and we were talking about what the future could hold for him. The conversation turned to Arteta and what he had been like as a teammate. 'I was the naughty one and he was the teacher's pet,' Wilshere said, laughing. And that was how Arteta was seen by many during his time at Arsenal. He wasn't disliked, by any means; he just took his football very seriously. He had very high standards and he wanted everyone to follow them. Even back then, the qualities of the future manager in Arteta were very apparent to those around him.

Emmanuel Frimpong was just becoming part of the first-team picture at Arsenal when Arteta joined, and he tells a good story of what sharing a changing room with the Spaniard was like.

'He was a player that liked to lead by example,' Frimpong told GOAL. 'He didn't talk much, but if you were doing something that he felt was wrong, he would have an opinion and tell you, "You should be doing it this way." At the time I used to think he was quite annoying, because I wanted people to let me do what I wanted to do. Arteta would come over and be like, "No, you should stretch like this." I used to think, This guy is busy, but he was just professional and wanted you to do the best to help the team. He's a serious guy who loves to win. He was somebody who used to take his training very seriously. After and before training he was in the gym, stretching and in the ice bath. He was a top professional. He was very dedicated to his craft.'

It's that type of professionalism and work ethic that has been the hallmark of Arteta's life in football. He has it as a manager and he had it back when he was a player. At the time of his arrival in 2011, Arsenal needed someone to come in and steady the ship. Wenger knew he couldn't replace Fàbregas, but he could bring in someone who could calm things down and offer a bit of control and experience to a team that desperately needed it. Arteta did that, and he did it very well. He wasn't spectacular, but he was effective and he had the respect of his teammates.

One of those teammates was Bacary Sagna. The French defender had been at Arsenal for four years by the time Arteta signed, and the pair grew very close following the Spaniard's arrival. They spent a lot of time together off the pitch, with Sagna often going to Arteta's house to watch European football on the television with the likes of Santi Cazorla and André Santos.

'He was very involved in the lives of the team, not only on the pitch, but everything that surrounded the players,' Sagna told me during a conversation about Arteta's impact behind the scenes at Arsenal. 'He always made sure we had a good vibe around the squad. He had that trust as a captain to be able to bring the team together and I think he realised the importance of us living well together away from the pitch. He used to organise lots of dinners for the players and their wives. He understood the vibe had to be positive.

'You will always hear people say that you don't have to be friends on a football pitch. I would always say to that, "Why not?" Because at some point, especially when you need that extra 10 per cent, the social side and emotional side of the game will become important. If you see your friend struggling and you have a good relationship with him, you will try and help him a bit more. If you don't have that connection, you won't do that little bit extra. But if it's your friend, it's different, the commitment is different. That's why it's very important to have that vibe in the squad and Mikel understood that. He was an amazing human being and an amazing player.'

Arteta's relationship with Arsène Wenger made him the natural choice to replace Thomas Vermaelen as captain on a permanent basis in the summer of 2014. He was already vice-captain and had worn the armband on countless occasions due to the amount of time the Belgian centre-back spent on the sidelines due to injury. Arteta and Wenger were on the same wavelength and would spend hours together at London Colney talking about tactics and the philosophy of the game. 'Mikel was the soldier of Arsène,' Sagna told me.

When Wenger wanted to get his point across to the changing room, it would be Arteta who delivered it. The way Arteta trained, his dedication to his craft and his professionalism were qualities Wenger admired. There was no partying, no drinking. Arteta would be one of the first to arrive at the training ground every day and would be one of the last to leave, even during his final couple of years at the club when his playing time was limited because of his injury issues.

'Mikel has a huge influence even when he is not playing,' Wenger said during a press conference in 2015. 'He is super-conscientious – every morning, two hours before training, he prepares, and that is absolutely right. Just through his behaviour, his focus on getting everything right in the team, he has a huge influence. He has great experience and is respected throughout the squad.'

Arteta's approach was not always universally popular. As Emmanuel Frimpong said, there were occasions when some of his teammates found him hard to deal with. He had his standards, and when they weren't met he was not afraid to let others know. Jack Wilshere's view of Arteta as a 'teacher's pet' may have been somewhat in jest, but there were certainly others that saw him the same way. On the whole, however, he was a well-liked figure and a popular captain.

'He was honestly one of the best professionals I've seen,' said Sagna. 'He took care of everything and he took it all very seriously. Young kids have to learn from experienced players, that's a fact. The older players have been through a lot, they know more. Jack was already a big player when Mikel came, he was in the national team. Mikel identified Jack as one of the best young talents in the world and he paid more attention to these players because he knew it was not easy for them to keep their heads straight. I think Mikel took the role of big brother for Jack. He had to be honest, maybe sometimes be a bit straight with him. Not just with Jack, but with all of us. He was the senior player and if he identified something he thought could make us better, he had to tell us. If he was unhappy about something, he would just say. Many times he would come to me and say, "You are too nice, you don't talk enough. You need to make statements." This is probably why Arsène got him, because we lacked experienced players.'

The FA Cup win of 2014 was Arteta's finest moment as an Arsenal player. He played the full 120 minutes of that absorbing final against Hull City as Wenger's side fought back from two goals down to win 3–2 thanks to Aaron Ramsey's dramatic extra-time winner. The relief around the club after that win was palpable. It was Arteta's first major honour outside of Scotland, where he had won a league title and a League Cup with Rangers, and it's a success that he still holds very close to his heart now. It was the pinnacle of a playing career that then started to go into decline. Injuries limited him to just 11 appearances the following season, and he only managed a further 13 in the 2015–16 campaign before taking the decision to retire.

Those final two years were very difficult for Arteta. He knew he could no longer perform to the standards he had previously set, and that was tough to take for a player who always demanded the best from himself and those around him. But what his time away from the pitch did do was allow him to slowly switch his focus towards coaching.

Ask anyone who played with Arteta and they will tell you that he was destined to become a coach. He was always thinking tactically, asking questions and looking to learn, whether that be from Wenger, David Moyes or even Alex McLeish, who was the man who first brought Arteta to British football when he signed the 20-year-old for Rangers in 2002.

I had a chat with McLeish in 2018, when Arteta was originally in the running for the Arsenal job, before he was eventually overlooked in favour of Unai Emery. McLeish told me how Arteta had arrived in Scotland as a somewhat 'timid' boy, but quickly grew into a big dressing-room influence despite still being so young and having come from abroad. He was constantly absorbing information and taking on leadership responsibilities. 'I knew then he had great ambition,' McLeish said.

It was that ambition that made Arteta's transition from player to coach slightly easier. Despite missing so much football over those final two years of his playing career, he kept himself busy by working towards his coaching qualifications. In 2015 he started on the Football Association of Wales' UEFA A Licence course, and as part of that he would regularly lead sessions with the Arsenal youth teams at London Colney. One of the players he coached back then was Reiss Nelson, a rising star at the club's Hale End academy, and those sessions made a lasting impression on the winger, as he explained in an interview with the Athletic in 2023.

'Mikel was my coach when I was 12/13 years old,' Nelson said. 'Even at that age, I felt he was going to do certain things because there were other player-coaches there, but they weren't really engaging as much. Mikel was one of the ones who would run a one-v-one drill with a defender and me attacking them, and he'd be giving me little coaching advice like, "When you get too close to a defender, use this foot," or, "Use the outside of your body to move like this."'

As the end of the 2015–16 season approached, rumours were rife that Arteta was going to call time on his playing career and make the permanent step into coaching. Pep Guardiola had just taken over at Manchester City and wanted him on his staff, while Mauricio Pochettino – with whom Arteta had played at Paris Saint-Germain – was floating the idea of joining him at Spurs. At Arsenal there were also internal discussions about keeping Arteta at the club, either by placing him in a role within the academy set-up or by creating a position on Wenger's first-team staff. Arteta held meetings with Wenger as he weighed up the decision, but ultimately the Frenchman told him that he felt his career would be best served by severing ties with Arsenal and starting somewhere afresh.

'I think the biggest favour Arsène ever did for Mikel was to say no,' Dick Law told me. 'Arsène knew that Mikel's best pathway forward was away from the club. He said, "For you to grow, you have to go someplace else." We knew he wasn't going to go to Spurs, he was smart enough not to do that. We always thought he would go to City.'

And on 3 July 2016 – just three weeks after playing his last game for Arsenal – Arteta did just that, joining Guardiola's staff at the Etihad as an assistant coach.

Arteta's relationship with Guardiola is, of course, well documented. As he progressed through Barcelona's famous La Masia youth system, he idolised Guardiola, who was 11 years his senior and forging a glittering career for himself in the first team at the Camp Nou. Given that both were midfielders, there were comparisons drawn between the two players, which were difficult for Arteta to deal with at times. But that did not stop him looking up to his hero. As a 16-year-old he played with him during a pre-season friendly, and after the match Guardiola pulled the teenager aside to discuss and dissect his performance at length. 'To have that from someone like him, the best in that position, you cannot have anyone better than that helping you,' Arteta would later fondly recall.

While Guardiola starred as a player at Barcelona, Arteta would have to move on to Paris Saint-Germain to start his senior career. But the pair remained in touch and Pep always had an immense respect for the way his fellow countryman read the game. So much so that when his Barcelona side met Chelsea in the 2012 Champions League he called Arteta – who had joined Arsenal a year earlier – to pick his brains ahead of the match. Soon after, he floated the idea of his friend potentially joining his coaching staff. It was a request Arteta rejected, because he still felt he had a lot left to offer as a player, but it was a clear sign of the high esteem Guardiola held him in.

Having grown up at La Masia, both men share very similar footballing philosophies that are entrenched in the ways of Barcelona. The great Johan Cruyff had just returned to the Camp Nou as manager in 1988 when he first spotted a 17-year-old Guardiola playing for the club's B team. It wasn't long before he promoted him to the first team and made him a key player in his all-conquering Dream Team side that went on to win four successive La Liga titles, as well as the European Cup for the first time in Barcelona's history.

Cruyff's influence has always loomed large in Guardiola's coaching career, just as it has for Arteta. Unlike Guardiola, Arteta never played under the legendary Dutchman, but like every player who has come through the La Masia system, Cruyff's philosophy was instilled from a very early age. When asked during an interview with BT Sport about the player who first made him fall in love with football,

Arteta replied, 'It wasn't a player, it was a manager. It was Johan Cruyff and the way he set up the Dream Team at that time.'

When Arteta joined Guardiola at Manchester City, he had not even passed his UEFA Pro Licence. That would come a year later in a class that also included Thierry Henry and Freddie Ljungberg. City had spent big money to bring in Guardiola as a replacement for Manuel Pellegrini, and the expectation going into the 2016–17 season was huge. For Arteta it was a big step. Just a few months earlier he had been set to move to Los Angeles with his wife Lorena Bernal and their three boys, Gabriel, Daniel and Oliver, where she planned to explore acting opportunities. That had been the plan, at least, but Guardiola's call changed all that. Instead, Lorena and the boys went to Los Angeles, while he went to Manchester to join his friend.

Arteta's appointment came amid a time of change at the Etihad Stadium. Not only had Guardiola been secured after a four-year-long chase, but over £170 million had been spent on freshening up a squad that had slipped to a disappointing fourth-place finish in the Premier League the previous season. Gabriel Jesus and Oleksandr Zinchenko were signed, as were Ilkay Gündogan, Leroy Sané, Nolito and Claudio Bravo. John Stones also arrived from Everton for £47.5 million, which made him the most expensive defender in Premier League history at the time.

Given that level of investment and the presence of Guardiola in the dugout, a lot was expected of City that 2016–17 season, but after a bright start, which saw them win their first six league games, they struggled to live up to those expectations. In January they suffered a 4–0 mauling at Everton which left many questioning whether Guardiola, despite all his success with Barcelona and Bayern Munich, could succeed in the Premier League. Those questions only increased when they went on to finish third, 15 points behind Chelsea and without a trophy to their name.

Behind the scenes, however, there were no doubts. It was accepted that it would take a bit of time for Guardiola and his coaching staff to really instil his way of playing into the squad and for the players to truly understand what was being asked of them. It was a steep learning curve for Arteta as well. Given that he had walked into the City changing room at the start of the season with no real coaching experience under his belt, some of the players could have been forgiven for questioning his ability and the wisdom of the appointment. But there was none of that.

Bacary Sagna, who had left Arsenal to join City two years earlier, recalls those early days of Arteta's coaching career well. 'He fitted in directly,' Sagna recalled. 'He got the respect of the players straight away. We all knew him from his time as a player, so we knew he was very clever tactically and that he knew what he was doing. I think he fitted in perfectly to the role, and I know it wasn't easy for him because at the beginning he was alone in Manchester and that was tough. To just be able to see his family a few times, to not be able to see the kids as much, it was difficult. He was telling me, "It's very different from being a player. You spend a lot of time in the office, you have to make your reports, you have to analyse." But he was committed and obviously that paid off.'

While Sagna was impressed by the ease with which Arteta adapted to his new role, his former teammate's arrival on Guardiola's coaching staff did also present a bit of a problem, especially early on. It hadn't been that long ago that the pair would regularly spend time together while they were living in London. Sagna would go to the Spaniard's house for dinner and to watch football. They were friends, teammates – but now suddenly Sagna had to adapt to Arteta being in a position of power.

'It was a bit difficult,' Sagna admitted. 'I had that previous relationship with Mikel and I had to cut it off because he was my superior, he was my coach. It was a struggle at the beginning, I didn't know how to act. When we were both in the room I didn't know if I could talk to him or not. It was tricky, honestly. I wouldn't wish for anyone to be in that situation. I felt very uncomfortable at first.'

Arteta's role saw him take on a lot of individual work during that first season in Manchester. While Guardiola would run the main session of the day and, of course, have the final say tactically, Arteta would spend time working with players on a one-to-one basis, drawing up his own specific programmes for them, especially the attackers. But when Guardiola was forced away from the training pitch for whatever reason, he had no issue with letting Arteta run things in his absence. 'Pep had full trust in him,' Sagna recalled.

Raheem Sterling was one player to benefit massively from Arteta's influence at Manchester City. Sterling had struggled for consistency following his high-profile move from Liverpool in 2015. He scored just 11 goals in his debut season at the Etihad, but in 2017–18, having worked closely with Arteta to improve his finishing ability, that number rose to 23. The following season, Sterling's tally was 25. That improvement was something Guardiola directly put down to the work his assistant was doing with the winger during their one-to-one sessions after training.

'I think Raheem is enjoying scoring goals, he's not scared,' Guardiola said in November 2017. 'Now he realises, Wow, how fun and good it is to score goals. Now he is more focused on that. Mikel is working many, many days after training sessions for the last action, for the control in the last moment.'

After that initial season of disappointment at City under Guardiola, they quickly became the dominant force in the Premier League. They won 32 of their 38 games as they were crowned champions in 2017–18, becoming the first and only side to reach 100 points in the English top flight.

They would go on to retain their title the following season, while also winning the FA Cup and League Cup, becoming the first English side to win the domestic treble. It was a period of unprecedented success for City, but back at Arsenal things were not going so smoothly.

Arsène Wenger's 22-year stint in charge was over at the end of the 2017–18 season, leaving the club looking for a new manager for the first time since 1996. There were several names in the frame, including that of Arteta, who had only left the club as a player two years earlier. Despite his relative inexperience, he was for a long time considered the favourite for the job. He held talks with Ivan Gazidis, who was then chief executive, and Raúl Sanllehi, who had come in from Barcelona as head of football relations. Talks had progressed to such a stage early in the summer that all the noises coming out of the club were that it was going to happen, and City were certainly expecting him to.

'If he decides to move because he has this offer, this option, I will not say, "You don't have to go,"' Guardiola said. 'I want the best for my friends and he's a friend of mine. If he decides to go, I will be so sad, but I will understand his decision, because it's his career, his life, his family.'

But just when it seemed official confirmation was imminent, Arsenal had a change of heart, mainly because of the Spaniard's lack of experience. It was a surprise to everyone, including Arteta, who had even started to put a coaching team together that would join him in north London.

During the whole process there were plenty of names known to have held discussions with Arsenal about replacing Wenger. Patrick Vieira was one, Massimo Allegri and Luis Enrique were others. But then, almost out of nowhere, Unai Emery was appointed.

It was an appointment that caught the media and the fans unaware, and it's not often that happens. I remember sitting in the press conference room at Emirates Stadium waiting for Emery to be officially unveiled. The former manager of Sevilla and Paris Saint-Germain walked in alongside Gazidis, who sat down looking very pleased with himself.

'Today I'm really excited to announce the new head coach of Arsenal football club as Unai Emery,' he said. 'I know that came as a bit of a surprise, and perhaps there were one or two rewrites necessary. But as I said at the beginning of the process, those who know won't speak, and those who speak won't know.' Gazidis could always talk a good game. Unfortunately, he was never able to really back that up by achieving anything of note during his time at Arsenal.

Missing out on the job was a blow for Arteta, but one that was made easier to accept by the fact that he could just continue at City, where he would soon be promoted to assistant manager following Domènec Torrent's decision to take over at New York Red Bulls.

And besides, it wasn't long before Arsenal came calling again, with Emery's tenure proving to be far from successful. The initial signs had been good, but the wheels started to come off towards the end of his first full season in charge. Just one win from Arsenal's last five league games saw Spurs pip them to fourth by a single point, a capitulation made worse by a bruising 4–1 defeat by Chelsea in the Europa League final in Baku.

It was clear during the opening months of the 2019–20 season that things were not working out for Emery at Arsenal. The mood around the club had turned rotten. The football was poor, results were worse and fans were staying away from games. Emery's exit felt inevitable.

I was down at the training ground the day before Arsenal played Eintracht Frankfurt at Emirates in their final Europa League group stage game of that season. Journalists are allowed to watch training sessions for 15 minutes ahead of a match in a UEFA competition, something we don't get to do for Premier League fixtures. Usually, it's a totally useless exercise. You never really get any sort of insight, as managers understandably wait until the media leave before starting the proper session, to ensure they don't give anything away ahead of the game.

But that day before the Frankfurt game was different. Just standing on the pitch watching the Arsenal players trudge out for training, it was startlingly obvious to anyone who was there just how broken things had become. Emery just stood there by himself, holding his clipboard. It was actually pretty sad to look at. The players barely acknowledged him. He looked the epitome of a dead man walking. Arsenal lost that game, surrendering a 1–0 half-time lead to lose 2–1. It was a seventh straight match without a win. Emery would be gone within 24 hours.

Even if Arsenal had won that game, Emery would still have been out. The decision had already been taken well before Arsenal kicked off against their German visitors. Raúl Sanllehi and managing director Vinai Venkatesham had flown to America to meet with owner Stan Kroenke and his son Josh following the 2–2 draw with Southampton in the Premier League the previous weekend. The visit was pre-arranged, but Emery's future dominated the discussion, with Sanllehi and Venkatesham recommending that he be dismissed. The Kroenkes, who up to then had continued to back Emery, agreed and the decision was taken to sack him. But Sanllehi and Venkatesham did not inform Emery of that decision when they returned to London, and instead they allowed him to take charge of the game against Frankfurt on the Thursday night. He was eventually told the news when he arrived at London Colney the following morning, with Freddie Ljungberg placed in temporary charge while the club started the process of finding a replacement.

Again, talks were held with several potential candidates, but Arteta was always the man Arsenal wanted this time around. The process was relatively swift, albeit not without the odd hiccup. Embarrassingly, Vinai Venkatesham and contract negotiator Huss Fahmy were pictured coming out of Arteta's house in Manchester in the early hours of the morning. These photos were quickly circulated and splashed all over the newspapers the following day, much to the annoyance of Manchester City.

'We didn't think it was such a great deal,' Raúl Sanllehi would later say in Arsenal's defence. 'In terms of City and given the tight relationship between Mikel and Pep, we have been very careful, extremely transparent and very respectful.'

After missing out to Emery 18 months earlier, Arteta was adamant he wanted the job this time. And Arsenal agreed. The doubts about his lack of experience that had led to him being overlooked previously were put to one side, with the club hierarchy letting it be known that they had been blown away by the presentations he produced on the squad and his vision for the future during the interview process.

Arteta was officially appointed Arsenal's new head coach on 20 December 2019. I travelled up to the Emirates that day for his official unveiling. The biggest thing to come from it was just how impressive he was during that press conference. The way he spoke, the message he sent out, it was exactly what Arsenal fans wanted to hear after a series of fairly disastrous seasons.

'I've been preparing for a few years for this challenge to come,' he said. 'I know the expectations, I know the level and I know the stature of this club and what it deserves. I'm ready for that challenge.'

After the cameras had been switched off at the press conference, a few of us went upstairs to the directors' box, where we got the opportunity to sit down with Arteta and Sanllehi in a more relaxed setting. I asked Sanllehi if he regretted the decision to overlook Arteta a year earlier.

'No,' he said. 'I do not like to look to the past, I like to look to the future, and at that time we made a decision with the information we had – it is not time to regret. We made a decision conscious of what we wanted at that time and we are now conscious and convinced of what we are doing now.'

One of the big talking points was Mesut Özil, Arsenal's German superstar and highest-paid player. Özil had dominated the news agenda during Emery's time in charge and that wasn't going to change under Arteta. Could he be the man to get the best out of Özil again? The pair had been teammates just a few years earlier, but while Arteta had gone on to make a success of himself in his new career at City, Özil had flatlined at Arsenal. Things had not gone well for him under Emery and his lack of involvement was a constant source of debate. In fact, it was a distraction.

'He's a massive player for this football club,' Areta said at his unveiling. 'I work with him and I know when he clicks, what he can bring to the team. It's my job to get the best out of him, of course.'

It was clear from that first press conference that the circus around Özil was not going to go away. It was one of the many things Arteta was going to have to deal with if he was going to get Arsenal firing again. But what I took from that unveiling was that the club had appointed someone who knew exactly what he wanted. He could see the task that was in front of him. It was a big challenge and he knew it. But it was one he felt he had the capacity to take on.

It had been three and a half years since a teary-eyed Arteta had called time on his playing career and waved goodbye to the Emirates. As he made his way down the tunnel for the final time after that win against Aston Villa in 2016, he turned to his wife and vowed to return one day as manager. Even he would have been surprised, however, at just how quickly he fulfilled that vow.

PART TWO

NEW DAWN

(2019–JULY 2020)

The message Arteta delivered at that first press conference at the Emirates was clear. He knew that the club he had left behind just a few years earlier had lost something. The spark had gone, the belief had gone. He needed to bring that back if he was going to have any chance of turning things around. Ironically, his final game as Guardiola's assistant had been at Arsenal just a few days before he was appointed. So he had seen first-hand how bad things had become, not just in terms of the level of performance, but the overall mood around the club. City had cruised to a 3–0 win at an eerily quiet Emirates Stadium littered with thousands of empty seats.

'Last week when I was here I was a little bit down after the game when I felt what was going on,' Arteta said in the press conference. 'It wasn't only the performance, it was the atmosphere and energy that I perceived when I was working around the place. That worried me. I understand that they [the fans] are used to success and fighting for things, and at the moment it's difficult for them to swallow the situation. So let me help. We need the fans. We need to engage them, we need to be able to transmit with our behaviours, our intentions, what we want to bring to this football club. That is the only way. We give them a little bit, they give us a little bit, and suddenly we feel that connection, because when we plug these two things together, it is so powerful.'

It was impossible to come away from that first press conference and not be impressed. One of the big downsides of the appointment of Emery was his lack of communication skills. That, of course, wasn't his fault, and he did all he could to improve his English while he was at the club. But it was always an issue, with the players, the media and the fans. When he had a message to try to get across, he struggled to deliver it in a way that made much of an impact. But as soon as Arteta arrived that changed. His message couldn't have been clearer. He wanted everybody on board and he wanted everybody in line. That was the only way he believed he could get Arsenal firing again.

Arteta had met the players for the first time on the morning of his appointment at London Colney, but he deliberately avoided having too much interaction with them. Freddie Ljungberg was in temporary charge following Emery's dismissal and was preparing the squad for a game at Everton the following day, so Arteta didn't want to disrupt things too much on the eve of the match. He did tell the players what he would be looking for from them in terms of their individual performances, but aside from that he mainly left Ljungberg to it.

Arteta used that first press conference, later that day, to get his point across to the squad in a different way. He knew they would be watching from their hotel up on Merseyside, and he wanted to make it known what he was going to demand from them more than anything else. It was all about his famous non-negotiables.

'Everybody has to respect each other, first of all,' he said. 'I want people who are accountable for what I'm asking them to do. I don't want them hiding. I want people to take responsibility for their jobs, and I want people who deliver passion and energy in the football club. Anyone who doesn't buy into this, or that has a negative effect, is not good enough for this environment. We have to build a culture that has to sustain the rest. If you don't have the right culture, in the difficult moments, the tree is going to shake, so my job is to convince everybody that this is how we are going to live now, and if you are going to be part of this organisation it has to be in these terms and in this way.'

These comments went down well with the fanbase. There were understandably a lot of doubts over the appointment of someone who was so young and so inexperienced, but on the whole Arteta was well received. He was seen as an Arsenal man by the supporters. He had a reputation for being someone who was firm and who knew exactly what he wanted. And that was the type of figure Arsenal needed at the top after some painful times for the club on and off the pitch.

Arsenal went into that game against Everton at Goodison Park sitting ninth in the Premier League and having won just one game from their last twelve in all competitions. Morale was low, the fans had turned on the team and the players were disillusioned. Özil was an ongoing soap opera. Emery had left the German out on several occasions due to what he described as 'footballing reasons', which basically boiled down to the fact that he didn't believe the World Cup winner worked hard enough.

Arteta had been given a close-up view of the Özil issue during the game against City immediately before he was appointed. Ljungberg took the playmaker off early in the second half and replaced him with the teenager Emile Smith Rowe. As he walked off the pitch, Özil ripped off his gloves and kicked them up in the air in disgust. It was just another symbol of the overall mood around Arsenal at the time.

Özil was injured for the game at Everton, but in his pre-match media Ljungberg revealed that he wouldn't have picked him even if he had been fit. 'Mesut has something on his foot,' explained the Swede. 'He wouldn't have been in the squad anyway after what happened in the last game. I want to make a stance that it's not what I accept from an Arsenal football player. That's my decision. I won't make the decisions again, but that's what I think.'

It was a telling insight into what Arteta was going to be taking on at Arsenal. At Manchester City he had left behind a changing room that was working in perfect harmony behind their coach; at Arsenal he was taking charge of one that had spent the past few months in revolt. So he was under no illusions as to the challenge he had in front of him.

'The immediate impact is just to win,' he told us. 'If we want to start a slow process to build something, at the moment that's impossible. We don't have a pre-season or six weeks. We have to be focused on things that can have a great impact immediately, in the short term.'

Arteta watched the game at Goodison Park on 21 December from the stands. It was an awful match that finished 0–0. Ljungberg basically used it to send out a message about what he thought of some of the squad. Club record signing Nicolas Pépé was left on the bench, as was Alexandre Lacazette. He handed Smith Rowe a first Premier League start, Reiss Nelson came in, while Gabriel Martinelli and Bukayo Saka also made the 11. It was the first time Arsenal had started a Premier League game with three teenagers for 12 years.

After the game I was with a few other journalists outside the changing room, waiting to speak to some of the players. Arteta walked past us with Edu and went inside to speak briefly with the team. He had also gone in just before kick-off as well to say a few words.

'He didn't speak too much about quality or about tactics,' Bernd Leno came out and told us. 'He just said he wanted to see players who run, who support their team-mates and defend as a team. It was a good point that he pushed us. We understood the message.'

It seems pretty basic for a coach to tell his squad that he just wants 'players who run', but that was exactly what Arsenal needed at that time. The team had totally lost its way under Emery. It was about getting back to basics. That's what had to happen if results were going to improve.

The key thing early on was just about trying to calm things down a bit after so much disruption. Arteta knew that. On one of his first days at the training ground he gathered all the players together in a room. They walked in and saw chairs scattered all across the floor. No one had a clue what was going on. Arteta then pointed to the chairs and told the players that the scene they were looking at symbolised where the team was. 'Chaos,' he described it. But then he walked around the room picking the chairs up and placing them in a structured order, which showed how he planned to change things over the next few years. He was telling them to trust him, that he had a long-term plan to turn things around.

Arteta inherited a decent squad. Not many coaches would walk into a job and have strikers like Pierre-Emerick

Aubameyang and Alexandre Lacazette to call upon. Aubameyang had won the Premier League golden boot the season before, while Lacazette had been named Arsenal's player of the season. Between them they scored 50 goals in all competitions during Emery's first season. Özil was there, of course, as was £72 million club-record signing Pépé. In Bernd Leno, Arteta had a German international goalkeeper, and he had the experience of David Luiz at the back. Héctor Bellerin and Kieran Tierney were two strong full-backs, while in Bukayo Saka, Emile Smith Rowe, Matteo Guendouzi, Reiss Nelson and Gabriel Martinelli he had some top-level young talent.

He also had Granit Xhaka. But when it came to the Switzerland international, Arteta had a big job on his hands to try to resolve a situation that had happened a few months before. No one who was inside the Emirates against Crystal Palace on 27 October 2019 will forget what happened when Xhaka, who was club captain, was substituted in the second half. It was perhaps the moment when years of pent-up frustration at the club came pouring out. The Arsenal fans – who had seen their team throw away an early 2–0 lead – were furious at how long Xhaka was taking to walk off after being substituted. The boos were brutal, as was Xhaka's reaction. 'Fuck off!' he screamed as he ripped off his shirt and marched down the tunnel. It was an ugly incident that perfectly encapsulated how much of a mess Arsenal had become at that point.

By the time Arteta arrived, Xhaka had been stripped of the captaincy, replaced by Aubameyang. He had, however, slowly been integrated back into the team by Emery, more out of necessity than anything else. But Xhaka was still angry. He was angry at the way he had been treated, not just by some of the fans, but also by how the situation had been handled internally. He felt he had been hung out to dry and he was in no doubt that he wanted to leave. January was fast approaching and the midfielder had already sorted out a move back to Germany. It was a question of when, not if he would go.

But Arteta didn't want that. He had always liked Xhaka as a player. When he was with Guardiola at Manchester City the pair had even considered trying to sign him. He liked his personality and his character. He was the type of leader he wanted in his squad. So as soon as he arrived, Arteta put a lot of focus into convincing Xhaka to stay. It was not an easy task, given everything the midfielder and his family had been through at Arsenal, but it was one he succeeded in.

'My bags were packed,' Xhaka would later reveal in an interview with The Players' Tribune. 'The passports were out. I was done with Arsenal. Finished. There was a contract on the table from another club, and all I had to do was sign. But then Mikel began to talk about how I was a big part of his plans. I liked his warmth. He was honest, straight. Clear plans. I felt I could trust him. He told me to give him six months to prove me wrong, and then if I still wanted to leave, no problem. Normally I spend a lot of time making these decisions. I talk to everyone around me, I weigh up the pros and cons. But that day I broke my own rules. I told Mikel, "Okay." I called my wife: "We're staying. Unpack the bags."'

This was the first real example of Arteta's ability to get his players to believe in him. We've seen it countless times since, but this was the first and perhaps the most important. Arteta had just walked into the club as a young coach. There were players who would have questioned why someone so inexperienced had been given such a big job. Convincing someone as strong-willed as Xhaka to change his mind was a big statement so early in his tenure.

Convincing his players of his ability was always going to be a big challenge for Arteta. Just a few years earlier he had been a teammate of several members of the dressing room; now he was suddenly their boss. Bacary Sagna described the difficulties he experienced when Arteta became Guardiola's assistant at Manchester City, having been his teammate not long before. This was what was now happening at Arsenal, but on a larger scale.

Özil, Bellerin, Mohamed Elneny and Calum Chambers had all played with him during Arteta's time as skipper. Now they were suddenly having to adjust to him telling them exactly how they should play and how they should behave. It was going to be difficult for them, and it was going to be difficult for Arteta. But he did have some experience with him. Dutchman Albert Stuivenberg, who had worked alongside Louis van Gaal at Manchester United, came in as assistant coach to work alongside Ljungberg, who had decided to stay at the club following his brief role as interim boss. Steve Round, who was at Everton with David Moyes when Arteta was a player at Goodison, was also named on the Spaniard's staff, along with goalkeeper coach Inaki Cana.

Arteta's first game proper as coach ended in a fairly uneventful 1–1 draw at Bournemouth on Boxing Day. Arsenal fell behind in the first half but equalised through Aubameyang after the interval to earn a point. Arteta didn't make wholesale changes. It was still the 4-2-3-1 formation we had become accustomed to under Emery, with Özil operating in the number 10 role, Aubameyang playing off the left and Lacazette as the central striker.

A 2–1 defeat by Chelsea followed in what was Arteta's first game in charge at the Emirates. Aubameyang was again on target, giving Arsenal an early lead, but Chelsea turned things around to win thanks to two goals in the final seven minutes from Jorginho and Tammy Abraham. It was a result in keeping with how the season had gone, but there was plenty to like about the performance.

'I'm pleased with a lot of things that I've seen,' Arteta said afterwards. 'I'm pleased with a lot of things we worked on in training that actually happened in the game, and how they [the players] bought into this. But I'm disappointed to lose, obviously.'

The improvement in a short space of time was obvious, and that set things up well for the home game against Manchester United on New Year's Day. It felt a bit like a new dawn for Arsenal as they beat Ole Gunnar Solskjaer's side 2–0 to hand Arteta his first win as head coach. It was almost like they had put 2021 behind them, and the Emirates felt alive for the first time in a long time. Goals from Nicolas Pépé and Sokratis put Arsenal in front at half-time, and they saw things out in the second half.

'A lot of things that I demanded and wanted to see on that pitch actually happened today,' Arteta said afterwards. 'What we are trying to create, you could see that happening. I said to the players: "Without you guys, I won't be able to do it. You have to open the door and believe I can bring something different to the club." We need all the staff to believe as well. It will take a long time and the process will not be easy and there will be ups and downs, but they've bought into this. That is my feeling. They want to do it and they are starting to enjoy. Hopefully it is a start.'

You could really tell that the players were enjoying working under Arteta in those first couple of weeks. He'd brought a new energy to the place, a new way of doing things that was desperately needed. The fun had been sucked out of the club during those final months of Emery.

The powers that be really should have made the change earlier instead of letting it drift for a few extra weeks. It was so glaringly obvious that a new direction was needed. The whole club needed a lift and you felt that happen as soon as Arteta arrived. Even though they lost that game against Chelsea, the performance was different and the atmosphere was different. And this continued against United, but this time the team got the win that they deserved. David Luiz spoke to the press afterwards and his comments shed a light on the sudden shift in mood inside the changing room.

'In life, when you are happy, results can be totally different,' he said. 'If you sleep happy, you can sleep four hours and be better than sleeping sad for eight hours. If you work with happiness and believe in what you are doing it is totally different.'

Luiz would later expand on those comments during an interview with Arsenal club media. 'I stand by it,' he said. 'The result of people when they are happy is ten times better than when they are sad. For me, you have to have fun not just in football, but in life. That's the most important thing – and Mikel has brought that back.'

A lot of people took those comments as Luiz taking a dig at Emery. But he wasn't doing that; Luiz and Emery actually got on well. But Luiz still knew that a change was needed. The fun had gone out of Arsenal. No one was smiling anymore. Anyone who spent some time around the club during those last weeks before the change was finally made could see something had to happen.

Arsenal followed up their win against United with another success, this time against Leeds in the FA Cup third round. Three draws in a row then followed, against Palace, Sheffield United and Chelsea, before a 2–1 win at Bournemouth – again in the FA Cup. That was a game that saw Bukayo Saka score his first domestic senior goal. It was a rocket of a shot and just the latest example of why there was so much excitement about the way he was progressing at the club. He then went on to set up Eddie Nketiah for what proved to be the winner.

Saka was only 18 at that time, but it was still very obvious that he could be something very special. He had made the step up to senior football look so easy, something that was made even more impressive by the fact that he had done it having come into a team that was really struggling. He'd scored his first goal for the club in the 3–0 Europa League win at Eintracht Frankfurt earlier in the season. He also set up both other Arsenal goals that night. After the game the Arsenal media pack who had travelled to Germany all went downstairs to speak to him. Arsenal's press officer came over to us just before he brought Saka out and basically told us to take it a bit easy on him, as he was just a kid and had never really faced a big group of journalists before. But as soon as Saka walked out it was clear the press officer hadn't really needed to do that. Saka was so confident; it was like he'd done this sort of thing a hundred times before. The way he carried himself and the way he spoke made it clear this player was different. This wasn't your normal teenage footballer.

Arsenal completed the loan signing of Pablo Mari from Flamengo a couple of days after the win at Bournemouth, giving Arteta the left-sided centre-back he had asked for during the January transfer window. Experienced full-back Cédric Soares soon followed, arriving on loan from Southampton. It was not exactly the type of window that would transform an underperforming squad, but financially it was all Arsenal could do at the time.

Mari was a signing somewhat out of the blue. He had been a Manchester City player earlier in his career, having joined them from Spanish side Gimnàstic in 2016, but he never even met Guardiola during his three-year stay with the club. He instead had three separate loan spells, with Girona, Dutch side NAC Breda and Deportivo La Coruña, before making a permanent move to Brazil. His time in Flamengo was successful, with the centre-back winning the Copa Libertadores, but he still arrived at Arsenal as a relative unknown. Arsenal had also been looking at Mykola Matviyenko at Shakhtar Donetsk, but the Ukraine international was deemed too expensive to pursue.

So with Mari the defender they focused on, Edu flew out to Brazil to try to get the deal over the line. He returned to London with Mari, and I went to the airport to meet them when they landed. 'Yes, of course,' Mari said to me when I asked him if he was excited to be signing. But a couple of days went by and he actually ended up flying back to South America with the transfer in jeopardy because Arsenal and Flamengo couldn't agree on the deal. The Brazilian club were holding out for a larger initial loan fee, something Arsenal were reluctant to agree to. It was eventually sorted out, though, and Mari was given permission to travel back to London to join up with Arteta's squad. Arsenal agreed to pay £4.25 million to take the 26-year-old and had the option to make the transfer permanent in the summer if they wished.

It wasn't the most exciting of signings, but it did strengthen Arteta's squad and he was happy to get the centre-back through the door. 'He balances what I want to do from the backline,' Arteta said when Mari arrived. 'He gives more options, more solutions, he opens up the pitch more. He's a player we've been following for the last few months. We are really happy to have him.'

The decision to bring in Cédric Soares was one that raised eyebrows, not least because he was injured. The Portugal international was an experienced player, but he had not been in great form with Southampton and had endured a fairly miserable loan spell with Inter Milan a year earlier. But Arteta wanted another option at right-back, someone who could provide cover for Héctor Bellerin. Cédric was signed, initially on loan, but Arsenal had an option included to hand the Portugal international a four-year contract in the summer.

'He's a player who's got a lot of experience,' Arteta said. 'He's played in this league and knows what it means. He's very willing to go to another top club and he's got that desire, that commitment. I followed him a few seasons ago and I really like what he can bring. They were the right conditions for us as well to try to improve the squad.'

The big worry over Cédric was that he was another player who was represented by Kia Joorabchian, one of football's so-called super agents. Joorabchian had been the man who brokered the deal to bring Luiz to the club from Chelsea the previous summer, and several links had surfaced with other players he was connected to, such as Layvin Kurzawa at Paris Saint-Germain and Philippe Coutinho at Barcelona.

Since Arsène Wenger's departure, Joorabchian had become more and more of an influence at the Emirates Stadium. He was friendly with Raúl Sanllehi and had always enjoyed a close working relationship with Edu, although, as Arsenal were very keen to point out at the time, he was not the Brazilian's agent. Joorabchian would often be spotted watching games with Sanllehi and Edu in the directors' box at the Emirates, and it was becoming more and more clear that he was beginning to have a major say in the way the club were conducting their transfer business. That made a lot of people feel uneasy, especially the fans. Poor recruitment over the years had played a large part in the mess that Arsenal had got themselves in, so it was understandable that there was concern that the club appeared to be allowing one single agent to have such a powerful say over recruitment plans. Wenger would never have allowed that to happen.

February started with a draw at Burnley before there were wins against Newcastle and Everton, with a 1–0 Europa League victory at Olympiacos in Greece sandwiched in between. Having lost against Chelsea on 29 December, Arsenal had gone on a ten-game unbeaten run in all competitions. But they had been doing it amid a backdrop of ever-increasing uncertainty around what was happening globally. News of the coronavirus outbreak in China had been generating headlines since the turn of the year, but as March approached the severity of the situation was becoming clearer by the day. And when Olympiacos arrived at the Emirates to play the second leg of their Europa League tie, a chain of events began that would see football in the country grind to an abrupt halt.

Arsenal were beaten 2–1 after extra-time by the Greek side. It was an awful night. After falling behind in normal time, an acrobatic volley from Aubameyang looked to have done enough to send the hosts through, only for Olympiacos to snatch a winner right at the end to claim an away-goals victory, though not before Aubameyang had missed a golden chance to make it 2–2 in the final few seconds. It's not often you hear a sound that is just pure disbelief, but that's what you could hear around the Emirates in the few seconds that followed Aubameyang somehow slicing that shot wide from a couple of yards out. No one could believe what they had just seen.

It soon transpired that the real drama of the night wasn't what happened on the pitch, however; it was what was going on inside the stadium during and after the game. Olympiacos owner Evangelos Marinakis had watched the match from the directors' box and, as you can imagine, he was pretty happy with the result. I was down in the mixed zone after the game, waiting to speak to some of the players, and Marinakis was down there. He was celebrating with everyone he could see. His players, the Greek media, even some of the English media. He was shaking hands and hugging people. He had been in the changing room, celebrating with the squad. He had even been out on the pitch with the players, celebrating with the away fans. At the time you obviously thought nothing of it. But then, ten days later, on 10 March, Marinakis announced that he had tested positive for coronavirus.

That led to Arsenal's game at Manchester City, due to be played the following night on Wednesday 11 March, being postponed by the Premier League because several players and a number of club staff had been forced to go into self-isolation, having been in close contact with

Marinakis at the Emirates. Then, a day after the City game had been postponed, Arteta himself tested positive.

'Everything happened very fast,' Arteta would later recall, during an interview with Spanish television channel La Sexta. 'On the Tuesday afternoon I was feeling so-so and I went to see the doctor, but he wasn't there. I then got a call from the board of directors after training while I was in my car, and they told me the president of Olympiakos had tested positive and everyone who had been in contact was at risk. I told them that I wasn't feeling well and that we had a situation because we had lots of players who had been in contact. We had the game against Manchester City the next day and obviously we couldn't put lots of people at risk without saying anything. I had the test done and I was diagnosed on the Friday, when we had to communicate it to the Premier League that I had tested positive.'

Arteta was the first major figure in English football to contract the virus, and within 24 hours the Premier League was officially shut down, initially until 4 April, but it would in fact not resume until 17 June. It was a remarkable time to be covering the club as a journalist. We had all been with Arteta for his usual pre-match press conference a couple of days before it was announced he had tested positive. Immediately we were wondering if we had been in what was called 'close contact' with the Spaniard. We were all assured we hadn't, but the snowball effect from Marinakis's announcement just a few days earlier was so dramatic. It felt inevitable leading up to Arteta's positive test that football was going to have to stop. Arsenal had played twice in the period between the game against Olympiacos and the Marinakis announcement, once in the FA Cup, a 2–0 win at Portsmouth, and once in the league, a 1–0 home success against West Ham. All the talk in the press room before and after that win against West Ham was about how long it would be before we came back to the Emirates for another game. It turned out it would be four months.

And so football came to a close, with the country plunged into lockdown to try to slow the spread of the virus and protect the health service. All training stopped. London Colney was closed, as was the Hale End academy. It would be well over a month before the training centres opened again. Everyone had to stay at home. It was a really difficult time for Arteta. He'd only just walked into his first ever head coach role, and suddenly he was faced with a pandemic that had seen football – and the country as a whole – locked down. Everyone had to adapt to a situation that no one had ever experienced before.

Arteta worked with the club's medical staff to draw up individual fitness plans for every member of the squad. Most of the players had personal gyms in their houses, but those who didn't had equipment such as exercise bikes and weights sent to them. Dietary recommendations were sent out, with Arteta making it clear they had to be strictly followed. The players were also given homework. Arteta drew individual plans for each player in which he detailed the parts of their game that he wanted them to work on and improve. They were sent videos of themselves in action. They had to analyse clips, watch what they had done in certain scenarios and then report back what they could have done differently.

Arteta took this very seriously. He wanted to ensure the players stayed focused and busy and that they still felt very connected with the club and the staff, despite being at home. The technology that was used meant he could see who had downloaded and completed the tasks that he had set throughout the week. Everything had to be sent back to him to go through. He also held regular video calls with his players, using the down time as an opportunity to speak to his squad on a more personal level than perhaps he had done previously. That was the one positive he would often point to when reflecting on what was otherwise an incredibly difficult period. By the time the players were allowed to return to London Colney on 27 April, he felt he knew them better.

During the break there was also the highly contentious issue of wage cuts to try to deal with. With so much uncertainty around when the Premier League would restart and in what sort of form, Arsenal club executives had been looking to slash the wage bill to ease the financial burden during the crisis. Talks took place with the players over a 12.5 per cent cut, which would last for a year. There were incentives included in the offer, including one which stated that the players would be paid in full should they secure Champions League football the following season. Arsenal made it clear during the talks that the financial situation at the club would be grave should the season not be completed, or if it were to be finished behind closed doors.

The offer was met with scepticism from some players, and it was rejected following a vote on WhatsApp. The club needed the support of 75 per cent of the players for the proposal to be accepted, and while some agreed to the cuts, the figure was nowhere near high enough for it to go through.

Arteta was keen to find a resolution, so he held a video call with all of the squad and urged them to try to find a way around the impasse. During that call he made it clear that he was understanding of the players' position, but he also laid bare the financial situation that the club found itself in with football suspended and the prospect of behind-closed-doors games looming large. It was an important intervention from Arteta and another example of the sway he was already beginning to have on his squad, as two days later it was announced that the majority of the players, as well as his coaching staff, had agreed to take the voluntary 12.5 per cent cut in salary.

'The move follows positive and constructive discussions,' an Arsenal statement read. 'We are proud and grateful to our players and staff for pulling together to support our club, our people and our community in these unprecedented times which are some of the most challenging we have faced in our history.'

One of the players who didn't agree to the pay cut was Özil, which was of course something that generated plenty of controversy at the time, given he was Arsenal's highest-paid player on around £350,000 a week. It was big news and Özil got widely hammered for it. He had been willing to accept a deferral of his wages, but he didn't want to commit to a cut until the football and financial outlook was clearer. He, as well as a couple of other players in the squad, felt they were being rushed into making a decision.

'We needed more information,' Özil would later say during an interview with the Athletic. 'Many questions were unanswered. For anyone in this situation, you have a right to know everything, to understand why it is happening and where the money is going. But we didn't get enough details. It was far too quick for something so important and there was a lot of pressure. This was not fair, especially for the young guys, and I refused.'

This was the beginning of the end for Özil at Arsenal. He remained at the club for a further eight months, but he would never play again. It was far from the end of the drama, however, when it came to the German.

★ ★ ★

When training resumed for the Arsenal squad towards the end of April, the players returned to a very different set-up at London Colney. Only five players were allowed inside the entire training complex at one time, and they all had their allocated time slots for the week sent to them in a rota. Once they were inside, the players were kept apart at all times, with all ten training pitches being used to ensure there was no issue in terms of space or social distancing. Players had to arrive in their training gear, go from the car park straight to their allocated training pitch and then return to their car and drive home once their hour-long time slot had come to an end. No buildings on site were open at all. There were a small number of fitness and medical coaches present, and they were allowed to remain in earshot of the players to assist with their pre-planned training programmes. Each player had their own set of footballs that only they could use while they were on the pitch.

The decision to allow the squad back into London Colney to do fitness work was taken after several players held talks with Arteta and expressed a desire to return. At home they had been using exercise bikes, treadmills and weights to stay in shape, but a number of them had run into issues when they left their house to go for a jog around their local area. Fans constantly trying to stop them to ask for selfies despite the social-distancing rules was an issue that left many feeling uncomfortable. There had also been incidents of players being pictured breaking lockdown rules that were in place around the country. Nicolas Pépé, Alexandre Lacazette, David Luiz and Granit Xhaka all had to be warned by the club about their responsibilities after being featured in the press.

This is how things operated at Arsenal for three weeks before clubs were given the green light to push ahead with the first phase of the new training protocols that had been drawn up as part of the Premier League's Project Restart. This finally gave Arteta the opportunity to return to the training pitch with his players, although things were still very different. The squad had to be split into groups of a maximum of five during sessions, which were staggered throughout the day to avoid large number of players being on site at once. Up to three members of the coaching staff were allowed to lead the 75-minute sessions, including Arteta. But players and staff had to stay more than two metres apart as much as possible, with contact training still not allowed due to the social-distancing rules that remained in place. It was difficult for everyone to adjust to, but it's what had to happen to get football going again.

The Premier League finally announced on 28 May that the season would restart on 17 June, with Arsenal's game at Manchester City – which had been postponed when Arteta tested positive for coronavirus back in March – to take place that night. From that point on, preparations really started to step up at London Colney, but there were plenty of things going on behind the scenes that made it difficult for the focus to be purely on football.

There was the Özil situation, of course, but contracts for certain players also had to be sorted out. Loan players such as Pablo Mari, Cédric Soares and Dani Ceballos – who had arrived from Real Madrid the previous summer under Emery – had been signed on deals that were due to expire at the end of June. But because the season had been suspended for so long, it now had the potential to run into August, as the FA Cup final had been rescheduled for 1 August. For those players to see out the season with Arsenal, new deals had to be agreed with them and their clubs, which was far from easy.

Arsenal also had David Luiz, who was due to become a free agent at the end of June. Arteta was pushing for him to be handed a new contract, but the club hierarchy were unsure about the wisdom of giving the 33-year-old an extension amid such an uncertain financial outlook. It was an issue that proved to be a massive disruption in the build-up to the City game. Arteta was a big fan of Luiz and what he brought to the squad. He knew the Brazilian could make mistakes, but he wanted to keep him around. That situation was a growing problem behind the scenes, as it rumbled on without being resolved.

Press conferences started up again in the build-up to the Manchester City game, but this was now a very different world we were living in. Usually, a couple of days before a game, we'd all make our way to London Colney and pack into the media room to ask questions and get what we needed. But that, of course, couldn't happen anymore. We all had to get used to a new way of working: the wonderful world of Zoom.

I'll always remember the first time we all got together with Arteta to preview the game at the Etihad, looking at him on my computer screen while he sat there in front of that awful virtual backdrop. 'I hope everyone is there,' he said. 'I can't see anybody! But I hope you guys are all well, I miss you a lot.'

It was all very bizarre. Journalists were trying to ask questions while on mute, others were desperately trying to work out how they could raise a virtual hand to make sure they could ask a question. It wasn't great, but it was something we were all going to have to get used to. And it did at least mean that football – albeit in a very different form – was coming back. Given what was going on in the country at that time, we all desperately needed the escapism that only football can bring.

'We are really excited to be back doing what we want to do,' Arteta said. 'Hopefully we can do it in the right way and we can sustain it, so now it is really important that everyone does what is required.'

That excitement didn't last too long, however, as Arsenal's long-awaited return quickly turned into a bit of a nightmare against City. Pretty much everything that could go wrong in that first game back, did go wrong. It was a bit of a shambles. In defence of Arsenal, the last game you would want after going 102 days without a competitive match would be Manchester City away, even at an empty Etihad. But even so, it was an awful night. It was also one that laid bare some of the issues that really needed sorting at the club.

There was no Özil. He was left out completely. 'It was a tactical reason,' Arteta said afterwards – in a line straight out of the Emery playbook. Luiz, whose head was all over the place due to his contract situation, was left on the bench. But he had to come on midway through the first half following injuries to Granit Xhaka and Pablo Mari. Within 25 minutes, Luiz had gifted City their opening goal, given away a penalty and been sent off. It was one of the most calamitous Premier League cameos of all time. The only good thing to say about it all was that Arsenal only lost 3–0.

Luiz fronted up to the TV cameras after the game and his comments offered some good insight into all the uncertainty that was circling behind the scenes. 'It was my fault,' he told Sky Sports. 'I took the decision to play. I should have taken another decision in the last two months, but I didn't. It was all about my contract, whether I stay or not. I have 14 days to be here, and that's it. I want to stay, the coach knows, he wants me to stay. We are just waiting for the decisions.'

It was difficult for Arteta, and things didn't get any easier when Arsenal travelled to Brighton a few days later. Bernd Leno injured his knee in horrible fashion when he landed awkwardly after getting a shove from Neal Maupay. It was an injury that would rule the keeper out for the remainder of the season. Arsenal were furious with Maupay. Leno even managed to sit up as he was being stretchered off to scream at the Brighton striker as he went past him. Maupay then, of course, rubbed salt into the wounds by scoring a last-minute winner. It all kicked off at full-time, with Matteo Guendouzi grabbing him by the throat and pushing him to the floor. Little did we know then, but was the last time Guendouzi would ever be seen in an Arsenal shirt.

Somehow, Guendouzi didn't actually get a ban from the Football Association, but Arteta was far from happy with the midfielder. He'd already had some issues with Guendouzi in the past. While the midfielder was clearly very talented, he was not an easy guy to manage and you wouldn't get many people at Arsenal offering him a glowing reference. Arteta had dropped him for a game against Newcastle before lockdown, following an argument between the pair during a training camp in Dubai. They had a row on the training pitch, with other staff involved, and it continued when everyone got back to the hotel. Arteta just didn't like his attitude, and he was not the only one.

Guendouzi didn't face any official disciplinary action at the time for what went on in Dubai. Arteta felt that dropping him for one game was punishment enough. But when the Brighton incident happened that was the end of Guendouzi. It wasn't really about what happened on the pitch; it was what happened off it. Guendouzi stormed down the tunnel at full-time and started pushing things over outside the changing room – such as the dividers that had been put up as part of the social-distancing measures. From what I've heard a lot of the Arsenal youngsters were walking down the tunnel behind him at the time, players like Bukayo Saka and Gabriel Martinelli. They actually went round, out of embarrassment, picking up all the things that Guendouzi had shoved over.

The fall-out rumbled on for a couple of days. Arsenal called him in for disciplinary talks at the training ground and he didn't apologise. Arteta was not impressed with his attitude, and the player was told to train on his own with a fitness coach away from the rest of the squad.

This was the first real example of Arteta putting his non-negotiables into action. It was also a clear message to the rest of the squad about what would happen if they did not behave in the manner that he expected from them. This was simply one strike too many for Guendouzi. Arsenal liked him, they knew he was talented. But Arteta had made it clear when he walked in that he only wanted players who trained and behaved in a certain way. As he said in that first press conference: 'I want people to take responsibility for their jobs. Anyone who doesn't buy into this, or that has a negative effect, is not good enough for this environment. We have to build a culture. This is how we are going to live now, and if you are going to be part of this organisation it has to be in these terms and in this way.'

Guendouzi had proven he couldn't live by those terms, so he was done. Loans to Hertha Berlin and Marseille would follow, before he eventually made a permanent move to the south of France in 2022.

The drama over Guendouzi symbolised the way things had gone for Arsenal following the restart. There had been two defeats and there were injuries and chaos away from the pitch. So it was a big relief to Arteta when the uncertainty over Luiz's future was brought to an end with the announcement that he had signed a one-year extension, which would see him remain in north London until the end of the following season. It was also announced at the same time that a deal had been struck with Real Madrid to allow Dani Ceballos to see out the remainder of the now extended season, rather than having to return to Spain on the original contracted date. The loan deals for Pablo Mari and Cédric Soares, which had been done in January, were also turned into permanent moves. It provided Arenal and Arteta with some much-needed stability.

They won 2–0 at Southampton the following day, Thursday 25 June, thanks to goals from academy boys Eddie Nketiah and Joe Willock. That was a game I'll always remember for two reasons. One, it was burning hot and I got ridiculously sunburnt, as my allocated seat in the stadium was facing directly into the sun throughout the whole afternoon. Given that we were now watching in closed stadiums and had to be socially distanced, the media weren't squeezed together in the usual press boxes anymore. We were instead placed in random seats all throughout one of the stands and we weren't really allowed to move. We basically had to stay in our seats from the moment we arrived until we left a few hours later. It's safe to say I looked an awful lot redder when I walked out of St Mary's that afternoon than I did when I arrived.

The second thing I remember, which is perhaps far more interesting, is what Özil was like during that game. Unlike the match at Manchester City, the German had been included in the match day squad by Arteta, but was only named among the substitutes. He sat right in front of me the whole game and it was clear that he never once believed he was going to be brought on. You'll probably remember a picture of him watching this game. He was sitting holding a red umbrella, sheltering from the sun. I was tempted at times to shout down to ask if I could borrow it. At full-time everyone went down onto the pitch to celebrate and congratulate the players, apart from Özil. He just took a sharp left and went straight down the tunnel. Away from that soap opera, it was a much-needed win for Arsenal after the defeats at City and Brighton, and it took them into their FA Cup quarter-final at Sheffield United with a bit of momentum behind them.

Arteta's side had enjoyed a decent little run in the cup up to that point, quietly making their way into the last eight. They hadn't had the toughest of runs, beating Leeds, Bournemouth and Portsmouth before lockdown, but they were now just one game from a Wembley semi-final. It was a big opportunity for them, one they took thanks to a last-minute Ceballos winner at Bramall Lane. Given the season Arsenal had endured, languishing in ninth in the league, it was understandable that the cup suddenly took on real importance.

There were a few league games to navigate before the trip to Wembley, however. There was a 4–0 home success against Norwich, a 2–0 win at Wolves, a 1–1 home draw with Leicester and what ultimately proved to be a costly north London derby defeat at Spurs. It was Arteta's first game in charge against Tottenham, and Arsenal actually started really well and went in front through a Lacazette screamer. But a mix-up between Luiz and Kolasinac straight after allowed Son Heung-min to equalise, and Toby Alderweireld went on to score a late winner that saw Jose Mourinho's side move two points above Arsenal with three league games remaining.

The 4–0 win against Norwich at the start of that run saw Aubameyang score his 50th Premier League goal for Arsenal in what was just his 79th appearance in the competition. Only five players in Premier League history had hit that milestone quicker and none of them had been from Arsenal, not even Thierry Henry. That showed just how big an impact the Gabon international had made in north London following his move from Borussia Dortmund in 2018. He was vitally important and he was also now club captain, following Xhaka's meltdown earlier in the season.

The big issue around him, however, was that his contract was due to run out in the summer of 2021, and every goal he scored magnified the importance of getting a new deal agreed. There was a bit of breathing space, but not much, and no one at Arsenal wanted Aubameyang to get into his final year without the situation being resolved. It was a big story at the time that dominated most of the press conferences we were having with Arteta.

He had made it clear he wanted Aubameyang to stay and had spent a lot of time during lockdown trying to convince his skipper of the project he was looking to put together at the club. The pair spoke at length during video calls, and as the season wore on there was a growing belief that the striker would stay, despite interest from overseas. Inter Milan wanted to take him to Italy and Barcelona were certainly putting the feelers out about a potential move to the Camp Nou, although Inter's Lautaro Martinez was their main target at the time.

Arteta was always calm about the situation, though, and would often talk to Aubameyang about creating a legacy at Arsenal. That was how he approached his discussions with the forward. It was never really about contracts and money; it was about being part of the project.

'Auba knows really well what my thoughts are towards him,' Arteta said after his skipper had brought up his half century of Premier League goals. 'He knows the project I want to create. I am positive and I remain positive that we can keep him here for many years, but things have to progress. I hope he scores 100 goals for us.'

Aubameyang had arrived at Arsenal with a reputation for being trouble behind the scenes. He was certainly a flamboyant character. He had all the clothes, the vast array of flash cars and the entourage. But during those first couple of years he was very popular around the club. His goal record spoke for itself and the concerns over his attitude hadn't really come to pass. All of the young players loved playing with him. Saka would always tell us how great Aubameyang was with him. Eddie Nketiah was the same, so was Ainsley Maitland-Niles. Aubameyang wasn't your classic captain, but he was someone the team liked and looked up to. Time-keeping was still a bit of an issue, as it had been while he was at Dortmund. But as he was performing on the pitch, it was not seen as anything major.

I remember Aubameyang flying past me on the road outside London Colney one morning. I was on my way in for a press conference and he was clearly running late for training. I can imagine I was not the only person during his time at Arsenal to glance up in the rear-view mirror and see one of his supercars speeding towards them, before watching him disappear off into the distance following a quick overtake. That's just how he was. The main thing was that he was scoring goals – and lots of them. This was a squad that Arteta had largely inherited. They were not his players, but he was having to use them to try to get results. And with Aubameyang in the team, he had a better chance of doing just that.

Arsenal had returned after lockdown and shown some resilience about them. They were looking more organised, with Arteta having moved away from the 4-2-3-1 system he had been using, and now playing three at the back. With Özil now no more than a spectator, he had Aubameyang, Lacazette and Pépé playing as the front three, without a number 10 operating behind them. That definitely saw a drop in creativity, but there was a bit more stability within the team. Luiz, his new contract having been signed, was playing well, Ainsley Maitland-Niles was doing a good job as one of the wing-backs, and even the much-maligned Shkodran Mustafi was performing. Even so, few gave Arsenal any sort of chance of getting past Manchester City in the FA Cup semi-final at Wembley. Remember, it had just been a few weeks since City had thumped Arsenal at the Etihad in the Premier League. In fact, going into that semi-final, Arsenal had lost seven games in a row against City, conceding 20 goals in the process and scoring just two.

They had, however, just beaten Liverpool a few days earlier. Jürgen Klopp's side had long since wrapped up the title, but they still had the all-time Premier League points record in their sights when they arrived at the Emirates. Goals from Lacazette and Reiss Nelson earned Arsenal a 2–1 win and ended Liverpool's chances of reaching 102 points in a single season. In the end the Merseyside club had to settle for 99, one behind City's record total of 100 set two years earlier. The game was the perfect warm-up for the semi-final at Wembley. Liverpool dominated in terms of shots and possession, especially in the second half when it was basically one-way traffic, but Arsenal held firm amid that pressure. It was a classic backs-to-the-wall type of victory.

Interestingly, Arteta used that win against Liverpool to send a message to the powers that be ahead of the summer transfer window. He knew it was a good result, but he also knew that the way Arsenal achieved it was not something they could continue to do long-term. He was not the type of coach who wanted to have to continue surrendering possession to the opposition in the hope that his team could do something on the counter-attack.

'The gap between the two teams is enormous,' he said during his post-match interview with Sky Sports. 'I think it's pretty clear that we need to strengthen the squad.' Arteta was then asked whether he was confident he would have money available to do that. 'I don't know,' he added. 'It's a big concern. You need it to build a squad. It's not magic. You need to improve with quality players in the squad and you need bigger squads to compete in this competition. There's the challenge.'

It was interesting timing from Arteta. He backtracked a bit in his next press conference, insisting the comments were not a direct challenge to the Kroenkes. 'That was misinterpreted,' he said. 'It wasn't my intention. It's not about sending a message. We all have the same objective, which is to try to bring the club back as quickly as possible.'

But Arteta is a very intelligent guy and he knows how powerful his words can be. We see it all the time in his press conferences. When he doesn't want to say something he won't say it. It doesn't matter how many times you ask the question or how cleverly you attempt to slightly reword it in the hope he might be tempted to bite, he will just smile and move on. So the fact that he chose that moment, after an excellent win, to very publicly call for investment felt very telling.

Arteta had arrived at Arsenal with a very clear picture in his mind about the direction in which he wanted to take the squad. He had been at the club for more than six months now and he knew that the only way he would be able to do that was with some high-level investment. He'd even spoken about it in the build-up to the Liverpool game, when he pointed towards what Jürgen Klopp had achieved and the money he had spent in key areas to transform his team.

'Financially, they had a big backing and made some big signings, which completely changed the club, in my opinion,' Arteta said. 'You get one of the best defenders in the world [Virgil van Dyke] with the best goalkeeper in the world [Alisson] with one of the best holding midfielders [Fabinho] and you change it pretty quickly. That is the way that I believe a team has to be built.'

Obviously the pandemic had completely changed the financial landscape of football. Arsenal were haemorrhaging money while having to play behind closed doors, and no one knew when fans were going to be allowed back in. There was huge uncertainty about what sort of cash would be available to strengthen the squad in the upcoming transfer window. This was a very timely reminder from Arteta about the need to be backed by the owners.

The semi-final against City was a huge game. City, who had Champions League football secured, could approach it with their focus purely on the silverware. Arsenal, who sat ninth in the Premier League, knew that winning the FA

Cup was now their best route into the Europa League the following season, something that would give them the chance to add around £30 million to their budget. Given that finances were expected to be very tight and there was so much to do in terms of transfers and contracts, the potential prize money European qualification offered almost felt more important than the cup itself.

'We don't know exactly what is going to happen or what we are going to be able to do or not do, to keep players or not keep,' Arteta said ahead of the Wembley showpiece. 'It will depend a lot on what we do on the pitch in the next three or four games.'

There was a real sense of uncertainty at Arsenal going into the match. Talks with transfer targets had been put on hold, with the club waiting to find out whether European football could be secured before proceeding, so there was a lot riding on the outcome of the game. Few gave Arsenal any hope of winning. But they did, and they did it relatively comfortably thanks to an Aubameyang brace.

It was a tactical masterclass from Arteta against Guardiola, a case of the apprentice getting one over his master. He went with a back three and had his wing-backs, Maitland-Niles and Bellerin, drop deep whenever City were in possession. Arsenal were happy to funnel Guardiola's side into the congested central areas all afternoon. City had 71 per cent of the ball but barely tested Martinez in the Arsenal goal because they were unable to find any space to create clear-cut chances. It was a victory straight from the training ground and every single player played their part. You could see they had been well drilled and they all knew exactly what they needed to do to give themselves a chance of shutting out City at one end and punishing them on the counter-attack at the other.

Defensively, Arsenal were excellent, limiting City to just one shot on target. David Luiz had his best game for the club, rewarding Arteta for the faith he had shown in him just a few weeks earlier during his contract stand-off. And going forward Arsenal were ruthless when their chances arose, with Aubameyang scoring in either half to take his tally for the season to 25.

Both goals were excellent, with the first particularly eye-catching. It featured 18 passes and involved 10 of Arsenal's 11 players in the move. Eight of the passes were actually made in Arsenal's own penalty area as they sucked City in before springing forward on the counter-attack. Lacazette, who was excellent throughout, found Pépé, who picked out Aubameyang perfectly at the back post to score. It was the type of goal that we would come to expect from Arteta's Arsenal, but at the time it was one we hadn't really seen much of before.

That goal and Arsenal's all-round performance clearly demonstrated the progress that was being made under the Spaniard. It was just a shame no one was inside Wembley to see it.

I'll always remember how this was the game that really made it hit home for me how rubbish football was without fans. I'd been to nine matches since the Premier League had restarted, but it was something about Wembley that made this one feel different. I walked up Wembley Way about two hours before kick-off. Usually it would have been a sea of colour, half red and half blue. But it was completely empty. I didn't see a single person. It just felt so wrong. Then inside the stadium it was really odd; because Wembley is so huge it just seemed to swallow everything up with no fans inside it. It was just a really strange experience that sucked so much of the joy out of what should have been a very special day.

For Arsenal, though, it was a huge moment. In the space of a week they'd beaten Liverpool and Manchester City, the top two teams in the country. It was the sort of week that gave everyone real confidence that things were beginning to get on track under Arteta. Tactically, the improvement was obvious, and the players were starting to believe in themselves. Aubameyang was at the top of his game, Pépé was finishing his debut season in England in fine form, and the likes of Xhaka and Luiz were showing why Arteta had fought so hard to keep them at the club.

In goal the form of Emi Martinez was a great story. Bernd Leno, Arsenal's regular keeper, had arguably been Arsenal's player of the season until Arsenal travelled to the Amex to play Brighton. When he was stretchered off with what was clearly a serious knee injury, there was under-standably a real belief that his absence could have major consequences on the remainder of the campaign.

The club had a lot of faith in Martinez, who had been back-up to Leno all season but had never been given a prolonged run of games in the top-flight. But no one really knew what to expect from him. I'd gone to meet Martinez the season before, while he was on loan at Reading in the Championship. The thing that struck me about him was how confident he was in himself. He'd been at Arsenal for nearly ten years at that point, but aside from the odd appearance he had never got close to being a first-team regular. That would have broken a lot of players, but not Martinez. It was obvious he still believed he was good enough to make it.

At the time of the interview, Petr Cech had just announced he would be retiring at the end of the season, and Martinez saw that as a potential opening for him at Arsenal. He was determined to go back and have a chance, and if he wasn't given one he was going to leave.

'If they don't trust me or buy a new goalkeeper, then my future has to be somewhere else,' he said to me. 'I don't know what they are going to do but I'm sure that if week in, week out I was able to play at Arsenal that I could be one of the best. I just need a chance. I promised my dad I was going to make it and I will make it. I believe I have everything that a keeper needs to play for Arsenal. If they don't trust me, then I will have to move away and the Arsenal fans will understand. But I believe I should have the chance to show how good I am at Arsenal.'

There had been plenty of interest in Martinez before the 2019–20 season started because of how well he had performed at Reading. But he decided to stay for one more year to fight it out with Leno for the number 1 spot. He did get to play in the cup games under Emery, but until Leno's injury he hadn't made a Premier League appearance. It was the chance he had been waiting for, and to be fair to Martinez he backed up all those confident words with performances. He was excellent after coming into the team. He had a real presence about him and you could tell how much the defence liked playing in front of him.

The victory against City at Wembley was a massive moment for him. I remember when the full-time whistle went, you could hear this roar echoing around the stadium. It came from Martinez, who had just fallen to the floor in his penalty area in floods of tears.

'I was emotional,' he said later on. 'Not because we beat City, but because of how much I have been fighting to play in a final with the club I love. I always believed that I could do it, and I had done it.'

Arsenal still had a couple of games to play in the Premier League before the final, which would be against Chelsea, the same opponents as three years earlier when Wenger won his seventh and final FA Cup. Arsenal went to Aston

Villa and lost 1–0, dropping to tenth in the table in the process. It was a defeat that meant whatever happened against Watford on the final day of the league season, they would finish outside the top six in the Premier League for the first time in 25 years. After the high of beating City, this was a real low.

The game was also notable for a group of Arsenal fans paying £1,700 to fly a plane over Villa Park. It was pulling a banner with the message 'Back Arteta, Kroenke out' on it. This wasn't the first time we'd seen something like this with Arsenal. Who could forget that day at West Brom in 2017 when there were two planes pulling banners over the Hawthorns, one calling for Wenger to go and the other showing support for the club's legendary manager. But this was the first time it had happened on Arteta's watch, and it was a clear indication of how sections of the fanbase felt towards the owners and where they believed the blame lay for such a disappointing league season.

The banner was a bit embarrassing for Arteta because it came hot on the heels of those comments he made after the Liverpool game about how much money would be available to spend in the summer. It was pretty obvious that the message from the fans was a direct result of what the Spaniard had said, so it was no surprise that he came out and defended the owners.

'I have full support from the Kroenkes,' he said. 'We are putting a very strong plan together to try to do as much as we can in the shortest period, because at the end of the day the league table doesn't lie and we now have the gap we have to fill in. We are on board and trying to do everything together.'

What the banner did do, however, was serve a bit of a notice of how the fans felt about Arteta. The fact that the message was an anti-Kroenke one, rather than anything negative about the coach, showed the support he had within the fanbase despite the relatively underwhelming form in the league. Things had definitely improved since he'd arrived, in terms of the performances and the general atmosphere around the club. But when Emery was sacked Arsenal were eighth and eight points adrift of the top four. The defeat at Villa left them tenth with one game to go, nine points outside the Champions League places. So while there had been improvements under Arteta, they hadn't really led to any great upturn in results in the league. That could have led to questions being asked of him. Of course, it didn't hurt that the fans had an FA Cup final to look forward to.

The defeat at Villa meant the final took on extra significance, as it meant Arsenal now had no other chance of securing European football for the 2020–21 season. Victory over Chelsea would guarantee Europa League qualification for Arteta's side. Defeat, meanwhile, would leave them with nothing but domestic matters to focus on for the next 12 months. So there was plenty at stake at Wembley, but

Arsenal still had to finish off their league campaign first, which they did with a 3–2 home win against Watford, a result that relegated the Hornets. Aubameyang was once again the star of the show, scoring twice and setting up the other goal for Kieran Tierney. That double saw the Gabon international finish with 22 league goals for the season, just one behind golden boot winner Jamie Vardy. The win brought the curtain down on Arteta's first league season in charge and saw Arsenal finish eighth, ten points outside the top four.

'I think we have progressed in many, many things,' Arteta told us after the game. 'The most important thing probably is we have changed the context and environment of the football club. A lot of issues that were happening, now hopefully they are gone. The spirit is there, the energy is there. You can start to see what we want to do, and as well I think we have brought some stability back to the club and some belief. The fact we are in a final as well shows how much we have gone to a different level. Now we have to win it.'

The build-up to the final was dominated by Aubameyang and his future. Publicly, Arteta remained insistent that he believed his captain would stay. The feeling was, however, that if Arsenal were to lose to Chelsea and miss out on the extra revenue that European football would bring, it might be hard to keep hold of the striker.

There was so much riding on the game for Arsenal. It really felt like the result would completely shape how the summer would go. Plans were already being made for the transfer window, but nothing had been set in stone. Arsenal had been in talks with Willian, who was about to become a free agent at Chelsea, and the club had other firm ideas in mind in terms of players they would try to sign, one of which was Thomas Partey at Atletico Madrid, but they needed to know what the budget would be before putting those plans into action.

'It is a reality that financially it would be really helpful,' Arteta said ahead of the final when talking about what European qualification would mean. 'Obviously in the sporting side as well, because to play in Europe for this club is a must and we have the opportunity to do both.'

But, of course, it wasn't just about the money. A 14th FA Cup was up for grabs for the club and Arteta had the opportunity to become the first person to captain and manage Arsenal to an FA Cup final victory. It was the chance to make history a little over seven months into his first job as a manager. He also knew what a trophy at this stage of his tenure would do for him in terms of power behind the scenes. The rebuild he had been planning since he first walked through the doors at the Emirates back in December hadn't even really started yet. It would be huge for him to be able to lift a trophy so early on.

'It generates trust when you win a title,' Arteta said in his pre-match press conference. 'It brings everybody together and you have good memories. It's about winning and winning a trophy. That is so positive for any club and when you are in a process, obviously that makes it even more important. We have a great opportunity, so let's go for it.'

The win against Manchester City in the semi-final gave Arsenal some real belief going into the game against Chelsea, as did the recent victory against Liverpool in the Premier League. They knew they had a game plan that could see them beat the best teams in England. They just had to stick to it. And while Chelsea were a decent side, they weren't City or Liverpool – and Frank Lampard certainly wasn't Pep Guardiola or Jürgen Klopp. Arsenal were confident going to Wembley.

Arteta once again went with a back three, as he had in the semi-final, with Kieran Tierney playing as the left-sided centre-back alongside Luiz and Rob Holding. Ainsley Maitland-Niles was once again preferred over Saka at left wing-back, despite the teenager having made such impressive strides throughout the season, with Héctor Bellerin on the opposite flank. Dani Ceballos and Granit Xhaka were the midfield pairing, with the usual front three of Nicolas Pépé, Alenxandre Lacazette and Pierre-Emerick Aubameyang ahead of them.

There was no Matteo Guendouzi or Mesut Özil, of course. Arteta told the German in the build-up to the game that he wouldn't even be in the squad. Covid rules meant that only ten non-playing club members were allowed to attend the final, so Arsenal gave Özil permission to fly to Turkey a few days beforehand. This was a big move from Arteta, a really clear sign that he just did not want Özil around the place, especially in the build-up to such a huge game. Matt Smith, a teenage midfielder from the youth team who had never made a senior appearance before, was named among the substitutes instead.

The final was not a classic; it was never going to be in an empty Wembley. But it was still a contest full of drama. And at the end of it all it was absolutely no surprise that Aubameyang was the difference between the two teams. Chelsea actually started really well. Christian Pulisic scored after just five minutes and caused Arsenal real problems throughout the first half, but Arteta's side slowly got themselves into the game. They levelled before half-time thanks to an Aubameyang penalty he had won himself after being tripped by César Azpilicueta. Pépé then saw an excellent finish ruled out for offside. It was a real shame because it would have been a superb cup final goal. Pépé actually played really well, as he had in the semi-final against City. The way he ended that season suggested he could really flourish under Arteta.

Just after half-time Pulisic did his hamstring and had to go off, which was a big moment. He was the one player that Arsenal were struggling to deal with. As soon as he went off, it felt like Arsenal were the most likely winners.

And that's how it proved, with Aubameyang getting the winner in the 67th minute. It was a brilliant goal: the run from Bellerin, the pass from Pépé and then the skill from Aubameyang to beat Kurt Zouma before clipping his finish over the onrushing Willy Caballero. It was all just pure quality.

The one good thing about behind-closed-doors football was that you would occasionally hear some funny little nuggets from the players during games, and this was definitely one of those occasions. As Aubameyang squares Zouma up and beats him just before the goal, you can hear an anguished cry coming from the backtracking Jorginho. 'Ah, Zou!' he says. He knew what was coming. Everyone did.

There was only one place the ball was ending up when Aubameyang got himself one on one with the keeper. It was a fabulous goal, Aubameyang's 29th of the season, and there was no coming back from it for Chelsea. For the 14th time in their history, Arsenal had won the FA Cup. In doing so, Arteta had become the first manager to win a major trophy for the club in his first season in charge since George Graham in 1987 and the first person ever to captain and manage the club to an FA Cup final win.

'It's even better considering everything we've been through since I arrived,' Arteta said afterwards when comparing it to winning the trophy as a player. 'I have to thank the players big time because they have really been right behind us since the day we jumped through the door, all the staff for their incredible work, and the people upstairs for believing in me and giving me this big honour and this incredible opportunity, and to the fans. I love this club so much and I know how much it means to them, so hopefully we made them happy and proud.'

It's tough to portray just how big an achievement winning the FA Cup was for Arteta in that season. For an untested head coach taking on his first ever top job, to walk into a club that was quite frankly in tatters and do what he did was pretty remarkable, especially when you add the pandemic into the mix. Those first few months could have broken an experienced coach, let alone a novice. But he just got on with it despite all the obstacles. Obviously it was far from plain sailing and there wasn't massive improvement in terms of the league form. But he'd ended the season with a trophy and ensured that Arsenal would be playing in Europe once again. In a short space of time he'd reinvigorated a squad through quality coaching and exceptional man-management. Emery had lost the changing room; Arteta came in and got all the players that he wanted back in the palm of his hand. They believed in him and what he was trying to do.

'He's a man who has given us a structure,' Emi Martinez said. 'He's given us hope and given us a game plan in every single game, so when you are on the pitch you see that the game plan that he does in training actually works. He's a great manager. He's been here six or seven months and he's already won his first trophy. He should be really proud of himself.'

That cup success was the result of months of hard work from Arteta and his staff. From the moment he arrived he'd set about installing a new type of mentality at the club. Players had definitely had it easy at times under Wenger and there was a lack of respect for Emery; not from everyone, but from some. That was quickly stamped out. There was a ruthlessness to Arteta that hadn't really been seen before at Arsenal, certainly not by that group of players, anyway. He'd warned them during his first press conference in the job that they would not be around very long if they didn't follow him or behave and work to the standards he expected. And they had all seen first-hand the way he had managed the situations with Özil and Guendouzi; they knew he was not bluffing. No matter who you were or how much you were being paid, you would quickly be on the outside of things if you didn't meet his expectations.

The celebrations on the pitch after the final were great to see. Aubameyang dropping the trophy was hilarious. When Arteta finally left the pitch after doing all his media duties, he walked into the changing room banging the trophy and then started dancing in the middle of the players, who were all spraying him with champagne. It told a real story of what he and his staff had managed to create in such a short space of time at the club. As did two simple words that Aubameyang typed on his phone during those changing-room celebrations: 'My manager!' This was the message Arsenal's captain put out on social media before he had even left Wembley. It was a post accompanied by a picture of him and Arteta standing arm in arm while holding the trophy between them. Nothing had been signed by that point, but it was very clear where the talks over Aubameyang's future were now heading.

There were a lot of positives to take from the way Arsenal ended that first season under Arteta, and not just the cup final success. In the closing weeks of the campaign they had won away at Wolves, who were a tough nut to crack under Nuno Espírito Santo, especially at Molineux. They had beaten Liverpool, who had cruised to the league title by 18 points. A defence and midfield that had looked pretty much uncoachable just a few months before had started to look like a well-drilled unit. The work done behind the scenes had been impressive, especially amid the backdrop of the pandemic, when Arteta was having to deal with difficult and potentially damaging talks over wage cuts with his players. For a new and inexperienced coach, discussions as sensitive as those could have been tough to handle, but he was the one who broke the deadlock in the talks. That showed how he had already earned the trust of the majority of the squad.

The scenes after the full-time whistle at Wembley, when every one of his players made a beeline for him to celebrate, highlighted once again the impact he had made. He had revitalised players like David Luiz. Even Shkodran Mustafi had been playing well up until he got injured in the semi-final against City and had to miss the last couple of weeks of the season. And then there was Granit Xhaka, a player who quite simply had no future left at the club until Arteta walked through the doors.

'Mikel turned me around and gave me a second chance,' the midfielder said after the final. 'He showed me he trusted me and I have tried to give him everything back. Since Mikel came to this club a lot of things have changed. He has changed the mentality, the spirit, not only for us players, but in the group. Everyone knows exactly what their job is. We have a clear game plan. We come to training with happiness.'

The thing that really stood out at the end of that season was the feeling of excitement around the club about what was to come. The cup win was great. It was a trophy, after all, which is what it's all about at a club like Arsenal. But it wasn't really the silverware that had generated the excitement; it was the work that had gone to get the team in a position to actually win it. Suddenly there was real optimism around the place again. You could really feel it. Arteta had brought the belief back that had slowly been sucked away over the past few years.

The FA Cup win in 2017 had felt very different. That was an incredible day and an unbelievable win against a very good Chelsea side. But it did feel like a bit of a one-off. You didn't leave Wembley that day thinking it was the start of something new for Arsenal. In fact, you left – or I certainly did, anyway – feeling that it was just more of the same. You knew it was going to lead to a new contract for Wenger and you knew that ultimately it would mean Arsenal would just trundle on, doing what they had been doing for the past decade. That was not the case this time around.

Arsenal now had someone in charge who was just getting started. One of the questions put to Arteta during his press conference after the final was whether the win was just the first step of his project. 'Yes,' he answered. 'This is the first one, let's enjoy it and know that there is still a long way to go.'

That was the exciting part of it. Arteta wasn't going to settle for this. This was just the very beginning of the rebuild. It was a trophy won using players signed by other managers. Now he was going to get the chance to bring his own players in, new signings who could really fit into his philosophy and play the way he wanted to play. You knew, for example, that the three-at-the-back system was not going to be a long-term thing. Once he got the players on board that he really trusted, he was clearly going to phase this system out at some point. So it was an exciting end to what had been a remarkable season on so many levels, not just for Arsenal but for football as a whole.

The issue now was that due to the 2020–21 campaign running into August, the start of the 2021–22 season was just a matter of weeks away. Arsenal won the FA Cup final at Wembley on 1 August and they would be back to take on Liverpool in the Community Shield on 29 August. It didn't leave much time to celebrate. Arteta's first full season in charge was just around the corner.

PART THREE

RESPECT

(2020–21)

The FA Cup win sent Arsenal into the summer in buoyant mood, but it wasn't long before the atmosphere around the club shifted once again. This wasn't because of anything that was happening on the pitch, however. Just a few days after the high of Wembley, the club confirmed that it was proposing 55 redundancies due to the 'significant and long-lasting' financial implications caused by the coronavirus pandemic. The news was announced in a joint statement released by Raúl Sanllehi and Vinai Venkatesham.

'We do not make these proposals lightly and have looked at every aspect of the club and our expenditure before reaching this point,' the statement said. 'We know this is upsetting and difficult for our dedicated staff, and our focus is on managing this as sensitively as possible. These proposed changes are ultimately about ensuring we take this great football club forward, creating the right organisation for a post-Covid world, and ensuring we have the resources to return to competing effectively at the top of the game here and in Europe.'

The announcement saw Arsenal come in for widespread criticism, especially as it was made clear that the redundancies would not halt any planned investment in the team going forward. New signings would still be made and new contracts would still be handed out. The message we got from Arsenal at the time was that the hierarchy were of the belief that the team had to improve for the club to remain financially secure. So it would mainly be commercial and administration roles that would be impacted by the cuts.

'Our main sources of income have all reduced significantly,' Sanllehi and Venkatesham explained in the statement. 'The pandemic represents one of the most challenging periods in our 134-year history and we have responded promptly by implementing wide-ranging measures to reduce our costs.'

It was a huge PR own goal for Arsenal. They were not the only club to make lay-offs during the pandemic, but when your owner is worth around £6.3 billion it becomes very hard to defend. Stan Kroenke could have comfortably covered the wages of all those staff if he'd wanted to during such uncertain times, but he chose not to, much to the disgust of some of the fans and to the frustration and disappointment of members of the first-team squad. One of the big reasons for the players being asked to agree to their year-long pay cuts just a few months earlier was that the money saved would go towards protecting the jobs of other club staff. Mesut Özil, who was one of the players who'd refused to take the pay cut and had not played a single minute since making his decision, would speak to the Athletic a few days after the announcement.

'Possibly the decision affected my chances on the pitch,' he said. 'I don't know. But I'm not afraid to stand up for what I feel is right – and when you see what has happened now with the jobs, maybe I was.'

What made the whole situation look even worse for Arsenal was that it was happening just as the club were closing in on their first signing of the summer. Talks with Willian, who was a free agent having been unable to agree a contract extension with Chelsea, had been going on for weeks. And it was becoming more and more clear that the Brazilian was going to be making the move to north London. So, at a time when the club were laying off 55 members of staff, which was around 10 per cent of their workforce, they were about to hand a 32-year-old player a three-year deal worth well in excess of £100,000 a week, as well as a hefty signing-on bonus. But Arsenal were adamant that they had to continue to spend on the squad, despite the dismal financial outlook, as it was the only way they could protect the club financially for the long term.

The Willian signing was an interesting one. Obviously it turned out to be an unmitigated disaster. Just hearing the

Brazilian's name now is enough to send a shiver down the spine of most fans. But at the time it felt like quite a smart piece of business by Arsenal. Willian was another Kia Joorabchian player, which again added to the concern over how much influence he was wielding at the club, but he had enjoyed an excellent time at Chelsea and his final season at Stamford Bridge, ending with the FA Cup final defeat by Arsenal just a couple of weeks earlier, had been a good one. He may have been 32, but he didn't appear to be a player who was well past his best. He had scored nine league goals in the 2019–20 campaign, more than he managed in any other league season for the west London outfit. He also provided seven assists, a number which equalled his highest previous tally. Chelsea had also wanted to keep him. It wasn't like they had bombed him out. The only reason he left was that they were only offering him a two-year extension, not the three-year one he had been pushing for.

Arteta was also a massive fan of the player. It wasn't a signing that was handed to him. It wasn't a Nicolas Pépé, for example. Whereas Unai Emery had little say in the matter when it came to transfers (he wanted Wilfried Zaha, but the club signed Pépé instead), Arteta did. He wanted Willian and pushed very hard to sign him. It was Arteta's passionate plea to the player to reject the advances of other clubs and join his project at Arsenal that proved decisive in convincing him to sign.

'I believe he's a player that can really make a difference for us,' Arteta said when the transfer was announced. 'We had a clear intention to strengthen in the attacking midfielder and the winger positions, [and] he is a player that gives us a lot of versatility. I have been really impressed with all the talks I have had with him and how much he wanted to come.'

The Willian deal was one that was done via the contacts book. The relationship Sanllehi and Edu had with Joorabchian made it a relatively easy one to get over the line. A contacts-led approach to transfers was certainly the route Arsenal had gone down following Sanllehi's move to the club from Barcelona. Willian's arrival meant that three of the club's last four signings had been Joorabchian clients, after the earlier captures of David Luiz and Cédric Soares. Willian's official signing photographs were actually taken at Joorabchian's house, a clear sign of just how comfortable things had become between one of football's most powerful agents and members of the Arsenal hierarchy. It certainly led to increased scrutiny in terms of how Sanllehi was operating. It was clear through conversations I was having just how surprised people working within football were at how reliant Arsenal seemed to have become on a narrow selection of powerful intermediaries. Arturo Canales, Pablo Mari's agent, was another. Canales had played a key role in Emery's sudden appointment back in 2018 and never seemed to be far away when it came to potential deals.

Arsenal had also just ripped up their scouting network, which only added to the narrative of growing agent influence at the club. Several key figures within the scouting department were told they would be losing their jobs at the start of the summer. At the time it was reported that the departures were part of the proposed 55 redundancies that had been announced, but that was not the case. They were in fact the result of a review that had been carried out by Edu, who was looking to implement his own blueprint on the recruitment department. There was real shock at the time, as it was a huge change in how Arsenal had operated in the market. Arsène Wenger had carefully built up Arsenal's scouting network during his long stay in charge, with Francis Cagigao absolutely integral to that. It was a network that was respected around the world, as was Cagigao, who had started scouting for Wenger in 1996. He was responsible for so many success stories during his time at Arsenal. Cesc Fàbregas, José Antonio Reyes, Alexander Hleb, Robin van Persie, Santi Cazorla, Emiliano Martinez, Carlos Vela, Héctor Bellerin and Nacho Monreal all arrived on his recommendation between 2003 and 2013, a period which saw Cagigao take on the role of head of south Europe and South America scouting before eventually being promoted to head of global scouting. So when it emerged that Cagigao had been let go, as well as other senior scouts – such as Brian McDermott, Peter Clark and Ty Gooden – there was a sense of real bemusement within football circles at the direction Arsenal were heading in under Sanllehi and Edu.

Edu's reasoning was that he wanted to move away from what he felt was an old-fashioned outlook to recruitment. Rather than having a network spaced out all across the world, he wanted to work more closely with StatDNA, Arsenal's internal data and analytics company, and to have a smaller team that was based around him in London.

'It is clear for me,' Edu explained. 'I want to work with less people. I want them to be very close to me. I want to create a group of people working together. I don't want individual people working in one area or for one country. Less people with much more responsibilities. That is my vision and for me in this process the most important thing is that everyone is very clear on the responsibilities which everyone has, to make the right decision.'

This was Edu looking to stamp his authority on the club. So for Cagigao and others, it was time to move on. I was one of the first journalists to speak to Cagigao following his sudden departure and I asked him whether he was worried about the route Arsenal were going down. 'No comment,' he replied, with a smile. He did admit he felt that relying purely on data would have made it 'impossible' for Arsenal to discover someone like Fàbregas when he was progressing through La Masia aged just 15.

'The best combination is when you have the experienced trained eye, with data and modern-day technology for player analysis,' he said. 'That combination is the perfect combination in a football club. I'm not talking about Arsenal, I'm talking about any football club. Of course each club needs to tailor its resources to their financial situation and to what their needs are. But I don't think there is any debate between one or the other. I think it's perfectly established that all of these are components that are needed within scouting and recruitment. There is no debate for me.'

Although Cagigao left at the start of summer, his influence would still play a major role in what Arsenal would go on to do during the transfer window. But there was yet more drama to come before any further signings arrived, with Sanllehi suddenly axed from his role as head of football on 15 August.

This was a big moment in terms of how Arsenal had evolved as a football club during the past few years. Sanllehi had been appointed by Ivan Gazidis in 2017, originally as head of football relations. He had spent 14 years at Barcelona prior to his move to London and had arrived with the reputation of a bit of a fixer. He was viewed as a man who could get things done thanks to his negotiating skills and his vast range of contacts around the globe. He quickly became a very powerful figure at Arsenal. Gazidis's shock exit to AC Milan in the summer of 2018 created a power vacuum and it was Sanllehi who benefitted the most. Sven Mislintat was Arsenal's head of recruitment at the time and Sanllehi had been brought in to work alongside the German as Arsenal looked to move away from the recruitment model Wenger had implemented at the club. But when Gazidis left, a new leadership structure was introduced, with Sanllehi promoted to head of football to work in tandem with managing director Vinai Venkatesham.

Sanllehi then led a process to appoint a technical director. Mislintat applied for the new role but was overlooked, a decision that saw him quit just 14 months after he had arrived. The German was an interesting figure. He'd often be seen out having a pint around the ground after games. He wasn't your classic club executive, but he certainly had a good eye for spotting talent. His track record at Dortmund proved that. He believed he had been promised the technical director role, but once Gazidis left his power vanished overnight and Sanllehi very much positioned himself as the top dog on the ground at Arsenal.

He brought Edu to the club in July 2019, but only after missing out on his top target, Monchi, earlier that year. The Spaniard had built an excellent reputation as one of the best sporting directors in the game during his time at Sevilla, where he worked with Emery between 2013 and 2016. Monchi made the move to Roma in 2017 but never really settled in Italy. Arsenal were very keen to bring him to England to work with Emery once again, and at one stage it looked very likely to happen. But after leaving

Roma in March 2019, he ultimately decided to return to Spain and to Sevilla.

Sanllehi was a charismatic guy. He'd often come into the media room at the Emirates and do the rounds before games, chatting to some of the journalists. Whenever we spoke the conversation always got around to the academy. He'd always tell me how much he wanted Arsenal to try to replicate the success Barcelona had enjoyed during his time there, when they reaped the benefits of the constant supply chain that would emerge out of La Masia. Publicly, his image was very strong. I remember before a game at Anfield, I was walking up to the stadium and he got out of a car behind the Anfield Road End, where there were lots of Arsenal fans milling about. He was actually with David O'Leary, yet the Arsenal fans all made a beeline for Sanllehi, asking him for selfies. A Liverpool fan came up and tapped an Arsenal supporter on the shoulder right next to me and asked who Sanllehi was. 'That's the guy who finally spent the money,' the Arsenal fan replied. It was just after the 2019 summer window when Arsenal had shocked pretty much everyone by signing Nicolas Pépé from Lille for a club record £72 million. Pépé was hot property back then, coming off the back of a season that saw him score 22 goals in France. Plenty of clubs wanted him, but it was Arsenal who got him. So, initially, there was real excitement about the signing. But it soon became very clear when watching Pépé that he was not a £72 million player. He wasn't even close to it. He was a good player and he did make a decent impact during his first couple of seasons at Arsenal, especially in the run to the 2019 FA Cup win. But his ability was certainly limited and not what was required of a £72 million investment from a club that was always very careful with its money.

The Kroenkes appointed Tim Lewis to the board in July 2020 to lead a financial review at the club amid the pandemic. Lewis, who was a partner at the London-based international law firm Clifford Chance, had worked with Kroenke Sports & Entertainment (KSE) throughout their time at Arsenal, first in 2007, when Stan bought his initial 9.9 per cent stake from ITV plc, and then again in 2018 when KSE completed their full takeover at the club after finally seeing off Alisher Usmanov in their long-running battle for total control at the Emirates. Lewis was a man that the Kroenkes trusted implicitly, and within a month of his appointment as a non-executive director, the 55 proposed redundancies were announced. Then, just a couple of weeks later, Sanllehi was gone.

Arsenal were always adamant that the decision was not down to Sanllehi's dealings in the transfer market and were also insistent that there was no internal investigation looking specifically at Pépé's transfer fee and the structure of the deal that had been agreed with Lille. The line was that the decision was down to nothing more than Sanllehi's role becoming unnecessary with Venkatesham and Edu now in place. It was put down to streamlining and club sources were very keen to point out that the parting of the ways had been amicable. But Sanllehi certainly did not want to go.

It wasn't really a big shock to see him leave, but the timing was hardly ideal, given that it was the middle of the summer transfer window and Aubameyang's new deal remained unsigned. But Arsenal were confident the targets they were pursuing at the time could still be completed with Edu and contract specialist Huss Fahmy leading the negotiations. For Edu it was a massive opportunity; his power at the club grew thanks to Sanllehi's exit, and the same could be said of Arteta. With another layer of bureaucracy removed, the Spaniard's take on football matters would now hold even greater sway than they already did. This was really the start of the partnership between Arteta and Edu that would go on to make such a big impact at the club over the next few years.

But at the time Arteta couldn't really focus too much on what was going on behind the scenes, because he had such a short turnaround that summer to get ready for the 2020–21 campaign. Arsenal had the Community Shield to prepare for against Liverpool at the end of August, just a matter of weeks after the FA Cup win. The extended 2019–20 season, combined with the pandemic, meant that there was no usual pre-season. All Arsenal could do before the big curtain-raiser with Liverpool at Wembley was squeeze in a couple of behind-closed-doors friendlies. One of which was at Milton Keynes Dons and was notable because it saw William Saliba start a game for the first time in an Arsenal shirt.

Saliba had signed from Saint Etienne a year earlier but had spent the 2019–20 season back on loan with the Ligue 1 club. There was a lot of excitement when Arsenal signed him. He was hot property at the time and Spurs did their best to try to get him at the last minute. But Arsenal won the race, thanks in large part to the work done by Francis Cagigao and his recruitment network. Senior scout Brian McDermott was heavily involved in the process to sign Saliba, as was Ty Gooden, who was Arsenal's chief scout in France at the time. They were the ones who put together all the reports on Saliba and watched him in action for Saint Etienne. It was just another example of the work that the recruitment team did before it was dismantled and the key figures were let go. Everyone was expecting Saliba to make a big impact on the season following his return from Saint Etienne, so all eyes were on him during that friendly with MK Dons. He played the opening 45 minutes in a 4–1 win, but that would be his last senior appearance for Arsenal for two years. No one knew that at the time, obviously, and he was named on the bench for the Community Shield final against Liverpool a few days later.

Arsenal went into the game at Wembley as underdogs, but it was Arteta's side who again came out on top, adding a second piece of silverware to the trophy cabinet just a few weeks after the FA Cup win. Aubameyang was again the hero. The Arsenal captain produced a wonderful goal to open the scoring and then struck home the decisive penalty in the shoot-out after Takumi Minamino had equalised for Liverpool in the second half. It was another impressive win for Arsenal and another excellent tactical performance from Arteta's side. There were no new signings on show, with Willian not included, so it was a display in keeping with what we'd seen prove so successful in the build-up to the FA Cup win. Defensively they were solid and Aubameyang made the difference in attack.

There were a couple of interesting team selections from Arteta for the game. Ainsley Maitland-Niles started at wing-back, while Emiliano Martinez was given the nod over Bernd Leno in goal. Both players were being heavily linked with moves away at the time. Wolves were pushing quite hard for Maitland-Niles and they made a couple of bids that summer – the second of which was over £20 million, which Arsenal rejected. Maitland-Niles had been excellent in the wins against Manchester City and Chelsea in the FA Cup, and he was impressive again against Liverpool in that Community Shield success. He could play in a number of positions and it appeared that Arteta really liked him. So rejecting Wolves' offers seemed like a sensible decision. Maitland-Niles was popular, home-grown and he brought real versatility to the squad. His form had also seen him earn an England call-up. He looked set to go on and have a big season. Within six months, however, he would be sent out on loan to West Brom.

One thing you often hear when you talk to people close to the Arsenal squad is how Arteta can struggle to interact with certain players. If you are in favour and in the team, there is no issue. But if you drop out of favour – and that can happen quickly with Arteta – you can find yourself out in the cold all of a sudden. Arteta is not really the type of person who will put his arm around a player, or go and have a quiet word with them to explain why he has made a decision or why they are not in the team. It's an area many feel he needs to improve as he continues to develop as a coach and it's something that has cost Arsenal a bit in recent years. Maitland-Niles is a prime example of that. Arsenal could have banked around £20 million for him when Wolves came knocking, but Arteta said no. Yet within a few months he had basically stopped using him and Maitland-Niles's value started to plummet as a result. It was similar with Matteo Guendouzi, although that situation was slightly more difficult to manage.

But the fact that Arsenal were willing to turn down such money for Maitland-Niles was a show of faith in Arteta, and an even bigger one was to come just ahead of the new Premier League season, when the club announced that he had been given a promotion. He wasn't head coach anymore; he was now first-team manager. This was a massive shift in direction from Arsenal and a clear sign of how impressed the owners and board were with Arteta. When Wenger left, the club purposely moved away from a model that had seen one man wield so much power over the club. The process started by Gazidis and continued by Sanllehi was for shared responsibilities. It was done to modernise the club's way of working, to bring it in line with how the majority of other top clubs across Europe operated, and to ensure there was as little disruption as possible should the head coach have to leave the club, for whatever reason. So reverting back to a model that had a powerful first-team manager rather than a head coach was a big thing. It wouldn't have happened had Sanllehi still been running things, something he would later admit in interviews.

But the owners and Venkatesham were well aware of the work Arteta had been doing since his appointment, and they had been really impressed with how he'd handled himself during such difficult circumstances throughout the pandemic. He was so hands-on in areas right across the club and they felt it was only right that his job title should represent his workload. A few of us sat down with Venkatesham and Edu – via Zoom, of course – after the announcement about Arteta's promotion was made and they explained the thinking behind it.

'Mikel joined as head coach and, I think as you all know, he hasn't been a head coach from the very first day he walked in the door. He has been doing much more than that,' Venkatesham told us. 'So this is really recognition of what he has been doing. He has walked into probably the toughest nine-month period this football club has had in its 134-year history.'

The decision was a major show of faith in Arteta so early in his tenure. He had shown he wasn't afraid to make big decisions, had worked through extremely trying circumstances and he had delivered a major trophy on top of it all. He had also forged an excellent working relationship with Edu, which would be vital if Arsenal were going to successfully rebuild a squad that was desperately in need of a major shake-up. Arteta did lose Freddie Ljungberg from his coaching staff just ahead of the new season, with the Arsenal legend deciding to leave so he could pursue a head-coach role elsewhere. Andreas Georgson arrived from Brentford, however, as a specialist set-piece coach. The Swede had only been with Brentford for a year, but he was lured away from the west London club after talks with Arteta.

'I had been coaching in Sweden my whole life,' Georgson told me. 'If there was one area that I was interested in, but never really felt like I'd got this depth of knowledge, it was the tactical side of the game, and Spanish coaches, the best ones, they just have such a deep level of knowledge in that. In Mikel's case he combined it with a very big CV as a player and then a complete winner's mindset. He has this complete dedication to improve so that he will win. Mikel has this fire in his eyes. He's very grounded and has good confidence in what he does. But as soon as he sees an area that needs improvement, he's willing to dig deep in himself to make sure he improves whatever steps he needs to have a better chance of winning. This combination of knowledge and this fire made me think, OK, if I go there, I will learn these different aspects.'

So far that summer Arsenal had signed Willian on a free transfer, and they were boosted further ahead of the Premier League season opener at Fulham by the addition of centre-back Gabriel Magalhães from Lille. The Brazilian defender was a key target for the club and they had spent a lot of time working on the deal. Bringing in a left-sided centre-back had been a priority and Gabriel was the player Arteta and Edu had identified to come in and strengthen the defence. He was a player who had been on the radar for a while. The previous recruitment team had recommended him, and Edu did well to get the deal over the line, as there were plenty of other clubs across Europe interested in the player.

'He has many qualities which will make us stronger as a defensive unit and as a team,' Arteta said. 'He has proved with Lille that he is a defender with many outstanding attributes and we are looking forward to watching him grow as an Arsenal player.'

The expectation at the time was that Gabriel and Saliba would go on and form a new-look centre-back partnership at Arsenal. We all went to Craven Cottage for the Premier League season opener against newly promoted Fulham expecting to see the pair of them in the starting XI. But when the squad got off the coach before the game, Saliba was not there. We initially thought his absence was due to injury, but it soon became apparent that was not the case. Arteta had chosen to leave him out.

'I think it's going to take him some time to adapt to our way of playing and get adapted to the language, the rhythm, the physicality of the country,' Arteta explained. 'We have to bear in mind as well that he didn't play much football last season with all the injuries he had. So I think we have to be patient, picking the right games with the right environment.'

Saliba's absence didn't matter, as Arsenal cruised to a 3–0 win. Gabriel scored on his debut and Willian picked up two assists, with Aubameyang and Lacazette also scoring. It was the perfect start to the season for Arsenal and built on the momentum from the Community Shield win. It also became very clear around that time that Aubameyang's new contract was going to be announced. There hadn't really been any doubt that it was going to happen, but it was still a big boost when confirmation did finally come through. It was a big contract for Aubameyang and at the time it looked well-deserved. He'd scored so many goals since his move from Dortmund and was absolutely crucial to Arsenal's chances of success. He'd almost single-handedly won them the FA Cup just a few weeks earlier, so no one really questioned the wisdom of giving him such a big contract at the age of 31. Arsenal had been burnt by doing something similar with Özil, who was of course still around despite not getting a look in under Arteta, but no one could envisage that happening again with Aubameyang.

'It was important for Pierre to stay with us,' Arteta said. 'He's a superb player with an incredible mentality. He's an important leader for the team and a big part of what we're building. He wants to be up there with the best players in the world and leave his mark. He can achieve that here.'

Arsenal followed up their opening day win at Fulham with a 2–1 victory against West Ham at the Emirates, making it six points from a possible six to start the season. Eddie Nketiah scored the late winner, finishing from close range after being set up by Dani Ceballos, who had just returned to Arsenal from Real Madrid for a second loan spell with the club. A couple of days before that West Ham game Arsenal had agreed a £20 million deal with Aston Villa for Emi Martinez. It was a shame to see him go, given the impact he had made at the end of the previous season. But Martinez wanted to be a number one. He'd spent so long being farmed out to various clubs on loan and having to be understudy to various different keepers that he just didn't want to do it anymore. Arteta had always maintained that he didn't have a number one and that he would select whichever keeper proved to him in training that they deserved to play. But despite Martinez starting at Wembley in the Community Shield, it was Leno who started at Fulham when the Premier League got under way. Martinez's move to Villa was already in the works at that point and it was confirmed soon after.

It was a transfer that sparked plenty of debate. It was good money for a player who had only made a handful of senior appearances for the club, but there were plenty who believed the Argentine was a better keeper than Leno. It was very difficult for Arsenal to keep both players, though, especially given the financial outlook at the time, with football still being played behind closed doors. They had to sell one of the keepers and there was certainly a larger market for Martinez than there was for Leno. Arsenal would soon bring in Alex Rúnarsson as number two keeper, the Icelandic international arriving from Dijon in France. For all of Arsenal's good work in the transfer market, this turned out to be a disaster of a signing. It didn't take long to work out that Rúnarsson was nowhere near the level needed to play for a club like Arsenal.

The start to the season was quite mixed. After the wins against Fulham and West Ham, Arsenal lost at Liverpool and Manchester City, with a win against Sheffield United sandwiched in between. There was also a penalty shoot-out success at Liverpool in the League Cup, following on from a win at Leicester in the previous round, and also a couple of group-stage victories in the Europa League. But arguably the biggest thing to happen during those opening weeks of the season was the signing of Thomas Partey on transfer deadline day.

Central midfield was a position they really wanted to strengthen and Partey was always the priority target. It was a transfer that dragged on all summer. Arsenal had done a lot of groundwork with Partey's representatives long before the deal was done. Cagigao had recommended the club sign the midfielder on several occasions in the years prior, and a detailed dossier on the Ghana international had been passed on to the club hierarchy by Cagigao's recruitment team. The player himself had been very keen to make the move from Atletico to north London for some time. But Atletico were adamant they were not going to sell. That was the message they made very clear to Arsenal throughout the summer.

Arsenal knew Partey had a release clause of £45 million in his contract, so they were happy to play a waiting game to see if Atletico's stance would soften as the summer dragged on. As deadline day approached, however, it became pretty clear that Atletico were not going to budge and that left Arsenal with a decision to make. The Sheffield United game took place at the Emirates the night before deadline day, and the word we were getting was that there would be no more business done. I went home expecting a relatively quiet end to the window, but the next morning I started to get word from a couple of different sources that something could be happening with Partey. I was told by one source that the club was about to trigger his release clause, and then another source told me that the club's legal team had got together at London Colney and were working on the last-minute transfer.

When you break transfer news, especially in the world of social media, it's always a pretty big thing, and I remember how nervous I was when I was about to tweet the news out to the world. I wasn't nervous about the story, because I knew my information was legit and I'd had it all confirmed. But when it comes to social media that doesn't really matter. There was still a long way to go in terms of completing the transfer, and if something went wrong and it didn't happen I knew I would be the one who ended up getting pelters over it. That's just how it works on social media.

I broke the story and in the end Arsenal did beat the clock to sign Partey that day. It was a massive signing for the club, one that Arteta had really pushed for. He knew that a powerful central midfielder was absolutely integral to the rebuild he was planning at Arsenal and Partey had all the attributes to be a game-changer in the Premier League. Technically he was excellent and he had the physical stature that appeared to be perfectly suited to playing in England. He was a big-game player, someone with Champions League experience. It was a genuine statement signing from Arsenal, one that was met with massive excitement at the club.

'He brings something different to the team and is a player with an enormous talent,' Arteta said about Partey. 'He's also someone that can transform the team in the way we want.'

The dramatic late capture of Partey capped an interesting first summer window for Arteta and Edu. Obviously, Sanllehi had been heavily involved prior to his sudden departure and had led the majority of the negotiations for Willian and Gabriel, but Edu had picked up the pieces and got the deals over the line. Arsenal had also held strong interest in Lyon playmaker Houssem Aouar, but after having some offers rejected by the Ligue 1 side, Arsenal backed away. This meant that the big arrivals that summer were Partey, Gabriel, Ceballos and Willian, reinforcing the spine of the team and the overall strength of the squad. Arteta was starting to put together a group of players he felt could fit into the way he wanted his team to play.

This was when you could really start to see that a changing of the guard was happening at Arsenal. The summer additions had given the team a bit of a new look, but the issue was that although new faces had come in, the old faces were still there, even the ones Arteta was not using. And that was not a good thing, especially behind the scenes. When it came time to name his 25-man squad for the Premier League on 20 October, Arteta knew he had too many players so he had to leave two out. Özil and Sokratis were the two to make way, and both players were also left out of the squad for the Europa League group stage. That meant neither player would be able to play until February at the earliest.

'I explained the reason why and it was really difficult for me to tell them,' Arteta said. 'But they have to respect that decision and try to train the best possible way, help the team how they can in that moment and see what happens.'

Leaving Özil out was obviously a huge story. He was the club's highest-paid player, yet for the next few months he was going to be sitting at home with his feet up every single weekend, unable to play competitive football. It was a story made even bigger when Özil took to social media to react to the news.

'I'm really deeply disappointed by the fact that I have not been registered for the Premier League season,' he wrote in a statement. 'Upon signing my new contract in 2018, I pledged my loyalty and allegiance to the club that I love, Arsenal, and it saddens me that this has not been reciprocated. As I have just found out, loyalty is hard to come by nowadays.'

Özil was such a divisive figure among supporters. He was a player with a hugely loyal fanbase across the world. While there were plenty of Arsenal fans who agreed with the decision, there were lots who were furious with the way that Özil was being treated. They felt the playmaker was being punished not just for refusing to take the pay cut that the club had been pushing for at the start of the pandemic, but also for a social-media post he had sent out in December 2019, criticising China's treatment of the Uyghur Muslims in Xinjiang. The post led to a furious backlash against Özil in China. The Premier League's two broadcast partners in the country refused to air Arsenal's match against Manchester City. When games were eventually shown, commentators refused to say Özil's name. His avatar was even removed from video games. Arsenal tried to limit the damage in terms of its business interests in China, releasing a statement on Chinese social-media site Weibo.

'Regarding the comments made by Mesut Özil on social media, Arsenal must make a clear statement,' it said. 'The content published is Özil's personal opinion. As a football club, Arsenal has always adhered to the principle of not involving itself in politics.'

The issue Arsenal had – and one that Özil supporters seized on – was that the club's statement was made to look somewhat hypocritical due to other incidents that took place around the same time. There was a tweet from Aubameyang in October 2020 showing his support for protests in Nigeria against police brutality. Arsenal didn't distance themselves from Aubameyang's comments; in fact, they responded by sending their own tweet of support. 'To our Nigerian fans,' it said. 'We see you. We hear you. We feel you.' Then there was Héctor Bellerin, a player who often spoke out on issues he felt strongly about. He took to social media on the day of the UK general election in December 2019 and urged voters to vote out the Conservatives and Prime Minister Boris Johnson. 'Today's the chance for all the British people to influence what your future and those living here holds #FuckBoris #GoVote,' Bellerin tweeted. It doesn't get much more political than that. Yet again there was no public comment from Arsenal distancing themselves from Bellerin's views.

This all added to the sense of injustice that Özil's fans were feeling about how he was being treated. 'I can promise you that this hard decision won't change anything in my mindset,' Özil said in the statement he made after being left out of the Premier League squad. 'I will continue to train as best as I can and wherever possible use my voice against inhumanity and for justice.'

Arsenal were adamant, however, that Özil's exclusion was nothing to do with anything other than football. Sources consistently denied that his social-media comments had anything to do with him being left out and they pointed to the fact that Özil was still a consistent presence in the team in the months following his post criticising China. He made 13 starts for the Gunners in all competitions in the three months that led up to the coronavirus-enforced lockdown in March, including starts in all 11 of the league games Arteta took charge of.

'It is nothing related to any behaviour or the pay cuts,' Arteta said defiantly when pushed on his reasons. 'It's my decision. What I can say from my side is that it is just a football decision. My conscience is very calm because I have been really fair with him.'

The simple fact was that Arteta wanted to move on from Özil. He didn't like the way he trained. Arteta felt he'd given Özil more than enough chances to show he was prepared to work the way he was demanding and viewed the whole thing as an ongoing distraction. But it had turned into a messy PR war, and that was a game Özil and his entourage were very good at playing. Nothing summed that up more than the story that unfolded around Gunnersaurus, the Arsenal mascot. It had emerged that Jerry Quy, the man who had played the role of Gunnersaurus for the past 27 years, had been made redundant during the cutbacks and Özil swiftly stepped in with a very public offer to pay his wages – posting it across all of his social-media pages. Obviously it was a nice gesture, but it was one Özil and his team knew full well was going to infuriate the Arsenal hierarchy and cause the club untold amounts of bad publicity, especially as it came just a day after they had signed Partey for £45 million.

The whole thing was crazy. It was portrayed as if the club were making Gunnersaurus redundant rather than the man inside the dinosaur suit. Arsenal had taken the decision because there was no job for Quy to do at that time, due to football being played behind closed doors and with social distancing still in place. There was no need for the mascot, whose main role on a match day was obviously to interact with the crowd and the younger fans. But Gunnersaurus was always going to come back at some point. When he did, of course, it was seen as a major win for Özil – even though Arsenal never took him up on his offer.

On the pitch, inconsistency was a running theme throughout the start of the season. Things were going well in the Europa League group stage, but in the Premier League wins and goals were proving hard to come by. After a home defeat to Leicester, however, Arsenal went to Manchester United on 1 November and won 1–0. Partey dominated the midfield and Gabriel was excellent in defence in a really impressive team performance, and Arsenal got their rewards thanks to a second-half penalty from Aubameyang.

It was the first time since 2006 that they had won in the league at Old Trafford. It was also the first time they had won away at one of the so-called 'big six' since a Santi Cazorla masterclass inspired them to a 2–0 victory at Manchester City in 2015. They'd had 29 attempts at ending that run since, but all had proved unsuccessful until the triumph at Old Trafford. The fact that the club's two big summer signings were so integral to it made it all the more encouraging. Arsenal had gone into the window looking to improve the spine of their squad and the indications at Old Trafford were that they had done just that.

'We knew since the beginning that we had to trust the process,' Aubameyang said after scoring the winner at Old Trafford. 'Mikel is bringing something very nice and everyone wants to follow him.'

Despite that win at United, however, it was becoming increasingly clear watching Arsenal that they were struggling as an attacking force. Aubameyang's penalty was his first league goal since he scored at Fulham on the opening day of the season. For someone who had been so prolific from the moment he'd arrived at Arsenal, it was somewhat worrying. The goals were drying up and the team were struggling to create chances, which, of course, saw Arteta's handling of the Özil situation come under even more scrutiny. When the team were winning, it wasn't an issue. But when they were losing and struggling for creativity, Özil's absence was always going to come under the spotlight. And after the victory at Old Trafford, Arsenal did start losing. A lot.

They were hammered at home 3–0 by Aston Villa. It was a horrible performance, one that was made even worse by Thomas Partey limping off injured. They then drew 0–0 at Leeds before losing three league games in a row. Wolves beat them at the Emirates, Spurs beat them 2–0, and then

Burnley claimed a 1–0 success in north London thanks to an Aubameyang own goal. This was the fourth home league game in a row that Arsenal had lost, something that had not happened in 61 years. When the full-time whistle went, Arteta's side had gone 12 hours and 32 minutes without scoring a league goal in open play. It was desperate stuff. They did at least claim a 1–1 draw against Southampton next time out, but then went and lost 2–1 at Everton on 19 December. This is the game that I look back on as Arsenal hitting rock bottom under Arteta.

It was a seventh defeat in their last ten league games and it meant that they had taken just two points from a possible 21 since beating Manchester United at the start of November. Arsenal ended that weekend fifteenth in the table, just four points above the relegation zone. It was the club's worst start to a season since 1974–75. This wasn't just a blip, it was a full-blown crisis – and the worrying thing was that you just couldn't really see how Arteta was going to turn it round. Arsenal had scored four goals in their last ten league games, two of which had been penalties. That's how bad it was.

This was the first time I thought there was a chance Arteta could lose his job. Behind the scenes we were constantly being told that he was safe and that the club weren't even considering a change. There was nothing to suggest that wasn't true, but when you are manager of a club like Arsenal you have to get results. You can't just keep losing. No matter how strong the club's resolve was to stick with Arteta and keep faith in their long-term project, he had to start finding a way to win games – and quickly. I asked him after the game at Goodison Park whether he understood why many would view his job as untenable if results didn't improve.

'I understand that,' he replied. 'My energy and my focus is only on getting the team out of this situation. It's not good enough and it's not acceptable for the standards of this football club. This is the challenge and the fight that we are against.'

There was so much wrong with the team at this point. There was no energy, no creativity, no goal threat. After producing that excellent performance in the win at Old Trafford, Partey had been out injured. Willian had been horrendous; his first-half display in the defeat at Everton was up there with the worst individual performances I'd ever seen from a Premier League player. Something had to change if Arsenal were going to get themselves out of the mess they were in. Arteta needed to do something different to try to find a spark. And when Chelsea arrived at the Emirates on Boxing Day, he did just that.

Arteta made six changes to the side that had been beaten at Goodison Park. Bukayo Saka started, as did Gabriel Martinelli. And Emile Smith Rowe came in for his first league start in more than a year. Suddenly a team that had looked so lethargic in attack looked vibrant. There was movement, pace and creativity. Between them Smith Rowe, Saka and Martinelli provided Arsenal with the type of attacking intent that Arteta's side had been missing all season. Arsenal won 3–1 thanks to goals from Lacazette, Xhaka and Saka. It was a first win in eight league games.

'We really needed that,' Arteta said afterwards. 'This was a big day for us. I saw a lot of things I really liked from the start. The courage we had to play, the energy that we showed, how aggressive we were without the ball and the energy the team was transmitting. We were very direct when we were attacking. The right spaces were always occupied and there was a lot of movement. It depends on the players and it depends on the opponents, but it was close to what we want, for sure.'

That win against Chelsea really felt like a big turning point for Arsenal and Arteta. Not just in terms of that season, but for the wider project. It was the day he turned to youth and was rewarded. The team felt like the blueprint for a more exciting future. The inclusion of Smith Rowe in the number 10 role gave Arsenal a link between the midfield and attack that they had been missing. Finally there was someone willing to drive forward and get ahead of the ball and the striker.

'Emile gives us something different,' Arteta said. 'He's got different qualities to any other midfielder.' Fans had long been calling for Smith Rowe to get a chance ahead of Willian, who had been a huge let-down following his move from Chelsea in the summer. The Brazilian was ill against Chelsea, which perhaps made Arteta's decision to start Smith Rowe an easier one. But given the way he played after being handed a start, the club's academy graduate surely had to stay in the team.

'The young players have been showing us in the last few weeks that they are capable of starting the games and I had no doubt they would respond,' Arteta said. 'We decided to play them because they fully deserved it. I think it's a message within the squad that everyone is important here and everybody is useful. It doesn't matter if you're a young lad or a senior player, everyone is here to contribute.'

Arsenal followed up that win against Chelsea with a 1–0 success at Brighton. They then went to the Hawthorns at the start of January and destroyed West Brom 4–0. Arteta's side were unrecognisable from the team we'd seen struggle all season. It had been a long time coming but Arteta finally seemed to have come up with a system that worked, and Saka and Smith Rowe were at the heart of it. Saka scored one of the goals against West Brom and Smith Rowe, playing as the number 10, picked up two assists. A lack of creativity had been Arsenal's issue since the start of the campaign, something that had been reflected by their meagre goal tally in the Premier League up until their clash with Chelsea on Boxing Day. But in the three league matches since Smith Rowe had been brought into the side, the Gunners had scored eight times – as many as they had in their previous 13 games leading up to the Chelsea match. It wasn't safety first from Arsenal anymore, it was pass and move. All of a sudden Arteta's side were up to 11th in the table, just six points off the top four. A season that had been in danger of complete collapse now looked full of opportunity.

With the January transfer window now open, Arsenal had a chance to strengthen the squad. But financial issues meant that any significant permanent moves were always unlikely. The dire financial situation was made clear at the start of the month when the club had to take a £120 million loan from the Bank of England to help ease cash-flow issues brought on by the pandemic. With that in mind, any business Arsenal did do in January was always likely to be a short-term thing. They wanted to get a goalkeeper to provide cover for Leno – the arrival of Rúnarsson in the summer was a mistake that needed rectifying. Arteta also wanted to try to bring in a creative player. But the priority going into that window was to try to move on the likes of Shkodran Mustafi and Sokratis, and to bring an end to the Özil situation.

'We have a large squad, we know that,' Arteta said ahead of the window. 'A lot of things that should have happened in the summer, we could not accomplish for different reasons. There are some players that are going to leave and that's the priority at the moment, because we can't sustain the numbers that we have in certain positions.'

Özil was still at the club even though he hadn't played since March, and that was something that had to be resolved. The club had been in discussions for a long time with Özil's agent, Dr Erkut Sogut, trying to come to an agreement over an exit for the playmaker. He still had six months left on his contract going into January, and publicly Sogut had always insisted the player would stay until the end of his deal. But that stance softened somewhat as the window approached, with Fenerbahce making it known they were very keen to take Özil to Turkey.

Arsenal were desperate to make the move happen. They had been trying to get Özil and his wages off their books for the past two seasons but had been unable to convince him to leave. There was a growing sense during the early days of the window, however, that a move could finally happen. Talks with Sogut over an agreement to cancel his contract early were progressing well, and the player had been given time off to travel abroad to try to move things forward. It didn't take long for an agreement to be reached, and on 17 January Özil said his goodbyes at London Colney before flying to Turkey to sign for Fenerbahce. Özil's seven-year stay as an Arsenal player was over.

For Arsenal this was a huge relief. Özil's contract, one that had been seen as a statement when it was signed in February 2018, had turned into a costly millstone around the club's neck. It had been a long and very public divorce, one that had grown more and more toxic as it rumbled on. It impacted on the fans, the club's finances and its ability to operate in the transfer market, and it caused problems at the training ground. For Arteta it was the end of a distraction and a chance to move on.

'He's a great footballer and a player who has done a lot for the football club,' Arsenal's manager said once the contract termination was finalised. 'But I want to take the team in a different direction. A player with such an importance that is not in the squad is a really difficult situation to sustain for both parties. If a player wants to play and we cannot give him the minutes, obviously that situation has to be resolved.'

Özil was not the only player who had his contract terminated by Arsenal in January. The club also came to an agreement with Sokratis and Mustafi before the end of the month. Sokratis would go back to Greece, signing for Olympiacos, while Mustafi would return to Germany with Schalke. Sead Kolasinac was also moved on, the full-back joining Mustafi at Schalke, albeit only on loan. Elsewhere, Saliba – who had still not played a single first-team game – joined Nice on loan, Maitland-Niles went to West Brom and Joe Willock left for Newcastle for the remainder of the season. It was a big clear-out by the club and the next stage in Arteta's drive to streamline his squad. He knew full well that having players around the place every day who knew they had no chance of playing wasn't helping anybody.

'We could not carry on with 31 players,' he said. 'This is unmanageable. When you have to leave some of the foreign players out, it makes it even more difficult. For a few weeks maybe it's okay, but to do it for months and maintain the health, ambition and the chemistry around the place it's really complicated. The important thing is that everybody feels involved and that they have a chance. When you're completely out of the equation, it makes it really difficult to find that motivation.'

Andreas Georgson, the set-piece coach recently arrived from Brentford, saw first-hand how tough a situation it was to manage. 'It wasn't easy,' he said. 'Conversations were going back and forth, weighing up decisions, finding the right timing. With all the players I always felt Mikel gave them a fair chance to really show that they wanted to commit to the team. But when does the point come when you feel that this player is not on board? I don't want to name any particular case, but in the beginning there were quite a lot that were not happy. They didn't get the playing time they thought they deserved. They weren't as important in training or games as they thought they deserved to be. When you get a group of these players, and of course they connect because they all share a disappointment, that's risky. So that was a tricky situation that was solved. But you never solve it in one week. It takes time. I think Mikel always dealt with any individual respectfully, but it was tough. These weren't decisions that grew overnight. It wasn't one angry reaction and then they were out. It was more that he was hoping that they would come around and prove him wrong, maybe, but then at some point drawing the line and thinking, I have to move on in another direction.'

Arsenal had broken this transfer window down into two parts. The first part centred around getting players out of the squad and freeing up some space; the second was about adding some quality. With phase one complete, the focus switched to phase two, and Martin Ødegaard was absolutely essential to that. Arteta knew he needed some more creativity. A struggle to score goals and create chances had been an ongoing theme of the season so far, and it was something the club were looking to rectify. They wanted to bring in a player who could be the link between the midfield and attack, someone who could provide the likes of Aubameyang and Lacazette with the opportunities they had been lacking all season. Smith Rowe had come in and made a big difference, but he was still just 20 years old, so Arteta knew he needed more depth in the attacking areas. He needed someone to come in and share the creative burden with Smith Rowe during the second half of the season.

One player that was discussed was Isco at Real Madrid, but the priority very quickly switched to Ødegaard, another player struggling for game time at the Bernabéu. Arsenal were aware that Ødegaard was frustrated at Madrid and wanted to leave. He had spent the 2019–20 season on loan at Real Sociedad and they were keen to re-sign him, but Arsenal quickly positioned themselves at the front of the queue. Talks with Madrid progressed relatively smoothly, with the player pushing for the move, and the loan deal was soon wrapped up, with Ødegaard arriving a few days before the end of the window. It was a significant coup for Arsenal, even if the deal with Madrid did not include a clause to make the move permanent in the summer.

The capture of Ødegaard was an exciting one. He was young, hungry and the type of player that you felt suited Arteta perfectly. I spoke to Lauren, Arsenal's legendary right-back from the Invincibles side, about the signing. He'd watched a lot of Ødegaard in Spain, where he'd worked as a pundit on La Liga games. He was convinced Ødegaard would make a big impact.

'The system that Arteta is playing, that 4-2-3-1, it will suit him because he is going to play behind the striker and in front of Granit Xhaka and Thomas Partey,' Lauren said. 'He should always be behind the strikers because he is a player who can link very well. He can get into the last third and score goals. He is a quality player who can see that final pass. An absolutely fantastic talent. If we give him those six or seven games in order to express himself, he's going to add many good things to Arsenal. I have no doubt.'

It was an injection of new blood into the team at just the right time. A lot of the dead wood had been removed, and with Ødegaard joining the likes of Gabriel, Saka, Smith Rowe and Martinelli in the squad, you could really start to see the direction that Arsenal were trying to head in. But there were still issues, as were made abundantly clear when Arsenal were knocked out of the FA Cup at Southampton just a few days before Ødegaard's arrival.

Arteta shuffled his pack for this game, making seven changes to the side that had just beaten Newcastle 3–0 in the league. Willian came in, as did Pépé, and both struggled yet again, as they had done all season. With each week that passed, the plight of both players was becoming a bigger and bigger problem for Arsenal. In transfer fees and wages, Arsenal had invested well over £100 million to bring both players to the club over the past two years, but the return had been minimal. There had at least been flashes of quality from Pépé, especially in the run towards the FA Cup success, but Willian had just been a complete disaster. Both players had been reduced to the status of bit-part players since Christmas, with Saka and Smith Rowe moving ahead of them in the pecking order. The youngsters had injected a vibrancy into Arsenal's attack, having come into the side against Chelsea on Boxing Day, inspiring a run of five wins from six games in all competitions. But with Willian and Pépé back in the side against Southampton, the performance Arsenal produced during a 1–0 defeat at St Mary's had all the signs of the stale and lethargic displays that had been the hallmark of their season up until Christmas. Having won the FA Cup so impressively just a few months before, this was a meek way for Arsenal to surrender their trophy and a clear indicator of how much work still needed to be done on the squad.

They had an immediate opportunity to make amends for that defeat when they returned to St Mary's a few days later to take on Southampton once again, this time in the Premier League. And they did just that, winning 3–1. Aubameyang was missing, as he had been given permission to leave the country to spend some time with his sick mother, so Pépé kept his place in the side despite his disappointing showing in the cup game. He responded well, scoring Arsenal's equaliser after Southampton had taken an early lead. Saka and Lacazette were also on target in the win. It was the first time Arsenal had come from behind to win in the Premier League all season. Arteta's side were now up to eighth, just five points off the top four. Given that they had been four points off the relegation zone exactly one month earlier, it was a remarkable turnaround.

Manchester United were next up at the Emirates and it ended in a 0–0 draw. Arsenal were again without Aubameyang for the game, as he was having to follow quarantine procedures after visiting his mother and hadn't yet been given the green light to rejoin the squad. Saka was also missing, as was Kieran Tierney, so this was a decent point for Arsenal against a United side who were second in the table at the time and hadn't lost away from home in the league for over a year. It was a game that also saw Ødegaard make his debut when he came off the bench late on to replace Smith Rowe. Arsenal ended January having kept five clean sheets in their last six league games and were unbeaten in seven league games.

With the transfer window now closed, the squad certainly looked in far better shape than it had when the window opened four weeks earlier. Arsenal had approached the window in ruthless fashion and that was exactly what was needed. Edu was still relatively new to the technical director role. He had done good things with the Brazilian national team before he arrived at Arsenal in 2019, but that position was very different to the one he had taken on at the Emirates. It was understandable that plenty of people would question whether he had the experience to take on such a big role at a Premier League club. But what he did during January certainly demonstrated that he wasn't afraid to make some big decisions, and it also showed that he and Arteta had the full backing of the owners. The club felt aligned for the first time in a while. There was a determination to right the ship, even if that meant having to pay players such as Özil, Mustafi and Sokratis to get out early. The relationship between Arteta and Edu was strong, and even though results on the pitch had been mixed, you could see there was a clear blueprint that they were working towards to try to turn things round.

'Probably in the last year or so I spoke to Edu more than anybody else in my life. That's what my wife says,' Arteta said, when discussing his working relationship with Edu. 'With all the things we've had to go through with the coronavirus as well as the transfers. We have a great relationship and a great understanding. We support each other in a great way. It's lucky at least that if you have to talk with someone many times throughout the day that the relationship is strong.'

A lot of the work Arsenal did in January was aimed at putting the club in a position that would allow it to attack the summer window in the best way possible. They had cleared the decks, which was what Arteta wanted, and now he could focus on the remainder of the season with a squad that was far more manageable.

First up for Arsenal after the window was a trip to Wolves, and for 45 minutes they produced their best performance of the season. Partey was back, fully fit, and was exceptional in midfield. Arteta's side were completely dominant and were deservedly leading thanks to a wonderful individual goal from Pépé. But then one last Wolves attack just before half-time saw Willian José race clean through with Luiz trying to get back. As Jose pulled his foot back to shoot, he clipped Luiz's knee and crashed to the floor. Referee Craig Pawson gave a penalty and sent Luiz off. It was a harsh decision. There was clearly no intent from Luiz to take the striker down – he didn't try to make a tackle. VAR really should have got involved, but it didn't and Luiz had to go. From then on it all went wrong for Arsenal. Rúben Neves scored the penalty and João Moutinho banged in a beauty early in the second half to make it 2–1. Leno then got himself sent off for a comedy handball outside his area as Arsenal ended the game with nine men. It was Arsenal's first league defeat since that awful loss at Everton before Christmas, which had led to Arteta shaking things up and bringing Smith Rowe into the side.

Arteta was understandably furious afterwards 'The way we lost the game really hurts, it's painful,' he said. 'To play with ten men for 45 minutes in the Premier League without your centre-back, against this opposition, of course, it changes the game. I've seen it ten times from different angles and I cannot tell you where the contact is.'

Arsenal immediately launched an appeal over the red card, but it was rejected by the Football Association, meaning Luiz was suspended for the following game at Aston Villa. 'We have worked really hard to overturn David Luiz's red card,' Arsenal said in a statement. 'We presented our case to the FA but are disappointed that our appeal has been unsuccessful.'

After going so long without being beaten in the Premier League, Arsenal's defeat at Wolves was a blow, and it was made even worse when they followed it up by going down 1–0 at Aston Villa a few days later. This time there were no red cards to blame; it was just a really tame performance and it meant that Arsenal had lost ten of their opening 23 league games of the season, something that had not happened since the 1983–84 campaign.

Despite the upturn in form after Christmas and the genuine signs of improvement within the squad, statistics such as this provided a stark reminder of just how turbulent the season had been up to that point and how much work still needed to be done to turn things round. A lack of consistency was still an issue. You never really knew what you were going to get when you turned up to watch Arsenal. They could be poor, as they were at Villa Park, or they could be excellent, as they were when they hammered Leeds 4–2 at the Emirates next time out.

Arteta handed Ødegaard his first start in that game, playing him in the number 10 role behind Aubameyang and with Smith Rowe and Saka either side of him. It was the first time the three of them had played together and they destroyed Leeds with their pace and clever movement. Arsenal's big problem that season, certainly up to Christmas, was that they were pretty easy to defend against. The build-up was slow and the striker, whether that was Aubameyang or Lacazette, was given very little to work with. But against Leeds, especially in the first half, it was the exact opposite. Saka, Smith Rowe and Ødegaard were excellent. It was a bit of a throwback to the days of Wenger, when he would pack his midfield with players such as

Samir Nasri, Cesc Fàbregas and Jack Wilshere. There was creativity, some slick passing and Leeds had no answer. Aubameyang scored a hat-trick, his first in the Premier League, and Héctor Bellerin scored the other. It was a really good response to the previous two defeats and it was exciting to see Ødegaard and Smith Rowe playing in the same side. When Ødegaard signed from Madrid, all the talk was about whether his arrival would stifle the development of Smith Rowe. Arteta was always adamant that they could play together and this performance certainly proved they could, which was really encouraging.

Arsenal sat tenth in the Premier League after that win, six points behind Liverpool in fourth. The improved results from Christmas onwards had at least given them a slight chance of a top-four finish, but the most likely route back to the Champions League always looked to be through winning the Europa League. They had cruised through the group stages earlier in the season and the knockout rounds were about to begin. Arsenal were drawn against Benfica and had the away leg first. Both legs had to be switched to neutral venues, however, due to Covid restrictions, as Portugal was still on the UK government's red list at the time, with a blanket travel ban to and from the country in place. The first leg was moved to Rome's Stadio Olimpico and the second leg was moved to Olympiacos' home ground, the Georgios Karaiskakis Stadium in Athens.

The game in Italy finished 1–1, with Saka scoring for Arsenal. And they just about did enough to go through in the second leg, although they had to survive an almighty scare before winning 3–2. After going in front thanks to an early Aubameyang goal, they suddenly found themselves 2–1 down on the hour mark. Benfica equalised with a gorgeous free-kick before a horrendous Ceballos error gifted them a second. That left Arsenal needing to find two goals in half an hour. They got one through Kieran Tierney, but that wasn't going to be enough due to the away goals rule. They needed another and with three minutes remaining Aubameyang provided it, heading in a sumptuous Saka cross to make it 3–2 on the night and 4–3 on aggregate.

It was basically the Europa League or bust for Arsenal at this point. The revival since Christmas had given them an outside chance of sneaking into the European places in the Premier League. But if they really wanted to salvage anything from their season they had to win the Europa League, which would see them qualify for the Champions League. Had they gone out to Benfica in the round of 32 it would have been a disaster, so there was a big sense of relief that they had managed to turn things round. For Aubameyang, it was a big night. He'd gone into the game under a fair bit of scrutiny. He'd missed some golden chances in the first leg to put Arsenal firmly in command of the tie, and the club had also been forced to launch an investigation into their captain after footage appeared on social media showing him getting a new tattoo. At the time UK government regulations stated that all mobile and static tattoo parlours had to remain closed due to the pandemic.

'We will speak to the player about this matter and establish what has taken place,' Arsenal said in a statement. It was yet another off-field issue that Arteta could have done without, so he was very happy to see his captain respond with two crucial goals in such an important game.

'I completely trust him,' Arteta said. 'In Rome he missed three opportunities that are normally three goals for him. He needed to react and it's great to see that the way he reacted is by being upset and trying to be better and not just feeling sad for himself. I am really pleased.'

After the win against Benfica, Arsenal picked up three points in an impressive 3–1 success at Leicester, before an awful Granit Xhaka error saw them throw away a lead and draw 1–1 with Burnley, a result that left them ten points off the top six with just 11 league games remaining.

'When you look at the league table it is not acceptable,' Arteta said. 'We are Arsenal football club and we should be nowhere near here. If somebody is happy with that he is in the wrong place.'

Next up was the Europa League last 16 first leg against Olympiacos, the side that had knocked them out of the competition a year earlier. Athens is never an easy place for a team to go, but this was made slightly easier given that the game was being played behind closed doors. Ødegaard's first goal for the club put Arsenal ahead in the first half. But, as had been the way several times in the weeks building up to this game, Arsenal gifted their opponents a goal, with a dreadful mistake from Ceballos being punished by Youssef El-Arabi to bring the sides level in the second half. However, Arsenal fought back and strikes from Gabriel and Mohamed Elneny sealed a 3–1 win.

It was a really good result away from home, but the individual mistakes were becoming an ongoing issue. A lot of it stemmed from trying to play out from the back. That's how Arteta wanted his team to play. They worked on it all the time on the training ground, but in a match situation some of them just didn't have the ability to do it. You could see how Arteta wanted the team to evolve, but it was still pretty clear that he didn't have the players that properly fitted his system or way of thinking. It was something he admitted himself.

'Very, very far,' he said, when asked how close the team felt from being his own. 'There's still a lot to improve, a lot of quality to add. More control of games, more defensive actions in the opponent's half, fewer giveaways in our own half, more clean sheets, more goals to score, more creativity. There's a lot to do.'

It had now been a year since Arteta had tested positive for coronavirus and those 12 months had been a remarkable period in Arsenal's history. It would have been tough for an experienced manager to deal with everything that had gone on, let alone someone who had just walked into his first ever senior position and barely had time to get his feet under the table before football – and the world – was turned upside down by a global pandemic. Given Arsenal's league position at the time, it was understandable that many questioned whether there had been any real progress made under the Spaniard. But people around the club were adamant that things were on the right track, and they were sure the work that had gone on had set the club up to come out of the pandemic in a strong position.

Arteta certainly believed that. 'I could never have imagined when I got tested, all of the consequences that this virus was going to have on all of us,' he said. 'After only being in the job for three months in normal conditions, to start to have a completely different context and framework to work in has been really challenging but, at the same time, it has made us, as a club, much stronger. We have created a really strong bond with our players, with our fans, with our staff, and that is going to pay some big tribute in the future when everything comes back to normality and we are able to work with some stability. I think this project is going to go bang! Sometimes it is difficult to see the moment now, but I'm sure where we are going.'

The thing with Arteta is that he always has full belief in what he is doing. He has his methods and he trusts them.

When he first sat down with the likes of Edu and the Kroenkes to talk about taking over in 2019 he mapped out the five-point plan he believed the club had to follow to get back to the very top of European football. He knew it wasn't a short-term thing and he made that clear. The first phases were going to be tough and there were going to be difficult decisions to be made that not everyone was going to agree with. But if everyone stuck to the plan, he had full belief that things could and would turn around.

'Trust the process' became a bit of a catchphrase. Some fans liked it, some hated it. In a way Arteta was quite fortunate during this stage of the rebuild that football was being played behind closed doors. Had there been supporters in the stadium during his first full season in charge, especially during the terrible run leading up to Christmas, it would have been interesting to see how they reacted to the performances and results. It was the fans that ultimately played a big role in Emery getting sacked. Thousands of them were staying away from games every week. You could see it by the number of empty red seats at the Emirates every time Arsenal played at home. It was a terrible look for the club and something the owners couldn't have failed to notice when watching matches back in the United States.

Arteta didn't have that problem to deal with and he can certainly count himself fortunate for that, because there were a lot of supporters who wanted him out during that bad run. There was real hostility towards him on social media from some sections of the fanbase. They felt he was too inexperienced to take on a club like Arsenal. They didn't want a project manager; they didn't want to trust a process. They wanted an immediate fix and that was understandable given the way Arsenal had fallen down the pecking order in England. But the club hierarchy were sure this was the way they wanted to go. They felt a reset was necessary and they had full belief in Arteta and the project they were all now working towards. They liked what he was doing and the way he was moving the squad forward.

Arteta had already shown during his short time in charge that he was not afraid to make big decisions, and he made a huge one a few days after the Europa League victory at Olympiacos, when he dropped Aubameyang to the bench for the north London derby because of a disciplinary breach. Aubameyang was due to start the game, but he turned up late to meet up with the squad.

It was not the first time Arsenal's captain had failed to arrive for something on time, and Arteta didn't let him get away with it. It was a massive gamble by the manager, one that could have easily backfired. Had Arsenal lost the game against their bitter rivals he would have got hammered for leaving out his top scorer. But Arteta wanted to make his point. Almost the first thing he did when he walked through the door at Arsenal was talk about his non-negotiables. He made it clear that everyone had to abide by them. If they didn't, they wouldn't last very long. And this was another clear indication of that. Aubameyang had already been spoken to by the club about the incident involving his tattoo, and earlier in the season he had been disciplined internally for missing a scheduled Covid test. This was one strike too many.

The interesting thing was that Arteta went so public with it. He could have just said before the game that Aubameyang had been feeling ill, but instead he went on TV and told the world why his captain had been left out. 'He was going to start but we had a disciplinary issue,' Arteta told Sky Sports ahead of kick-off.

Aubameyang didn't come on during the game, which saw Arsenal come from behind to win 2–1 thanks to goals from Ødegaard and Lacazette. He stayed firmly on the bench throughout the 90 minutes and left the stadium almost as soon as the final whistle went after his very public shaming by the manager. Arteta was still out on the pitch doing his post-match interviews when Aubameyang left. You could hear him go. The roar of his Ferrari speeding away from the ground echoed around the empty Emirates. It was unmistakable.

Arteta was well aware of the gamble he was taking by shaming a player of Aubameyang's stature so publicly. He knew the reaction that would have come his way had Arsenal lost the game, but of all the players in the squad that he wanted to set an example, his captain was at the top of the list.

'They are the foundations and the platform that will allow us to build something medium- and long-term that is sustainable; that can bring us joy and happiness,' Arteta said, when asked why his non-negotiables were so important. 'Without discipline, I don't believe it would happen. That's why I keep talking about it and acting on it. I made what I thought was the right decision. We have a process that we have to respect for every game and that's it. We have drawn the line. We know how important Auba is for us, for the club. But it's been dealt with, so let's move on.'

Arteta did bring Aubameyang straight back into the starting XI for the next game, which was the second leg of the Europa League last 16 tie with Olympiacos. Leading 3–1 after the first game in Greece, this was expected to be a comfortable night for Arsenal, but it was anything but. They were beaten 1–0, with Aubameyang missing several good chances, but the result was still good enough to send them through to the quarter-finals, where they would meet Slavia Prague.

The Europa League was now Arsenal's full priority. There was still an outside chance of securing European qualification through the Premier League, but a crazy 3–3 draw at West Ham and a 3–0 hammering by Liverpool made that very unlikely. Kieran Tierney picked up a serious knee injury during that defeat, one that would rule the left-back out for several weeks. It was a big blow at such a crucial stage of the season, and it meant Cédric Soares had to come in at left-back for the games against Slavia Prague.

Arsenal were big favourites going into the quarter-final, but the Czechs had a formidable home record, so Arteta's side were under a lot of pressure to produce a strong result in the first leg at the Emirates. It didn't happen. Arsenal were poor, they wasted several good chances, and even after Nicolas Pépé finally opened the scoring with just four minutes remaining they still found a way to let the visitors scramble in a stoppage-time equaliser. The result left the season on a knife-edge. Arsenal knew they had to go to Prague and score at least once. If they didn't, they were out and the season was basically over.

A comfortable 3–0 win at Sheffield United did at least lift confidence levels before the must-win second leg, but Arsenal suffered a worrying blow just ahead of the match. Aubameyang had missed the game at Sheffield United, with his absence just being put down to illness. But then, just ahead of kick-off in Prague, he posted a picture of himself in hospital saying he had contracted malaria while away with Gabon on international duty.

'This was the worst moment of being sick in my life,' Aubameyang would later reveal. 'I stayed in hospital for three days and I think I lost four kilos. It was a really bad moment and my family was a bit scared to see me like this. I am lucky that we took it in the end at the right moment because sometimes with malaria, if you don't treat it quickly, you can have some big problems.'

Aubameyang was a really popular member of the squad. We'd seen that by the way his teammates had reacted when his mother was ill earlier in the season. So this wasn't ideal preparation for the biggest game of the club's season, but they responded in emphatic fashion – blitzing Prague 4–0. Given the circumstances and the pressure they were under going into the game, it was a fantastic result. Pépé, Lacazette and Saka all scored within 24 minutes, and Lacazette wrapped things up with a fourth in the second half. It was a result that set up a semi-final with Villarreal, who were of course managed by Unai Emery, the man Arteta had replaced just 16 months earlier. You couldn't have scripted things any better if you'd tried.

In keeping with such a ridiculous season, Arsenal couldn't just concentrate on the build-up to that game, because the shameful episode that was the European Super League suddenly exploded onto the scene in such dramatic fashion. The Super League story had always been bubbling away under the surface, and Arsenal had always maintained that they were committed to the status quo in England and Europe but had to stay involved in the conversation to maintain their place as one of the leading clubs in world football. But then almost out of nowhere, a statement was released that confirmed they were one of 12 clubs – which also included Liverpool, Manchester United,

Chelsea, Spurs and Manchester City – that had agreed to form the breakaway league. In doing so they had resigned from the European Club Association (ECA) and Arsenal CEO Vinai Venkatesham had resigned from his position on the ECA board.

'Going forward, the founding clubs look forward to holding discussions with UEFA and FIFA to work together in partnership to deliver the best outcomes for the new League and for football as a whole,' the statement said. It was an announcement that sparked 48 hours of complete bedlam throughout football, both in England and abroad. The rest of the football world was in uproar at the plans. It was seen as nothing more than an attempt by the rich to get richer and to freeze everyone else out. Supporters of the clubs involved were furious and took to the streets to protest. Players – who had not been consulted about the plans – spoke out against them. UEFA and FIFA threatened to expel teams and players from their competitions. It was chaos. Arteta had no idea the announcement was coming until he was briefed just beforehand, and neither did the squad. The players immediately demanded a meeting at London Colney, with Venkatesham having to explain his and the club's thinking behind the plans. It was an absolute PR disaster for Arsenal and the owners. The Kroenkes had never been popular and this just stirred up the hornets' nest again.

Within 48 hours the club had to embarrassingly back down amid such a vehement backlash. They, along with the other English clubs involved, publicly apologised and announced that they had withdrawn from the project.

'The last few days have shown us yet again the depth of feeling our supporters around the world have for this great club and the game we love,' a statement from Arsenal said. 'It was never our intention to cause such distress; however, when the invitation to join the Super League came, while knowing there were no guarantees, we did not want to be left behind to ensure we protected Arsenal and its future. As a result of listening to you and the wider football community over recent days we are withdrawing from the proposed Super League. We made a mistake, and we apologise for it.'

It was yet another thing Arteta could have done without, especially with the Villarreal game looming large. It was so disruptive. Publicly he stopped short of criticising the owners and the club, but Stan Kroenke spoke to him directly via conference call to apologise for what had gone on.

Arsenal had a league game against Everton to prepare for ahead of the first leg with Villarreal, and they had to do it knowing there were going to be huge protests from supporters outside the stadium. The supporters' plan was initially to protest over the Super League, but once Arsenal pulled out of the project the focus switched to Kroenke. It was huge, the biggest protest seen at Arsenal in years. The fans wanted their voices to be heard – and they were heard loud and clear. They started to arrive three hours before kick-off and within an hour the numbers gathered outside the stadium had made it into the thousands. The match itself was a sideshow. It was so strange watching from inside the ground, with the noise of what was happening outside echoing around the empty stands. Arsenal lost 1–0 thanks to a calamitous Leno own goal. Never had a game summed up their miserable league season more. They dominated, wasted loads of chances and then shot themselves in the foot at the end yet again. It was a 13th league defeat of the season for Arteta's side.

Arsenal then headed to Villarreal for the first leg of the Europa League semi-final. It was a huge tie for the club and for Arteta, given the fact that he was going to be up against Emery in the opposition dugout. The narrative was there for all to see and it certainly added to the pressure. Emery had done a superb job since taking over at Villarreal. He was the most successful manager in the Europa League's history, having won the competition three consecutive times with Sevilla and also taken Arsenal to the final in 2019, when they were beaten 4–1 by Chelsea. And he was now looking to win the competition for a fourth time. The fact that he was now up against the club that had booted him out just 16 months earlier would have only added to his motivation.

Arteta wasn't helped going into the first leg by an injury to Lacazette. Aubameyang was back with the squad, but still wasn't fully recovered from his malaria scare. There was a lot of talk ahead of the game about what Arteta would do up front. The expectation was that Martinelli would come in, or Pépé would operate in a more central role. But instead Arteta threw a curve-ball, using Smith Rowe as a false nine. Trying something new is not a bad thing, but perhaps the semi-final of a European competition is not the best time to do it – especially when your season is on the line. It was a gamble and it backfired. Arsenal were two down within half an hour and then had Ceballos sent off. They were staring disaster in the face in the biggest game of the season. Martinelli did come on after an hour and Arsenal managed to grab themselves a lifeline through a Pépé penalty late on, somehow getting away with just a 2–1 defeat. It could have been much worse and Arteta understandably came in for lots of criticism for his decision to use Smith Rowe the way he did.

'It is the way we prepared for the game,' he said afterwards. 'It is the decision that I made, thinking that it was the best way to play.'

Despite his team losing, Arteta had got off relatively lightly in that first leg. The tie could easily have been out of sight. But there was no reprieve in the second leg at the Emirates. Emery set his team up to get the draw they needed to go through to the final and they did just that.

Arsenal had Aubameyang back in the starting XI, but he couldn't inspire the win they needed. He had the best chance of the game, hitting the post with a header in the second half. The match finished goalless, with Villarreal going through 2–1 on aggregate.

Emery had won the battle and Arteta now had to face the backlash. He really didn't do himself any favours in either game, experimenting with his formation in both. Arsenal just looked confused and devoid of ideas as a result. You expected a big performance in that second leg given what was at stake, but it never came. Arsenal looked like a bunch of individuals, while Villarreal looked like a team who were well coached and together. Arsenal knew they needed a goal to go through, yet they managed just two shots on target in the 90 minutes. It was a really poor performance that prompted more questions about whether Arteta was the right man to take the team forward.

The season had started full of optimism after the FA Cup win, but here we were in May with Arsenal out of Europe and sitting ninth in the Premier League. Lots of fans wanted Arteta gone, and had Arsenal pulled the trigger at this point he couldn't have had any complaints. Yes, a lot had gone on behind the scenes throughout the season, but it was hard to use that as an excuse. Results hadn't been good enough and neither had the performances. The big positive that he could point towards was the upturn since Christmas. There had definitely been a big improvement, and in Saka and Smith Rowe you had genuine reasons to be excited as an Arsenal fan. But that couldn't mask what had been a difficult campaign. Willian had been a disaster, Partey had spent more time in the treatment room than he had on the pitch, and Aubameyang had been a big disappointment after signing his huge new contract.

Arsenal did at least raise themselves to finish the league season with five straight wins, which was enough to see them finish eighth – matching their position from the previous season. But that still meant that they had failed to qualify for Europe for the first time in 25 years.

Arteta was defiant amid the criticism. He knew it wasn't good enough, but he was convinced that what had gone on during the campaign had left Arsenal in a much stronger position to go into the summer. The players he wanted to get out had gone and he felt the squad was much tighter as a result. It was telling when he was asked in the build-up to the final game of the season against Brighton what positives he could take from what had been a largely disappointing campaign, he pointed to the fact that the club had stuck together when people from the inside had been trying to hurt it.

'To keep together and block that and be so strong, I think is some achievement,' he said. 'Normally when that happens, it cracks and everything falls, but it didn't.'

The season ended with the manager under pressure, but there was never a sense that he was going to get fired. It had been a hugely challenging campaign for so many reasons, but with fans set to return to stadiums in 2021–22 there was a belief at Arsenal that they could move on to the next stage of the rebuild, even without European football. Arteta still had the backing of the owners and the board, and there was a plan in place to really attack the summer transfer window in aggressive fashion and continue to build a squad that could get the club back competing for the top four. At this point that still looked a long way off, but Arteta was convinced he had the long-term plan to turn things around.

'This club is even bigger than I thought and even better than I thought,' he said. 'I am prepared to do anything it takes to give the club the most success. I won't stop until I do that.'

PART FOUR

TRUST THE PROCESS

(2021–22)

This was always going to be a big season for Arteta. After such an up and down 2020–21 campaign, he had to show that things were moving forward to appease a fanbase that was growing impatient. There were plenty who still backed him and felt time was needed for him and the club to see the rebuild through, but there were others who, after successive eighth-placed finishes in the league, felt that results simply hadn't been good enough and a more experienced manager was needed to take the club on. That was understandable, but everyone at Arsenal was still fully behind the project and were ready for a summer that they hoped would really move the squad to another level.

There was a confidence within the club and the staff that everything that had gone on since Christmas – both on and off the pitch – had steadied things and made a real difference. Set-piece coach Georgson had just finished his first season with Arsenal. It would turn out to be his last, as he would soon opt to return to Sweden to take up a position with Malmo. But when he left he was absolutely convinced that the club was on the right track.

'We finished the season really strong in the league,' he said 'The results made it quite clear that we were on to something. We had started to build a stability in the team. I remember saying to journalists back in Sweden that if Arsenal gave time to Mikel then there was nothing that could stop very good development at the club. That was my honest belief when I was leaving. The results had been improving, but also the feeling around the place had changed. The buy-in from the players. Mikel had them completely on his side now. I don't think there was one doubt there.'

As ever, Arteta's belief was unwavering. This is one of his strongest traits. He has a vision and he sticks to it. It's easy to panic and veer away from a plan if things start to go wrong, but he doesn't do that. Everything he does has been carefully thought out and he doesn't mix his messages. One of the big positives from this is that the people who work with him, his staff or his players, know exactly what they have to do all of the time.

'Mikel is very serious,' Georgson explained. 'When he is working, there is no fucking around. But he has a sense of humour, for sure, and also he has a really good temperament. We were tested quite hard, especially during that autumn (in 2020–21), but there weren't many times I sensed anything different from him during the week, even after three defeats in a row. The atmosphere was the same, the trust in the staff was the same, the process was the same. It was very constant, no matter what happened to rock the boat. Mikel is a proud man, but he has a higher value and that is winning. So if that meant at some point he had to take advice from me, who had no background as a player in elite football and had spent only one year in England, he would be like, "Okay, bring it on." He gave zero prestige to who came up with the best idea and that is such a key thing to ensure you keep improving. There was no politics or status, it was just about getting better and that's what I really liked when I was working with him. He showed nothing but full trust in the process and gave me a lot of freedom to create things and time on the training pitch to do it. He never put pressure on. It was more about living up to his standards. When you look in his eyes you understand. You think, Wow, now I have to step up.'

Arteta has that aura about him. He demands a lot from his staff, but they want to deliver for him. When Arteta talks he is very convincing, and it's tough to come away from a conversation with him and not feel like what he has told you is right. Ødegaard summed it up well during an interview he gave with the Players' Tribune in February 2023.

'Honestly, I challenge anyone to come away from a meeting with Arteta and not believe everything he tells you,' Ødegaard said. 'He is next level. It's hard to explain.

He's passionate, he's intense and sometimes, yeah, he's a bit crazy … but when he speaks, you understand that whatever he says will happen, will happen.'

There was a lot of noise around Arsenal going into the summer, but Arteta, Edu and the club did their best to shut it out as they looked to prepare for the new season in the best way possible. They wanted to strengthen the squad significantly and they wanted to do it by bringing in young players. In previous windows, Arsenal had focused on more experienced names. The likes of Luiz, Cédric and Willian had come in on big wages, but the plan was different this time around. Arteta and Edu had agreed that the transfer policy had to change. Young and hungry players were going to be targeted. Players who could be developed.

Arteta was desperate to bring Ødegaard back on a permanent basis. The Norway international had been a huge success during his loan spell. On the pitch he had shown his quality and that he could handle the demands of the Premier League, and off it he had really impressed Arteta and all of the staff with the way he read the game and how he worked during training.

'We were all blown away by Martin's presence,' said Georgson. 'He shows such confidence. It's an odd combination because he's quite quiet and low-key. He's not loud at all, but at the same time he transmits such confidence in terms of self-esteem and also confidence on the pitch. I think that's what was striking from the first moment.

Mikel Arteta in his Barcelona days. Arteta came through the club's famous La Masia academy, sharing a dorm room with Pepe Reina, Victor Valdés, Andrés Iniesta and Carles Puyol. He left in 2002 without making a senior appearance.

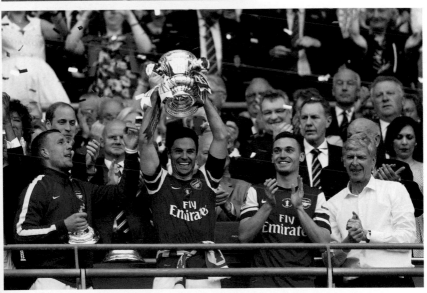

Arteta captained Arsenal to a dramatic 3–2 win against Hull City in the 2014 FA Cup final. It was a win that ended the club's nine-year wait for a trophy under Arsène Wenger.

After retiring as a player in 2016, Arteta took his first step into coaching, joining Manchester City as part of Pep Guardiola's coaching staff.

After just under three years at City, Arteta returned to Arsenal in 2019 to replace Unai Emery as head coach. Arsenal had opted against appointing Arteta in favour of Emery 18 months earlier.

Arteta guided Arsenal to the 2020 FA Cup final during his first season in charge. The Gunners took on Frank Lampard's Chelsea and the final took place behind closed doors at Wembley due to the coronavirus pandemic.

Two goals from Pierre-Emerick Aubameyang in the final against Chelsea earned Arsenal a 2–1 win and gave Arteta his first major honour as a head coach. It was Arsenal's 14th FA Cup success.

Arteta never played with Aubameyang during his time as a player at Arsenal, but he did play against him during a Champions League clash against Borussia Dortmund in November 2014.

Arteta and Aubameyang are all smiles after the striker signed his new Arsenal contract in 2019. Arteta played a major part in convincing the striker to stay, taking a personal role in the negotiations.

Arteta can't keep the smile off his face as he celebrates with Cédric Soares after beating José Mourinho's Tottenham in March 2021. It was the game that saw Aubameyang dropped to the bench for turning up late.

A dejected Arteta stands on the touchline during Arsenal's disastrous defeat at Brentford on the opening day of the 2021–22 season. Arteta's squad had been decimated by a coronavirus outbreak ahead of the game, but the club saw their appeals to have the game called off rejected by the Premier League.

Granit Xhaka heads for an early bath after being sent off in Arsenal's 5–0 defeat at Manchester City in August 2021. It was a defeat that left Arsenal bottom of the table after three games. Arteta's side had lost all three games without even scoring a goal.

After such a miserable start to the 2021–22 season, an Arsenal team boosted by new signings then went on an excellent run as they made a bid for a top-four spot. Arteta picked up two manager of the month awards during the season, in September and March.

Arteta tries to get a message across to Bukayo Saka during Arsenal's 3–0 defeat at Tottenham in May 2022. It was a defeat that helped Spurs pip their north London rivals to the final Champions League spot.

Bukayo Saka has been one of the stars of the new-look Arsenal to emerge under Arteta. The academy product has transformed from teenage prospect to world superstar in just a few years.

Arteta's passionate touchline antics have seen him criticised by people outside of the club, but Arsenal fans love his celebrations and his high-energy behaviour.

Eddie Nketiah heads home in a 3–2 win against Manchester United at the Emirates in January 2023. It was one of several memorable victories for Arteta's side during the 2022–23 campaign.

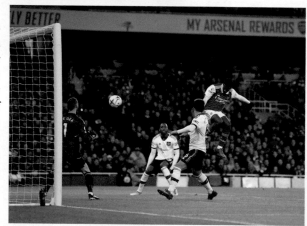

Arsenal captain Martin Ødegaard scored 15 Premier League goals during the 2022–23 season. The Norwegian, pictured celebrating one of his two first-half strikes during a 3–0 win at Fulham, is Arteta's leader on and off the pitch.

Martin and Mikel are quite different. In fact, they are very different in terms of temperament and the way they compete. They both compete, but they do it very differently. I could see straight away, though, the respect they both had for each other.'

Arteta and Ødegaard had an immediate connection. Arteta saw the Norway skipper as essential to the way he wanted his team to play. That's why he'd pushed so hard to bring him in from Madrid in January and why he was now determined to bring him back on a permanent basis. He fitted the age profile of the player that the club were looking to target and he had the hunger, the intelligence and work ethic that Arteta was looking for in any new signing.

'Martin is the perfect team player and role model,' Georgson explained. 'That is what Mikel wants to transmit to his players. A role model is a complete team player. Someone who always puts the team first and is professional from when he wakes up to when he goes home, someone who does everything they can to improve. Mikel lives that 24/7 and so does Martin. There's no question about it. If you talk about the team, but then you don't care about a teammate, or you are too big to carry the balls, then that kills the whole situation. But Martin is the perfect example of a team player. He treats everyone the same, he is always there when the team needs him, he is not bigger than anyone else in any way and he's always the most ambitious and professional person. And Mikel is the same. He never has behaviour that makes you doubt and that is a massive strength, I think, in an environment when you constantly get challenged about that.'

The issue that Arsenal faced in terms of bringing Ødegaard back, however, was that it was a transfer that wasn't going to be easy to wrap up quickly. One of the reasons Ødegaard initially left Madrid on loan was that he was not getting a look in under Zinedine Zidane, but the Frenchman had now been replaced by Carlo Ancelotti. So it wasn't clear what plans Madrid had for Ødegaard and that meant Arsenal would have to bide their time. That meant taking a bit of a risk. They had other players in mind in terms of an attacking midfield role. They liked Emi Buendia at Norwich, for example, and did hold talks with his agent about a possible move. But Aston Villa were also in the running, and when they made an official bid of £35 million for the Argentine, Arsenal had a decision to make. Were they going to match the offer or wait for Ødegaard? They opted for the latter and Buendia ended up at Aston Villa.

As well as a playmaker, Arsenal wanted to sign a goal-keeper, two full-backs and a centre-back. Luiz's contract had come to an end and it had been decided that he would leave as a free agent. The Brazilian needed replacing, and while Saliba was a potential option to finally come into the squad following his loan spell with Nice, it was unclear at that stage whether Arteta would use him. Saliba had done well in France during the second half of the previous season, but Arteta was still not convinced that he was ready for the Premier League.

Saliba's performances in training the previous summer had shocked a lot of people at Arsenal. There were mitigating circumstances. He'd lost his mother just before heading over to England and that was far from easy for such a young player to deal with in a new country. But no one at the club felt he was even close to being ready to be thrown into the first-team picture. I spoke to one agent of an Arsenal player who said that his client felt Saliba would struggle in the Championship from what he was seeing on a daily basis at London Colney. But a year had passed since then. The fans wanted to see him brought into the fold by Arteta, but the feeling at the start of the summer was that he would probably be sent out on loan again. And with Luiz having left, that meant a new centre-back would have to come in to play alongside Gabriel in the heart of the defence.

The transfer window was made more difficult because the European Championship was being held throughout the summer. It had originally been due to take place in 2020, but the pandemic had seen it pushed back a year. Arsenal had a number of players involved and some of their summer targets were also in action with their national teams. International tournaments always make transfer windows tricky to navigate. If clubs don't get players in before they begin, they then have to wait until they get knocked out, which can often stretch deep into the summer. And that's what happened with two of Arsenal's main targets, Ben White and Aaron Ramsdale, who both went away with England.

White, who was at Brighton, was identified as the centre-back that Arsenal wanted. At 23, he fitted the age profile of the type of player Arsenal were now targeting under Arteta and Edu, and he also had versatility. Technically he was very strong and he'd shown during a loan spell under Marcelo Bielsa at Leeds that he could play high-intensity football under a demanding coach. Arsenal pushed to try to get a deal done early for White, but had a £40 million bid rejected in mid-June. Talks continued and Arsenal were always confident of getting a deal done – but Brighton were adamant that they wanted £50 million. Eventually, Arsenal hit that figure and brought White in, but they had to wait until after the Euros to do it. Nuno Tavares and Sambi Lokonga were two of the other summer arrivals. Left-back Tavares, who was 21, joined from Benfica, while central midfielder Lokonga, also 21, was signed from Anderlecht. Both were viewed as players who could come in and improve the squad, rather than make an immediate impression on the first team.

It was a good start to the window for Arsenal, but far more needed to be done and, as the summer dragged on, frustration started to grow about the lack of business the club had finalised in the market. There were clear areas of the squad that needed addressing. A playmaker had to arrive and at that point it was still unclear whether it would be possible to bring Ødegaard back. There was lots of talk about James Maddison at Leicester, but while Arsenal did hold an interest in Maddison, they never bid for him, despite some of the reports that went around that summer. Ødegaard was always the man they wanted and the player they were waiting for. The club was also pushing to sign Ramsdale from Sheffield United to provide competition for Leno, but it was a saga that dragged on throughout the summer. When Arteta's squad returned for pre-season training, only Tavares and Lokonga had been signed.

Arsenal began pre-season with a short training camp in Scotland. They played two friendlies while they were there, losing to Hibernian and drawing with Rangers. The plan was to then travel to the United States to take part in the Florida Cup alongside Everton, Inter Milan and Colombian side Millonarios. But just before they were due to fly, a number of the travelling party tested positive for Covid and Arsenal had to withdraw at the last minute.

It was a nightmare for Arteta and plunged his pre-season plans into chaos. London Colney was shut and had to undergo a deep clean. Once that was done, players and staff who did not test positive were able to return to the training ground under 'controlled circumstances', but everyone else had to stay away. It left Arsenal scrambling around to try to find a couple of friendlies that could be squeezed in at short notice. They managed it, beating both Millwall and Watford 4–1 behind closed doors at London Colney. While that was a relief to Arteta, he knew those matches were not what was needed to get his players up to speed ahead of the new campaign. They now had just two friendlies left, against Chelsea and Tottenham, before the Premier League season opener at Brentford.

The good news for Arsenal ahead of those games was that they had finally completed the signing of White from Brighton. It had taken longer to do the deal than he had wanted, but Arteta was delighted to get the centre-back on board.

'Ben was a top target for us,' he said. 'Ben is an intelligent defender who is very comfortable with the ball at his feet and his style fits perfectly with us. He is still young, so his age and profile fits with what we are building here.'

This was a key signing for Arsenal. Arteta wanted a centre-back alongside Gabriel who could bring the ball out and progress it forward. Having centre-backs who could do that was essential to the way he wanted his team to play. Arsenal had looked at several options around Europe, but they had identified White as the defender they really wanted. At £50 million he was expensive – only Pépé and Aubameyang had cost Arsenal more – but Arteta and Edu were confident they had landed a young player who fitted the system perfectly and would go on to be a big success.

White made his debut off the bench against Chelsea. It was a game Arsenal lost 2–1 and one that saw Partey pick up yet another injury after a challenge by Ruben Loftus-Cheek, ruling the midfielder out until September. Arsenal then rounded off what had been a miserable pre-season by losing at Spurs a few days later. It meant that, aside from the two behind-closed-doors fixtures at the training ground, Arteta's side had failed to win a single pre-season game. With the opening match of the Premier League season at Brentford looming large, Arsenal did not look well prepared. They still hadn't signed a keeper and Ødegaard remained at Madrid. The signing of White was a boost, but there was a sense that the squad was well short of where it needed to be.

'We are talking about probably the most difficult transfer market in this industry over the last years,' Arteta said just ahead of the Brentford game. 'It's been a really difficult window. We've done a few things we wanted to do. There is still a bit to go, so I'm sure things will happen either way. The club, the owners and myself, we all have the same interests, which is to make this team much stronger and we know that we still have things to do to get what we want.'

It had been a difficult summer for Arsenal on a number of fronts. But if Arteta thought things couldn't get any worse, he was about to be given another huge reality check as Arsenal prepared to get the Premier League season underway at newly promoted Brentford.

In the days building up to the game, the curtain raiser to the new season due to be played on a Friday night, a Covid outbreak swept around the Arsenal squad at London Colney. Staff fell ill, as did a number of the players. Aubameyang tested positive, so did Rúnarsson, and then, on the day of the game itself, Lacazette also succumbed to the virus. Arsenal's preparations for the match were in complete turmoil. No one knew who was going to be next to test positive. All the players were having to be kept away from each other to try to limit the outbreak.

Arsenal were in constant dialogue with the Premier League and felt the game had to be called off, as they were in no position to play. But their appeals fell on deaf ears. The Premier League were adamant that the match had to go ahead. Arsenal were furious and felt the only reason they were being made to play was to save the league embarrassment. It was the first game of the new season, fans were finally being allowed back into stadiums and the eyes of the world were going to be watching. It was Brentford's big night, their first English top-flight game in 74 years and their first ever competitive match in their brand-new stadium. Sources at Arsenal remain adamant to this day that had it been any other scenario, the Premier League would have granted their request for the game to be called off. Things were so bad that hours before the match was due to kick off, Arsenal's players were still isolating in hotel rooms and were unable to even see each other while they were waiting for yet another batch of test results. No one knew for sure that the squad would even be able to leave the hotel until about an hour before the coach was due to depart for the stadium.

Arteta was furious, although he kept himself in check in front of the cameras, as Arsenal did not reveal publicly what was going on. All they announced before the game was that Aubameyang and Lacazette were ill.

'Instead of looking for excuses, you have to seek for solutions and that's what we try to do every day,' Arteta said ahead of kick-off. 'We have a really young team, full of excitement and energy, and that's what I want to see on that pitch.'

With Aubameyang and Lacazette at home and Eddie Nketiah injured, Folarin Balogun started for Arsenal as the central striker. It was his first ever league start. Lokonga started due to Partey's injury, while Gabriel was sidelined due to a knee problem he'd picked up while away with Brazil. That meant Ben White was thrown straight into the side at centre-back alongside Pablo Mari. Saka was with the squad, but only on the bench due to his late return from international duty following England's Euro 2020 final defeat by Italy.

Arteta had granted Saka an extended break after the Euros, so he had only returned to training the previous week. He could potentially have started, but Arsenal didn't want to take any risks with him. Arteta also wanted to ease him back in slowly due to what he'd gone through during the summer. Saka had been one of the stars of the tournament with England, but he had been the subject of vile racist online abuse after missing the decisive penalty in the shoot-out against Italy in the final. Arteta, and Arsenal as a club, had rallied round the young attacker in the weeks after the game at Wembley. Arteta spoke to him immediately after the final and he remained in contact with him throughout his break to ensure he was okay. Meanwhile, the club collected the thousands of letters of support that had been sent in for Saka and put them all up on a huge wall at the training ground and surprised him with them when he returned to Colney after his break. It was a gesture that meant a lot to Saka, and he was determined to get straight back out on the pitch and move on from what had happened to him while he was away with England.

Given what had been going on in the days and hours before kick-off, it was no surprise that Arsenal struggled massively on the night. Brentford were excellent and overpowered Arteta's side, winning 2–0 in front of a raucous home support. For Brentford and for the Premier League it was a dream opening fixture. For Arsenal, however, it was a disaster. Everyone at the club felt they had been completely let down by the powers that be. Understandably, the fans were in uproar. It was an embarrassing result and they had no real clue about the huge disruption the squad had suffered ahead of the game to give it any context.

Arteta could easily have let rip in his press conference after the match, but he didn't. He didn't say anything about it, aside from one line which gave a big indication into how he was feeling. 'I don't think tonight's game is one to [overly] analyse given the circumstances we had on the day,' he said as he walked out.

The reaction to the result was brutal. White was widely hammered for his performance. Jamie Carragher, who was doing commentary for Sky Sports on the night, singled him out. 'How do you describe Arsenal's defending? It's just Arsenal,' he said. 'Weak. Bullied. Men against boys – again. New season, same old story. People are going to watch tonight and think, Just play long balls on Ben White. He can't show his quality if he doesn't step in with the ball. He had two giants next to him at Brighton.'

Gary Neville, who was with Carragher on commentary, was equally scathing, but he went even further – questioning the club as a whole. 'I don't know what the plan is at Arsenal,' he said. 'The recruitment has been really poor. They are just poor at it compared to other clubs. I don't get the strategy and I don't get the direction.'

For all the criticisms you could have levelled at Arsenal at this point, Neville's was a bizarre one. Amid all the uncertainty and the poor results, the one thing that was clear was the recruitment strategy and the direction that the club were heading in. Edu had ditched the agent-first approach and figures such as Kia Joorabchian had been moved further away from the process. Arsenal had deliberately set out to target young players who could come in and be developed over time. All of the summer additions had been of ages between 21 and 23. The strategy and plan was clear. Whether you agreed with it or believed it was what Arsenal needed was another thing entirely, but the direction was obvious and there was further evidence of this in the days following the defeat at Brentford, when both Ødegaard and Ramsdale were finally signed.

Next up for Arsenal was Chelsea at home. It was the first game at the Emirates to be played in front of a full ground in 16 months. But injuries and Covid issues left Arteta down to the bare bones once again. Aubameyang was available, but he was only fit enough to be on the bench. White, however, had to miss out after testing positive for Covid just before the game. Ødegaard was also unavailable due to visa issues following his move from Madrid.

Arsenal lost 2–0 and were well beaten. Chelsea barely had to break sweat, with Romelu Lukaku absolutely destroying Pablo Mari and Rob Holding.

'It's really challenging at the moment,' Arteta admitted after the defeat. 'We are missing nine players – and the majority of them are big senior players. It's what we have. Credit to the boys. They are playing with a lot of courage in this situation, which is tough. They are trying their best – but at the moment it's not enough to win football matches.'

The pressure was really mounting on Arteta. The full-time whistle against Chelsea was met by a chorus of boos from supporters. Up to that point they hadn't been able to make their feelings known about results and performances, but now they were finally back inside the stadium again that was all going to change.

'We'd be fooling ourselves [as] a club with this rich history, if anybody is going to be happy with that [performance],' Arteta said in response to the boos. 'When players get back, I think it will be completely different. Hopefully we will see a different squad, a different level in the way we can play – and different results. Then the story can change.'

The problem for Arteta was that Arsenal's next fixture was away at Manchester City. Another defeat felt inevitable. They were thumped 5–0, with Xhaka getting himself sent off in the first half. Arteta's side had just 19 per cent of possession and they failed to muster a single shot on target for the first time since before the 2003–04 season, when Opta records began. Arsenal had played three league games and lost them all, scoring no goals and conceding nine. It was now the worst start to a league season in the club's 134-year history.

'I don't think today is the day to talk about any process,' Arteta said after the game when asked whether fans should still 'trust the process'. 'I've always said I will be the one [to take responsibility]. I stand here today and I do exactly the same thing. It is [now] time to reflect, to look in the mirror, each of us, and try to change the dynamic straight away because we need to pick up results.'

There was an international break immediately after the defeat at City, and it certainly came at a good time for Arsenal. The transfer window also came to a close during that fortnight, with right-back Takehiro Tomiyasu arriving from Bologna on deadline day for £16 million. That took Arsenal's summer spending to around £145 million, the club's largest ever outlay on players in a single transfer window. A lot of players went out as well, although the only permanent deal saw Joe Willock sold to Newcastle for £25 million. Willian left right at the end of the window after he and the club agreed to terminate his contract two years early. Saliba joined Marseille on loan, Bellerin moved to Betis for the season and Reiss Nelson went to Feyenoord. It was a busy end to a dramatic window.

Arteta had started the summer by predicting that it would be 'unprecedented', and that's how it turned out. Given the age profile of all the players signed, it was far from clear whether they would be a success, but the squad was now really starting to feel like Arteta's. He had been heavily backed by the owners, and despite the poor start they were still very much behind him. You saw that briefly in a couple of clips from Amazon's *All or Nothing* documentary. Amazon had agreed a deal with Arsenal to document their season for their highly successful series, and the opening episode showed Josh Kroenke at the training camp during the opening weeks of the season with Arteta. At one point the pair are talking on one of the training pitches and you see Kroenke comforting Arteta and putting his arm around his shoulder when he admits that it's been a 'tough week' and that the 'clouds are dark'.

Arsenal's first game after the international break was against Norwich. It was a battle of the bottom two. Like Arsenal, Norwich had lost their first three games, but they sat above the Gunners because they had managed to score one goal during those three defeats. It was a game Arsenal simply had to win. They went into it under a lot of pressure and it was no surprise that it was a nervy contest settled by the odd goal. Aubameyang got it midway through the second half, tapping in from close range after Pépé had seen a shot hit the post.

It was a far from convincing success, but it did have the feel of something new to it. Ramsdale started in goal instead of Leno, White and Gabriel played together at centre-back for the first time, and Tomiyasu made his debut at right-back. It was a new-look backline for Arsenal. It felt fresh, which was what was needed.

Arteta's decision to start Ramsdale over Leno was certainly the one that raised the most eyebrows. When he arrived from Sheffield United the belief was that Ramsdale was very much coming in as understudy, albeit with the hope that he would one day replace the German once he had settled in. But no one expected it to happen as quickly as it did. 'We had to change something and Aaron has come here to try to make us better,' Arteta said. 'We needed a result and I decided to play him. That's all.'

Ramsdale kept his place in the team for the next game, at Burnley, and produced another clean sheet as Arsenal claimed a second 1–0 win, this time thanks to an Ødegaard free-kick. It was a battling performance. Gabriel and Tomiyasu were excellent, as was Ramsdale. Burnley tried to bully Arsenal. They pumped countless high balls into the box looking for an equaliser, but the visitors held firm and showed they were more than up for a physical battle. It was another important building block for this new-look Arsenal team, one that was vitally important ahead of the first meeting with Spurs of the season.

The north London derby is always important, but this one felt particularly big. While Arsenal had started the season with three straight defeats, Spurs had started it with three straight wins. Spurs were top of the table during that international break and Arsenal were bottom, much to the delight of their fans. But things had started to turn. Just three points now separated the sides going into the derby and Arsenal knew that a two-goal victory would see them move above their bitter rivals. It was also the first north London derby to be played in front of a capacity crowd since before the pandemic. The Emirates was rocking and it was expectant, but few would have predicted what was to happen during an incredible first half.

Arsenal were absolutely rampant. They blew Spurs away. They flew out of the blocks and were in front after just 12 minutes with a goal that was straight out of the club's Hale End academy. Saka was at the heart of it, driving towards the box before crossing for Smith Rowe to score. Smith Rowe then turned provider, launching a thrilling counter-attack which led to Aubameyang making it 2–0, before Saka raced through to add a third. Arsenal had scored 3 goals in 22 thrilling minutes. It was party time at the Emirates.

Spurs did pull one goal back in the second half as Arteta's side eased off the gas, but that did not take the gloss off a special win. If the narrow victories against Norwich and Burnley were the building blocks, this felt like the success that could ignite Arsenal's season. The performance had everything that Arteta wanted from his team. There was so much intensity all over the pitch. The forwards were pressing to win the ball high, and when they did the counter-attacks that followed were full of pace and intent. You could see and feel what the win meant to everyone, especially Arteta. The Spaniard had been under huge pressure during the early weeks of the season, and while the wins against Norwich and Burnley had eased that somewhat, he still needed something to really get the doubters on board. And nothing will do that more than a convincing win in the north London derby.

Arsenal had now won three league games in a row and sat just four points off the top four. After appearing to be in complete crisis just two weeks earlier, the club now felt like it was moving forward. There was a freshness about the side. There was the new-look backline, of course, while Partey was now back from injury and Ødegaard was pulling the strings in the final third, with Saka and Smith Rowe providing real energy and goal threat from out wide. The average age of Arsenal's starting XI in the derby was just 24, with Aubameyang the only player involved who was over 30. Even Lokonga and Tavares came on in the second half, which meant that all six of Arsenal's summer arrivals ended the game on the pitch together.

This felt like Arteta's team for the first time since he'd arrived. Aside from Aubameyang, every Arsenal player on the pitch at the final whistle had either been signed by Arteta or come through the academy. We'd always been told that this was a long-term process to reinvigorate Arsenal and these were the first real signs of it coming to fruition. Obviously it was still very early days, but the difference in mood around the club over such a short space of time was remarkable.

Rebuilding the relationship between the club and the fans was key to Arteta's plans when he first arrived at Arsenal. That proved to be impossible during his first couple of years thanks to the pandemic, with games being played behind closed doors. But now that fans were back inside stadiums he was determined to build that connection once again. Arteta had been shocked at just how broken the relationship had felt when he first arrived from Manchester City, and he always felt it would be impossible to turn things around at Arsenal without the supporters being fully behind the project. That's why the win against Spurs and the atmosphere it generated felt so significant. There was a feeling of togetherness there that had been missing.

One of the best things about the *All or Nothing* documentary was the insight it gave from inside the changing room, both before and after games, and Arteta's team talk before the Spurs match has become somewhat iconic. The drawings he did on the whiteboard of a heart and a brain have even been made into T-shirts. But the whole idea behind it was to symbolise to his players that if they played with both their heart and their heads, then the supporters inside the ground would give them the energy they needed to win the game. 'The moment you connect these three things, you are going to have a feeling on the pitch that you are invincible,' he said. 'That you are unstoppable.' That's certainly how things felt during that thrilling first half in the derby when Tottenham were simply blown away.

Two draws followed the derby success, against Brighton and Palace, before Villa were beaten 3–1 at the Emirates. That was the first of three successive league wins that saw Arteta's side move up to fifth in the table. One of those victories was against Leicester, a game that was notable not only for a fine 2–0 away success, but also a quite stunning save from Ramsdale to keep out a James Maddison free-kick. It was truly sensational, one of those stops that genuinely takes your breath away. It looked impossible for Ramsdale to even get a hand to Maddison's effort, which was heading for the top corner. Yet somehow he not only got a hand to it, but also managed to scoop it up onto the underside of the bar before the loose ball was eventually cleared.

That was one of eight saves that Ramsdale made in the game and it summed up the start to life he had enjoyed at Arsenal. There were a lot of question marks over him when he arrived for big money, some £24 million, but on the back of successive relegations, first with Bournemouth and then Sheffield United. Lots of fans didn't want him and Ramsdale actually had to deal with a lot of abuse sent his way via social media at the time.

'It was difficult,' he would later reveal, ahead of the *All or Nothing* launch a year after he signed for the club. 'I had a lot of negativity around the signing, with idiots online saying, "Don't sign!" Not necessarily death threats but threats saying, "We know where you live," and things like that, trying to scare me.'

It got so bad that Ramsdale had to turn off notifications and comments on his social media. But while there were some Arsenal fans who were far from convinced by him, Arteta was adamant that he was the keeper he wanted. He had been impressed by Ramsdale when the keeper had played against Arsenal for Sheffield United. But it wasn't just about his ability in terms of shot stopping, it was the personality that he played with, the character that came through on the pitch. He had the type of presence Arteta wanted. Getting the right goalkeeper was crucial to his way of playing. He needed someone who could play out from the back, who was comfortable with the ball at his feet, and Ramsdale ticked those boxes. No one had expected Leno to be moved aside so quickly, but the performances Ramsdale had produced since replacing him spoke for themselves. The clean sheet against Leicester was his fifth in eight appearances. He would go on to add another during a 1–0 success against Watford next time out, a win that made it nine games unbeaten for Arsenal in all competitions. Since being hammered in such embarrassing fashion at the Etihad before the international break, Arsenal had picked up 20 points from a possible 24 in the league, scoring 13 goals and conceding just four. Incredibly, they were now just six points behind leaders Chelsea.

There was a real sense of unity at the club again. The new signings had invigorated the squad and the young homegrown players like Saka and Smith Rowe had galvanised the fanbase. Belief was growing at Arsenal and that was a feeling Arteta was determined to harness. He wanted everyone pulling in the same direction. 'Without unity, you can't achieve what we want to achieve,' he said.

Connecting the club from top to bottom was something Arteta had worked hard on since his appointment. From his relationship with the owners right through to his dealings with Per Mertesacker at the academy, he wanted everything to be aligned. He had also pushed through big changes at the training ground. When he arrived he felt that the corridors around London Colney were too sterile, so he had pictures, murals and inspiring quotes put up on the walls throughout the complex. They were just little changes, but ones that he thought were important. For example, he had a huge club crest painted onto the walkway just before the main first-team training pitch with the phrase 'train to win' painted above it. It's the last thing the players now have to walk over before they start training each day. That kind of messaging is really important to Arteta. He also had a giant picture of Wenger put up right by the doors of the main building at the training centre. He wanted it to be the first thing the players saw when they walked into the building every morning. A quote from Wenger sits on the wall underneath it, which reads: 'Here you have the opportunity to get out the greatness that is in each of you.'

I asked Arteta once why he put that picture up and why having Wenger's presence at the training ground was so important to him. 'For me, it's something that we lost and we have to recover,' he said. 'I wanted that picture and a phrase that is very inspirational at the entrance because it was a big part of what he did at Colney and how everything started at the Emirates. You just look at his eyes and it's as if he's there. He has this capacity, he penetrates when he looks at you. The players really benefit from it. He had to be there.'

Arteta is big on that sort of thing. The motivational side of the game is so important to how he operates. One of his biggest strengths is his ability to get players to buy into his way of thinking. He wants them to feel like they are all part of the process. As part of the facelift he pushed through at London Colney, he moved out of the office that both Wenger and Emery had used, which was situated close to the entrance and away from everyone else, in favour of one that was next to the offices of other members of the coaching and management staff. He also started to hold meetings in an open space within the coaching area to try to build a sense of openness throughout the building, and he would regularly watch youth games and training sessions. That was something that insiders at the club would often criticise Emery for failing to do. Club legends were welcomed back, including David Seaman, who was brought in to help coach the academy goalkeepers. Arteta also opened the doors for Jack Wilshere to return, not as a player, but to train with the first team while he looked for a new club. Wilshere would also be given the opportunity to coach the academy sides while he was there so he could get his UEFA A Licence.

The win against Watford sent Arsenal into the second international break of the season sitting fifth in the table, just two points behind Liverpool in fourth, who they would play at Anfield after the break. It was a game that many felt would be an indicator of how far this new-look team had come in a short space of time. Arteta tried something different ahead of the game, which was shown in the *All or Nothing* documentary. In the days leading up to the match he had speakers wheeled out to the training pitch that played Liverpool's famous anthem 'You'll Never Walk Alone' loudly while the session was taking place. It was a tactic that certainly raised a few eyebrows. The idea was obvious, he wanted his players to get used to the sound of the crowd, but it did look a bit odd given that there were plenty of players in that squad who had experienced hostile atmospheres before.

Ødegaard later admitted he was a bit shocked by the whole thing and a few of us sat down with Ramsdale and Xhaka about a year later, and it was obvious what they thought of it. 'I'd never experienced speakers before,' Ramsdale laughed. 'I don't think they'll be coming back out.'

The whole idea came from a previous experience Arteta had endured at Anfield. It was when he was a player at Arsenal, during the 2013–14 season. Wenger's side travelled to Merseyside sitting top of the table but were blown away by a rampant Liverpool. The hosts were 4–0 up inside 20 minutes, and the game eventually finished 5–1, with Arteta scoring a late consolation penalty. It was a humbling result for Arsenal and an experience Arteta has never forgotten. He looks back on it as the only time in his career that he ever hid on the pitch. 'It's a regret that I live with,' he would later admit. 'I let myself down.'

He told his players this story during his pre-match team talk at Anfield, but it made no difference as Arsenal were hammered 4–0. They did bounce back with a 2–0 win against Newcastle but then a season that had just got back on track exploded during a dramatic fortnight.

Arsenal had two tricky away games in a row, at Manchester United and Everton. There was a lot of talk about the form of Aubameyang ahead of the game at Old Trafford. Arsenal's captain hadn't scored in four matches and had missed several good chances during that run. People were starting to question whether he warranted a place in the side, and those questions grew louder when he produced another anonymous display as Arsenal were beaten 3–2 at United.

It was getting harder to justify starting Aubameyang, so it was no surprise when he was left out of the starting XI for the trip to Everton. Things were going well for Arsenal at half-time at Goodison. They were leading 1–0 thanks to an Ødegaard volley, but Everton equalised late in the second half before Demarai Gray won it for the hosts in injury time. Arteta did throw Aubameyang on for the closing stages, and the striker had a great chance to equalise with the final kick of the game, but he dragged his effort wide.

After putting together a decent unbeaten run, Arsenal had now lost three of their last four matches. They were still just four points outside of the Champions League places, but the spate of defeats raised familiar questions. Arteta's side had crumbled amid a Liverpool onslaught at Anfield. They led against United, only to end up with nothing, and they did the same thing at Goodison.

'We have to do better when we have the lead,' Ødegaard said. 'I think it is [a mindset problem]. When you're leading 1–0 you get afraid to lose the win and, in my opinion, that's what we did wrong.'

It was a frustrating period for Arsenal, given the way they had been playing before the break, but things were about to get much worse. Arsenal's next game was against Southampton at the Emirates. The night before the match I started to get word that Aubameyang wasn't going to be involved. I put the feelers out, trying to find out exactly what was going on, but I couldn't get a proper answer. No one at Arsenal was saying anything and Aubameyang's camp was also staying silent. Someone suggested to me that he could be ill, but it felt like there was something bigger than that going on.

It didn't take long to find out. The next day we all travelled to the Emirates, and when the team was announced there was no Aubameyang. Arteta quickly revealed the reason why.

'Unfortunately, due to a disciplinary breach,' he said before kick-off. 'I think we have been very consistent that we have certain non-negotiables in the team that we have set ourselves as a club, and he's not involved today. It's certainly not an easy situation, or a situation that we want to have our club captain in.'

Arsenal won the game 3–0, but the match was a sideshow really. Arteta refused to go into any further details about Aubameyang in his post-match press conference. All he would say was 'it starts today' when asked whether Aubameyang's absence from the squad would be a long-term thing.

It soon emerged that the reason Aubameyang had been left out of the squad was because he had arrived home late after being given permission to travel to France to see his sick mother. Arsenal were understanding of Aubameyang's situation. They had allowed him to visit his mother the season before, even though that meant he missed three matches. So when he asked to do so again after the game at Goodison, Arteta and the club granted him special permission, even though they had banned all travel due to rising Covid cases throughout the country in the build-up to Christmas. It was made clear to Aubameyang, however, that he had to return on the Wednesday night so that he could train as normal on the Thursday ahead of the match with Southampton at the weekend.

Aubameyang did not arrive back in the UK until Thursday. Arteta felt that he had been let down by his captain, and what infuriated Arteta the most was that this wasn't the first time he'd had to take Aubameyang to task. There had been the incident before the north London derby earlier in the year when the forward was dropped for turning up late, the incident with the tattoo before that and the missed Covid test.

Some of Aubameyang's teammates felt he was being harshly treated, but Arteta was determined to show that everyone had to live by the same standards and that anyone who didn't, no matter how big a name they were, would be punished. Arteta felt he had to make a stand, and a few days after the Southampton game the club released a statement confirming that Aubameyang had been stripped of the captaincy.

'The decision that we have taken as a club is very clear,' Arteta said in the statement. 'It is because we believe that he has failed to be committed at the level that we all expect and agreed. That commitment and passion has to be there. Unfortunately, it wasn't.'

Arteta knew that Aubameyang was a popular figure within the squad. Just before the statement was released he gathered the players together at the training ground and told them what was going on. 'We have to set ourselves even bigger standards,' he said. 'The club and myself are not going to accept any behaviour like this. If we are going to change our culture and make sure we become a different club and team, we have to stand to those words clearly with anybody. This is the message I have to send you.'

Given the stature of Aubameyang, Arteta was well aware that his tough stance would divide opinion, especially with the fanbase. Aubameyang may have been struggling for form, but his goal record during his time at Arsenal spoke for itself. Taking your star striker out of the squad when you are trying to qualify for the Champions League was never going to be a decision that was universally accepted. Many felt Arteta was acting like a dictator, that he was using Aubameyang to show how strong he was. That was something Arteta was quick to deny, however.

'I don't establish my authority by being dictatorial or by trying to be ruthless,' he said. 'I'm not going to ask them to put the ball in the top corner every time they shoot, but I am going to ask them to do the right thing every single day for this club, that's for sure.'

Aubameyang was removed from the squad while talks continued about what would happen next. He was still allowed into Colney, he still parked in his same spot every day and he was still able to see his teammates around the complex. But he was not involved in training at all. He had two fitness coaches who would work with him to keep his fitness up, but that was it. He wasn't involved in team meetings and obviously didn't travel to games. It was an extremely difficult situation for everyone involved, but it certainly sent a message out in terms of exactly how Arteta expected everyone to behave. There's a great clip in *All or Nothing* which shows Mo Elneny and Rob Holding chatting in the canteen at London Colney about what was going on. 'The boss has balls,' Elneny says. 'Yeah, the boss has balls,' Holding agrees.

The reason Arteta felt so strongly about the whole thing was that he was determined to change the culture at Arsenal. He'd been working on that from the moment he'd arrived and felt that he was making good headway. So to have his captain consistently dropping below the standards he was demanding from everyone else was something he believed couldn't continue. He felt that if he didn't take action, it would send out the wrong message to people at all levels of the club. Not just to the first team, but all the way down to the youngsters who were coming through at the academy. The way he acted certainly left no room for any doubt. It was clear that if you wanted to succeed at Arsenal under Arteta, you had to work by his standards.

I spoke to Per Mertesacker, Arsenal's academy manager, about the impact Arteta had had across all levels of the club in terms of the way he operates. 'It makes it so much easier for me now,' he said. 'I can really ask the players the question: What will Mikel say about this behaviour going into the first team? Do you think from what you've just seen that Mikel Arteta will accept this behaviour? Not from what I'm telling you, but from what you've just seen? This is pretty impactful.'

Arteta kept a record of every incident involving Aubameyang. He detailed the dates and times that the striker had been late as well as the conversations the pair had had. This was evidence that the club made available to their lawyers while discussions continued over Aubameyang's continued absence from the squad. On the pitch, Arsenal were thriving without him. After beating Southampton 3–0, they won their next four games in a row, scoring 16 goals in the process and conceding just two. When they thumped Norwich 5–0 at Carrow Road on Boxing Day they sat fourth in the table and were just six points behind second-placed Liverpool. Goals were coming from everywhere. Saka was scoring, as was Smith Rowe. Lacazette had come in to replace Aubameyang as the central striker and was proving to be an excellent link man for the other attackers around him. Arsenal were in buoyant mood and the timing was perfect, considering they had Manchester City to play at the Emirates on New Year's Day.

But their preparations for that game were rocked when Arteta tested positive for Covid in the days leading up to it. Cases had been spiking across the country during the festive season and lots of fixtures had been cancelled. Arsenal had managed to stay relatively unscathed up to that point. But Arteta falling victim to the virus once again meant he had to stay at home, so he couldn't take training and wasn't allowed at the stadium for the game. He had a feed set up in his house so he could watch and speak to the players in the changing room as normal, but it was assistant manager Albert Stuivenberg who led the sessions at Colney and who was on the touchline for the match.

The Dutchman is seen as a relatively calming influence at Arsenal. A forward-thinking coach who is well respected throughout the game, both he and Steve Round are Arteta's chief assistants and have very different traits that work well together. Stuivenberg is seen more as the thinker, someone who operates more on the tactical side of things. He is known as AirPods Albert by the fans because he is always in communication with club analysts during games – standing next to Arteta with his AirPods in, receiving information and passing it on.

Round, meanwhile, is someone who has been in and around Premier League teams for years. He's someone who knows the league, knows what the players need and works with them to get the best out of them, not just physically but mentally as well. Arteta values both men highly and they are very popular with the players. Andreas Georgson worked with both during his year on Arteta's staff before moving to Malmo, and Arsenal's former set-piece coach believes Stuivenberg and Round are essential to how Arteta operates.

'They are very important and carefully selected,' he said. 'Mikel knew exactly what he wanted from those two closest to him because they are very different and have very different qualities. But they complement each other and they complement Mikel very well. He bounces one type of idea off one of them and a whole different type of idea or situation with the other. So there is no conflict of interest between them. There is no prestige with them, they are very well grounded in what they offer to the process and it's different things. It's not a coincidence that they were chosen. Mikel knew exactly what he would get and what he needed to be complemented with.

'Managing a Premier League team, you need so many different things. You need man management, you need to understand the psychology of the game. It's not so much to do with football, but dealing with a group of staff and players that are living under extreme pressure and expectation. And then the other side of managing is, of course, creating the next game plan, the next opponent analysis to get the right technical and tactical details in. Sometimes staff can compete over oxygen. Everyone wants to come up with the best tactical idea. I think it's good when one is more aware that this is his area and then it's also equally as important that one picks up on other things and treats a staff member that needs a hug or a bit of an uplift. It's a clever balance of this duo.'

Arteta is never shy when it comes to paying tribute to his staff. He has won several individual awards during his time at Arsenal and every one has been celebrated with a picture alongside the entire coaching team. That's something he is very keen on. It's all about the collective, not the individual. So he had no concerns over Stuivenberg taking charge for the game against City, which was something he was keen to point out before the match. 'He's someone who is very close to me and he's more than capable,' Arteta said. 'He's done it before, so in that sense I'm very relaxed about it.'

Given the form Arsenal took into the game against City, there was real expectation that they could give Guardiola's runaway league leaders a real game, even with Arteta at home watching from the sofa. And they did just that. For 57 minutes, Arsenal were electric. They were all over City and were thoroughly deserving of their 1–0 lead thanks to a superb Saka goal.

The first half was as good as Arsenal had ever played under Arteta. Martinelli and Saka were electric down the flanks and Partey was monstrous in midfield. City didn't even muster a shot on target before the break. For the first time in a long time Arsenal were playing the way they wanted to play against City. They weren't trying to simply contain Guradiola's side; they were taking the game to them, and that felt very significant.

But the match then changed completely during four crazy minutes around the hour mark. There was a Manchester City penalty awarded by VAR after a foul by Xhaka, a goal-line clearance from Nathan Ake, an open-goal miss by Martinelli and a red card for Gabriel. It was a remarkable passage of play that paved the way for a last-minute City winner from Rodri. It was a real smash-and-grab job by the champions and there was a huge sense of injustice in the stadium. Arsenal were furious at the decisions that had gone against them, as was Arteta back at home.

It was a defeat that started a dismal run that stretched throughout January. Arsenal went out of the FA Cup in the third round after producing an awful performance at Championship side Nottingham Forest, going down 1–0. They also went out of the Carabao Cup, losing a two-legged semi-final against Liverpool, and were held to a disappointing 0–0 draw at home to Burnley in the league.

They were also due to play at Spurs in the second north London derby of the season, but the game was called off after Arsenal requested a postponement due to a lack of players. Rules that had been brought in by the Premier League during the pandemic stated that teams could apply for a match to be called off if they had fewer than 14 players available (13 outfield players and a goalkeeper). Arsenal, due to a combination of injuries, Covid and players being away at the Africa Cup of Nations, had just 12 players who would have been able to feature. So the Premier League granted their request and the derby was postponed, with the official announcement coming around 24 hours before the game was due to kick off. It was a decision that caused considerable anger at Spurs. They felt Arsenal had used the Covid rules to their advantage.

'We are extremely surprised that this application has been approved,' Tottenham said in a statement. 'The original intention of the guidance was to deal with player availability directly affected by Covid cases, resulting in depleted squads that when taken together with injuries would result in the club being unable to field a team. We do not believe it was the intent to deal with player availability unrelated to Covid. We may now be seeing the unintended consequences of this rule.'

Spurs' frustration came because out of all the Arsenal players who would have been absent, only two were due to Covid. The rest were missing due to injury or being away with their national teams. Arsenal had also just chosen to send Folarin Balogun and Ainsley Maitland-Niles out on loan, which infuriated their rivals even further.

'Abusing the rules,' former Spurs midfielder Jamie O'Hara fumed on social media. 'Sent players on loan a week ago then ask for games to get called off. Disgrace from the Premier League, meant to set the standard for every other league and it's a shambles.'

O'Hara was far from alone in holding views like that. Arsenal were widely hammered for the ruling, with fans, pundits and sections of the media all having their say. The criticism was really harsh and Arsenal still feel bitter about it to this day. So many fixtures had been called off throughout December and January and there had never been a reaction like the one that greeted the Premier League's announcement over the Tottenham game.

Arsenal had only ever tried to have one match called off before this request, and that was the game at Brentford on the opening day of the season. On that occasion the Premier League pretty much forced them to play, even though they were in no real state to do so. Since then they had always just got on with it, even when an injury-hit Wolves had their match at the Emirates postponed just before Christmas or when a severely depleted Liverpool managed to have the first leg of the Carabao Cup semi-final called off when they conveniently managed to uncover what subsequently turned out to be a batch of false positive test results just ahead of the game.

'We didn't have the players necessary to have a squad available,' Arteta said in the face of fierce criticism. 'That is 100 per cent guaranteed. We know that we did the right thing. We will defend our club tooth and nail. We're not going to have anybody damaging our name or trying to lie about things that haven't occurred. We played against Forest when we had ten players out. We went to Liverpool and we played when we had many players out. We got to the point where we could not get a squad available as is required in this league to play a game. That's why we didn't play – as simple as that.'

Amid all the controversy, the January transfer window was in full swing, and as usual Arsenal were being linked with several names. Fiorentina striker Dusan Vlahovic was the player making all the headlines, with countless reports coming out of Italy about multiple bids from Arsenal. This was a tough story to follow. Arsenal's interest in Vlahovic was being widely reported by various outlets, but I was always adamantly told that while he was a player Arsenal had been looking at, the club were not actively pushing for him and that he wasn't a top target. So it was always one I steered away from. It just felt like one of those stories that was being driven by different parties. For Fiorentina it worked, because it allowed them to drive his price up amid interest from elsewhere. And from Vlahovic's camp it was never going to be a bad thing to have their client consistently mentioned in the same breath as Arsenal. I was not surprised when he ended up going to Juventus for big money towards the end of the window.

Arsenal did hold talks over a move for Juventus midfielder Arthur Melo and at one point it looked like a deal could happen. Melo's agent Federico Pastorello travelled to London Colney to try to get things over the line, but in the end Arsenal walked away. They wanted a straight loan deal until the end of the season, but Juventus wanted an obligation-to-buy clause inserted so that the move would be turned permanent in the summer. Melo stayed in Turin, which made for a quiet window for Arsenal in terms of incomings. Very little happened aside from striking a deal with MLS side New England Revolution which would see goalkeeper Matt Turner arrive in the summer.

The big thing that needed to be sorted out was, of course, Aubameyang. Arsenal's former captain was still at the club, and as the window ticked by there was little sign of him moving on. Arteta was coming under pressure – not just from the fans, but also the hierarchy at the club – to reintegrate him into the squad. There was a growing feeling that the situation could not be allowed to continue through until the end of the season. Arsenal were trying to qualify for the Champions League and it was clear that having Aubameyang sitting at home on a match day despite being paid well over £300,000 a week was not going to help with that. There is a clip in the *All or Nothing* documentary which highlighted this perfectly. Edu, Vinai Venkatesham and director of football operations Richard Garlick are all sitting in Edu's office at London Colney talking about the situation.

'He has to come back to the squad and help us until the end of the season,' Edu says.

'We're going to have to reintegrate him,' Venkatesham agrees.

Garlick then adds: 'There needs to be a conversation with Mikel, then.'

But Arteta was unmoved when that conversation did happen. He felt the trust between himself and the player had gone, and from his point of view there was no coming back from that. He was adamant that Aubameyang would not be brought back into the fold no matter the circumstances. That obviously left the club in a difficult position. They agreed to put all efforts into getting him out, but with transfer deadline day approaching there was still nothing concrete on the table. Saudi Arabian side Al-Nassr were interested, but Aubameyang did not want to go there. Barcelona were also keeping tabs on the situation, but the feeling was that they had to move players on before any deal could be discussed. It was a waiting game, one that eventually burst into life during the final 24 hours of the window. Barcelona called and made an offer for Aubameyang, but they wanted him on loan until the end of the season. That was not what Arsenal wanted. They knew that if they loaned him, the situation would just be repeated in the summer once he returned. For Arsenal the preference was to terminate Aubameyang's contract and get him out permanently.

Talks continued during a crazy final day of the window. Aubameyang even flew to Barcelona without the permission of the club. The first Arsenal knew about it was when videos started to do the rounds on social media of him arriving at the airport. The rest of the Arsenal squad were in Dubai at the time for a warm-weather training camp. Aubameyang was meant to be at London Colney keeping his fitness levels up. When Arsenal called his agents to ask what was going on, they were told that he had flown out for personal reasons, as his father lived there.

As the day progressed it started to look more and more likely that a deal would not be done. Both clubs had made their positions known and were refusing to budge. But then, with just a few hours remaining, Barcelona blinked. They agreed to cover Aubameyang's wages for the following season and that Arsenal could terminate his contract, allowing him to sign a three-year deal with the La Liga outfit. It was the dream scenario for Arsenal. It brought an end to a situation that was not helping anyone, took away the distraction it was causing and saved them around £20 million in wages in the long run. But it was also a huge risk.

Aubameyang was one of six January departures, which left the squad ending the month looking weaker than when it had started. With no new striker coming in, Arteta had just Lacazette and Nketiah to call upon for the second half of the season, both of whom were out of contract in the summer. It was a huge gamble with Champions League qualification on the line. Arteta could have put a plaster over his relationship with Aubameyang to try to secure a top-four spot, but he stuck to his guns and went down the other route, letting him go without signing a replacement. It was obvious that should things now go wrong, the finger of blame would be pointed squarely in his direction.

'I am extremely grateful for what Auba has done at the club, for his contribution since I've been here,' Arteta said following the striker's exit. 'The way I see myself in that relationship is the solution, not the problem, 100 per cent. I can look in the eye of anybody.'

There was at least a sense of relief at Arsenal that the soap opera had been put behind them. With the window shut and Aubameyang gone, the team could move forward without any distractions over the second half of the season. The squad returned from Dubai and all the talk was that it had been a very successful camp. Arteta and the coaching staff spent a lot of time running bonding sessions for the team while they were away, something he is very keen on. Arteta is a serious guy, but he knows he has to try different things to keep the squad switched on and motivated. He places a lot of demands on them when they are training, but when they are together in the team hotel he places a real emphasis on the group having fun together. Staging 'spot the difference' games is a particular favourite. Playing games of dodgeball is another.

The break in Dubai certainly seemed to help Arsenal. After enduring such a miserable January, they returned to pick up a hugely important 1–0 win at Wolves, the first of five successive league wins. Brentford were beaten, then Wolves were seen off again in thrilling fashion at a raucous Emirates, before six points were taken from Watford and Leicester. Liverpool ended the winning run with a 2–0 success in north London, but when Arsenal bounced back to win 1–0 at Aston Villa a few days later, they took a firm stranglehold on the race for the Champions League places. They were now fourth, four points clear of fifth-placed Manchester United with a game in hand and six points clear of Spurs. It felt like a huge win and it was a big day for the manager. It was the day the 'We've got Super Mik Arteta' chant was born. There were some fantastic scenes at the end when it was sung over and over again in the away end as the Spaniard and his players celebrated in front of the fans at full-time.

'That's what gives sense to everything that we do,' Arteta said in the press conference afterwards, when asked how it had made him feel. 'You realise it in those moments that those people have big emotions towards the club, and if we can make them happy then everything just makes sense. The connection that they show with the players and with me as well, we have to be very grateful because they have come on this journey and I think they believe in what we do.' Arteta had worked so hard on building that connection between the team and the fanbase and this was a day when you really started to see the results of that.

The win at Villa put Arsenal in such a strong position in terms of the top four and sent them into the final international break of the season in a confident mood. There was a real sense of momentum around the club. But that all came crashing down at Selhurst Park a fortnight later when Arsenal travelled to Crystal Palace to begin the end-of-season run-in. It was a miserable night in south London, one that would have dire consequences for Arsenal's season.

Just before kick-off we learned that Kieran Tierney was absent. He'd played for Scotland over the international break and had returned with an issue with his knee. At the time it was unclear just how serious the problem was, but it would ultimately rule him out for the remainder of the campaign. He was replaced by Nuno Tavares at Selhurst Park, and the summer signing from Benfica had a nightmare evening and was hauled off at half-time by Arteta.

By that point Arsenal were already two goals behind and things got even worse after the interval. Wilfried Zaha added a third for the home side from the penalty spot, but in the build-up to the goal Arsenal lost Partey to yet another thigh injury. It would soon emerge that Partey, like Tierney, would not play again all season. Coming away from the ground that night it felt like the injury issues were more harmful to Arsenal's chances of securing qualification to the Champions League than the result itself. Tierney and Partey were so integral to Arsenal's team that losing one would have been bad enough, but to lose both at the same time was disastrous.

Arsenal had Brighton next and Arteta opted to use Xhaka at left-back instead of Tavares. It was a big call, especially as it meant both Xhaka and Partey would be missing from central midfield. Sambi Lokonga came in to partner Elneny there and Ødegaard was asked to play in a much deeper role than he was usually accustomed to. The plan didn't work. The changes left the side looking unbalanced and Arsenal really struggled again, losing 2–1. Brighton, who went into the match having scored just one goal in their previous seven games, were deserving winners.

It felt like a body blow for Arsenal. They now found themselves fifth, three points behind Spurs, although they did still have a game in hand. The back-to-back defeats had sucked the life out of their top-four bid and the injuries to Tierney and Partey had left an already small squad looking woefully short of what was going to be required during the final eight games of the season. With games against Chelsea and Manchester United looming large, you felt Arsenal had to go to Southampton next time out and get a result if they were to have any chance.

Arteta needed to find a system that made up for the loss of two of his most influential players. Xhaka had to come back into midfield and Ødegaard had to return to his role higher up the pitch because Arsenal were now looking toothless up front. They had lost three of their last four league games and had only scored twice during that run. It was a statistic that brought firmly back into focus the decision to let Aubameyang leave without bringing in another striker. It had now been four months since Lacazette had scored from open play. His only goal during 2022 had come from the penalty spot against Leicester. Meanwhile, Aubameyang had scored ten goals in his first 14 games at Barcelona.

'Laca's contribution to the team in many other ways has been phenomenal,' Arteta said in defence of his stand-in captain. 'Of course we want the strikers to score goals and we know we require them to do that. But Laca has a really important quality, which is that he makes the people around him better.'

The big issue now, though, was that even Lacazette's link-up play had let him down. Following the defeat at Everton on 6 December and up to the win at Watford on 6 March, he contributed seven assists in ten games. But he had now gone five matches without one, and during the 90 minutes against Brighton he only made eight passes and had just 22 touches. It felt like something had to change, and it did at Southampton, with Arteta leaving his skipper out and bringing in Eddie Nketiah as the central striker. It seemed like the correct call, as did restoring Xhaka to the midfield and bringing Tavares back in at left-back. Arsenal were much improved, but they lost again. They dominated, had 23 shots to Southampton's nine, but couldn't score. A Jan Bednarek strike just before half-time made it three defeats on the spin for Arteta's side, who now looked down and out. It had been a nightmare few weeks for Arsenal and they now faced back-to-back games against Chelsea and United in the space of just three days.

This was last-chance-saloon territory for Arsenal. Spurs had lost at home to Brighton on the same day that Arteta's side had been beaten at Southampton, which did at least give them a chance. But they still travelled to Stamford Bridge sitting sixth in the table, three points adrift of their neighbours and also behind United on goal difference. You felt that Arsenal had to win at Chelsea or their chances of a top-four spot were all but over.

It was a huge night and Arsenal produced an excellent performance. Arteta brought Elneny back into the side after dropping him for the defeat at Southampton, and the Egyptian was exceptional alongside Xhaka in midfield. White was also shifted out to right-back in place of Cédric Soares, with Rob Holding coming in to partner Gabriel at centre-back. Arteta again started with Nketiah instead of Lacazette, and the young striker, who had been released by Chelsea as a teenager, scored twice. Smith Rowe also scored, as did Saka, who slotted home a penalty in the final minute.

This was a big moment for Saka. It was his first ever penalty for Arsenal and it was the first spot kick he had taken since he missed the decisive penalty in the Euro 2020 final for England against Italy. The online abuse that Saka had to endure after that miss at Wembley a year earlier had been utterly shameful. As a club, Arsenal had rallied around Saka, and the way he handled the whole thing was yet another example of what an impressive young man he is. But there was still a huge sense of closure when Saka scored that penalty at Stamford Bridge. You could see exactly what it meant to him when he celebrated in front of the travelling Arsenal fans.

'I thought that Gabi [Martinelli] was going to take it,' Arteta said afterwards. 'When I saw Bukayo, honestly, the first thing that I thought was back to the summer and what happened. But, I said to you guys, when that happens to Bukayo, that happened for a reason and he learned so much and he matured so much, that's why he's having the season that he's had. For him to have the courage to say "I'm going to take it again", because I'm sure it was in the back of his mind, for me it's *chapeau* even if he had missed it.'

The win sent Arsenal into their game with United a couple of days later with renewed belief. The top-four dream felt like it was over after Southampton, but now there was a sense it was on again and victory over United would only add to that. United still had an outside chance of fourth themselves, but really had to win in north London to give themselves a chance during the final few games. That only added to the occasion at a cauldron-like Emirates.

It was a thrilling game. Tavares and Saka scored early on – Saka's once again from the penalty spot – then Cristiano Ronaldo pulled one back for United. Bruno Fernandes missed a penalty in the second half to equalise and Arsenal took advantage when Xhaka thumped in one of his trademark strikes from distance to seal a 3–1 for the home side and spark wild celebrations. It was a special moment for Xhaka. No one would ever have imagined he would still be at the club to enjoy a moment like this after he had stormed off the pitch to that chorus of boos and abuse against Crystal Palace less than three years earlier. He had come full circle, much to the delight of Arteta.

'I was dreaming of that because he deserves it,' the manager said after the game. 'If every fan, or individual, spent five, ten minutes with Granit – or even two minutes is enough – they will understand the person that he is and how much he cares about the club. He feels loved [now], so thank you to everyone, to the fans for showing that dedication to him, because I know how much that means to him.'

Arsenal were now two points clear of Spurs in fourth, a gap they maintained when they went to West Ham the following weekend and won 2–1 thanks to goals from Gabriel and Holding. Arsenal had seen Spurs beat Leicester earlier in the afternoon so were under real pressure to win at the London Stadium. It wasn't the best performance, but they showed a lot of fight to battle it out. The way they had responded to the successive defeats against Palace, Brighton and Southampton was hugely impressive and they were now just two wins away from securing qualification to the Champions League. They had Leeds and Spurs to come. Win both and a top-four spot would be assured with two games remaining. It was that simple.

Arteta signed a new contract just ahead of the Leeds game, committing himself to the club until 2025. There was some surprise about the timing of it. Many felt Arsenal should have seen how the season was going to pan out before making a decision. But there was never any doubt at board level or from the owners about Arteta, so they didn't think they needed to wait. They felt he deserved a new deal and they wanted his future secured.

'It provides stability and clarity for the future and helps us all move forward together effectively,' Josh Kroenke said. 'Mikel's commitment and passion are clear for everyone to see. We are confident that, as we move forward, he will get us back to competing for the top trophies in the game.'

Arteta was happy to commit and he believed the timing was right, as it sent a message not just to players already at the club, but also those who were being targeted as potential new arrivals for the summer. He didn't want any uncertainty about his future to become a distraction.

The build-up to the Leeds game was dominated by a song that had become a bit of a social-media phenomenon. Louis Dunford is an Islington-based singer, an Arsenal fan who grew up in the shadow of Highbury and the Emirates. He'd been having a few pints with a mate a couple of weeks before the Leeds match and was watching a video clip of himself performing one of his songs at a gig he had done at the Union Chapel in Islington. The song was called 'The Angel' and it was a homage to his north London neighbourhood.

'We were sat in the pub and my mate was going to me, "They've got to play it at the Emirates,"' Dunford told me during an interview at the time. 'So, as a genuine joke, I tagged Arsenal on Twitter and said "Play 'The Angel'. The people want it." I was just thinking that my small following of Twitter fans would think it was funny. And then, the next day, I woke up and it had exploded overnight. I had over 1,000 retweets. I couldn't understand what had happened. Over the next couple of days I went from having 2,000 followers to 10,000, then 15,000, then 30,000. I was like, "Fucking hell, all this over a drunk joke!"'

The online reaction to the song was genuinely remarkable. It struck an immediate chord with large swathes of the Arsenal fanbase and within days the track had reached number two in the iTunes chart; only Lady Gaga kept it off top spot. But Dunford's *Popham* EP, which 'The Angel' is on, went one better and topped the album chart. 'It was fucking mad,' Dunford said. 'I was looking at the chart and I was above Ed Sheeran and Harry Styles.'

Arsenal were being swamped by requests from fans for the song to be played at the Emirates. Arteta himself received thousands of messages calling for it to happen and he seized on it. He'd spent so much time trying to connect the club from top to bottom since his arrival and that work had really started to pay off during this season. For the first time in a long time the supporters were watching a team they really felt something for. You could feel it at every game, home or away. Arteta had built such a likeable team. It was young, it was vibrant. There were homegrown players, there were players like Ramsdale and White who had that personality on the pitch that fans just loved. As the season wore on you could sense that something was growing at the club. It felt new, it felt fun again and Arteta was determined to harness that.

He knew how important it was to embrace the crowd, something he'd made clear from his first ever press conference when he was appointed in 2019. He'd been searching for a long time for a song that could potentially become a club anthem, to be played at the Emirates before kick-off and which would bring the fans and team even closer together. So when 'The Angel' suddenly burst onto the scene he was all over it.

Arteta played it to the players at the training ground during a team meeting and Dunford was then invited to London Colney. He met Arteta and the team and then he was a guest of the club for the game against Leeds. He sat in the directors' box as his song was played just ahead of kick-off as the players formed their pre-match huddle. Despite the popularity of the song and the social-media movement that it had generated, you still weren't quite sure what to expect when it was played. Would the fans in the stadium join in? Would they know the words? Would they even care? These were all questions that were answered emphatically as thousands belted out the chorus with their arms aloft and their scarves in the air. It was the moment Dunford officially handed over ownership of his song to the Arsenal fanbase.

'I'll never forget what you lot have done for me and this song over the last couple of weeks,' he tweeted after the game. 'Whatever happens – the song belongs to you now. Thank you. North London Forever!'

Arteta would describe it as an 'emotional moment', and it was. Arsenal had tried and failed with club anthems in the past. The Elvis hit 'The Wonder of You' had been trialled years earlier, but it had all felt very forced. This time was different. It was the fans who were driving things this time. They wanted it and Arteta and the club were happy to oblige.

'So many things came together at the same time and it just struck a chord,' Raymond Herlihy of the prominent Arsenal supporters group REDaction said. 'Everyone loves a sing-along chorus and I think that clip that they play before kick-off is absolutely perfect. I'm hugely proud to be from that area of London and obviously a lot of other people are. But we've also got the global fanbase and the people that come to matches can come down to north London and get to sing about it. It was the perfect storm really and that is where Mikel really gets it. He understands that connection and how important it can be. As much as I loved Arsène Wenger, very rarely would he mention the fans, the connection, or the atmosphere. Obviously we had some great teams back then and they didn't always need us. But having been involved in fan groups for a long time, there was always something missing. Arsène didn't really mention it, but Mikel has gone very, very heavy on that. You can see he believes in that connection and the importance of it.'

Two goals from Nketiah were enough to give Arsenal a 2–1 win against Leeds. They were now just 90 minutes away from the promised land. If Arteta's side could go to Spurs and win, they would be guaranteed fourth, no matter what happened in the final two games of the season. North London derbies are always huge occasions, but this was monumental for both teams with Champions League football at stake. Given how Arsenal had started the season, it was remarkable really for them to be in the position they were now in. There was talk of a relegation battle when they began the campaign with those three painful defeats without even scoring a goal. But since then, with Arteta's new-look team firmly bedded in, they had won 21 of their 32 league games to turn things around completely and leave themselves one more victory away from returning to Europe's elite club competition for the first time since 2017.

'We don't have to explain the importance of the match,' Arteta said, when looking ahead to the trip to Tottenham. 'Everybody is aware of that. We have the opportunity now against them to do it and all our mood and our energy is going to be directed in that way. Let's go for it.'

This was a north London derby that was four months in the making. It should have been played in January but was, of course, postponed amidst huge controversy after the Premier League agreed to Arsenal's request to have it called off due to a lack of players. Spurs were fuming at the time and that anger hadn't really died down in the four months that followed.

You could feel that extra hostility when you arrived at the stadium. Spurs had to win. Even a draw would have left Arsenal only needing to pick up one victory from their final two matches. It was win or bust for Antonio Conte's side. Arsenal knew they would have another chance should the result go against them, but with a very difficult trip to Newcastle on the horizon they wanted to get the job done there and then.

The atmosphere was incredible and Arsenal actually started pretty well. But then Tottenham were given an incredibly soft penalty following a challenge by Cédric on Son Heung-min and the game changed completely. Kane scored the penalty and then within a few minutes Holding had picked up two quick bookings and was sent off. It was calamitous stuff and there was no way back from it. Kane scored a second before half-time and then Son made it 3–0 soon after the interval.

In the end Arsenal were fortunate to get away from the ground with just a 3–0 defeat. It felt like the occasion was too much for them and Holding's red card was a symbol of that. He was too highly charged and couldn't keep his emotions in check. It felt like a hammer blow for Arsenal. It wasn't just the defeat, it was the manner of it. Mentally, you knew it would take its toll and that it was going to be incredibly hard to bounce back from it in the four days they now had before the Newcastle game. Gabriel had also limped off before the end, and with Tierney and Partey sidelined, White having not played since the win against United thanks to a hamstring injury, and Holding now suspended, it was the last thing Arsenal needed.

Arteta tried to pick his players up. He defended them after the Spurs defeat, but there was no defending them after Newcastle. Spurs had beaten Burnley 24 hours earlier to move above their neighbours into fourth, so Arsenal knew they had to win at St James' Park. With Tottenham travelling to already-relegated Norwich on the final day, there was simply no room for error. But Arsenal never even looked like winning.

Gabriel and White were patched up and paired together at centre-back, but they were clearly not fit. Tomiyasu started but did his hamstring inside half an hour and had to be replaced. It was one game too far for Arsenal. Despite everything that was at stake, they couldn't compete with a Newcastle side that blew them away on the night. It was 2–0, but it could have been far more. Arsenal's Champions League dream was now all but over; it had been crushed in the space of four traumatic days. The disappointment was palpable. 'Mathematically it was in our hands,' Arteta said. 'That feeling will take some time to go away.'

Arsenal went into the final game of the season two points behind Spurs. The only way they could snatch fourth place was by beating Everton at the Emirates and hoping bottom of the table Norwich could somehow beat Tottenham at Carrow Road. No one really believed it would happen. Arsenal did their job, thumping Everton 5–1, but Tottenham also hit five as they brushed Norwich aside 5–0.

So it was a fifth-placed finish for Arsenal, which certainly represented progress having finished eighth in the previous two seasons. Internally, the club's target at the start of the campaign had been to finish in the top six and bring European football back to Emirates Stadium – something Arteta had achieved comfortably. So in that context, he had done exactly what he had been asked to do. And there was no doubt he had created an atmosphere around the club that hadn't existed for a long time. There was a carnival-like atmosphere inside the Emirates during the victory against Everton and that was very telling. While parts of social media may have been its usual sea of toxicity after the Newcastle capitulation, there was no sense of negativity or division inside the stadium on that final day.

'They can see what we're doing,' Arteta said. 'They can see what the players want to do, how they represent the club and who we are as a group.' Arsenal had given supporters so much to enjoy during the past ten months and they had done it with the youngest team in the league. As disappointing as the finish was, the progress was clear. The squad had been overhauled, the wage bill had been slashed, the age of the squad had been drastically reduced, and a new and vibrant young team had established a connection with match-going fans that had been almost totally lost.

It felt fun to go to the Emirates again. For years it had felt like a bit of a chore, as if you were going to games because you had to, rather than because you actually wanted to. But that had changed. It was exciting to watch Arsenal again. The fans had a team that they believed in, that they really felt something for. Never was that more evident than on that final day against Everton.

The key thing now for Arsenal was to build on the progress they had made. There was no time to feel sorry for themselves after letting the Champions League slip through their fingers. The club had a big summer ahead of it. They wanted to be aggressive in the transfer market and were already in talks with Gabriel Jesus over a move from Manchester City.

'We will take the club to the next level,' Arteta said. 'That is the ambition. In order to do that we have a very clear plan again.'

PART FIVE

PASSION

(2022–23)

There was understandably a real sense of disappointment at Arsenal about how the season had ended. Having had Champions League qualification in their hands and then to throw it away right at the end was always going to take a while to get over. But with no international tournament taking place over the summer, the players had a chance to properly wind down. Arteta did as well, taking his wife and three sons to spend some time with his older sister in Majorca, like he does most summers.

Family is a huge part of Arteta's life. He tries as hard as possible to shut things out and devote as much time to his wife and children as he can, although it's something he admits he still needs to improve on. When you have a work ethic like he does, it can be very difficult to switch off.

Arteta married his wife Lorena in 2010, but they met back in San Sebastian when they were just 19. 'I fell in love very quickly,' Arteta revealed during an interview with the

Telegraph. 'As soon as I saw her I think I knew she was for me. But I had to work hard, she did well on that.'

The family now live together in London, but it was not always like that. When Arteta was appointed in 2019, Lorena and the children were still living in Los Angeles, and that was a difficult period for the Arsenal boss. He values his time at home highly. He loves to entertain and barbecue, spending time building the fire with his children. It's one of his favourite ways to wind down after a difficult day. Even in the depths of winter he will be out in his back garden doing it. The barbecue is one of the central features of the house. It is engraved with his and Lorena's initials along with the quote '*Que nunca se nos apague el fuego*', which translates as 'May the fire never go out'.

Hosting barbecues has always been a big part of Arteta's life. As Arsenal captain he would often have teammates round. Santi Cazorla, André Santos and Bacary Sagna were regular visitors to have some food and watch the football. The Spaniard would host El Clásico nights whenever Barcelona played Real Madrid.

'The first thing he would tell me before I could even say hello was about the formation the teams would play,' Sagna recalled. 'I had not even been in the house for a minute and he was already hammering me. "What do you think? Will they play 3-5-2?" All I was doing was just looking for the snacks. But this is something you want from a football lover. He always lived football.'

It's that devotion to the game that made Arsenal's end of season collapse so difficult to take for Arteta. Those who work closely with him say how difficult he finds it to shake off a defeat. He knew what securing a top-four spot would have meant to the club and to the wider project at Arsenal, so he felt the pain of missing out more than anyone. But he and Edu were still determined to push through the plans they had in place for improving the squad in the summer.

Bringing in Gabriel Jesus from Manchester City was seen as an absolute priority. Lacazette had now come to the end of his contract and wasn't being offered an extension, so he was on his way out. Nketiah did sign a new deal following his fine end to the 2022–23 season, taking on the club's famous number 14 shirt in the process, but Arteta knew he had to sign at least one new top-quality forward to take the team to another level. Arsenal had scored just 61 goals during the 2021–22 season, a number Arteta knew was not enough. He felt his team had to score between 90 and 100 goals if they were going to be able compete towards the top of the table. So he wanted more firepower, a player who could come in and score goals but also get even more out of the likes of Saka and Martinelli. And Jesus was a player he believed could do exactly that.

Arteta had obviously worked with Jesus during his time at City and knew the Brazilian well. He felt he was perfect for the system he was now playing at the Emirates and was determined to get him. A big reason behind Arsenal opting not to panic and sign someone for the sake of it in January following Aubameyang's departure was that the club were already working on getting Jesus through the door. City were willing to let the Brazilian go, as they were signing Erling Haaland, but they would not allow it to happen until the end of the season. Arteta and Edu were willing to bide their time to get their number one target.

There were other forwards considered, though. Discussions took place with the agent of Napoli's Victor Osimhen, but they didn't go very far due to the money the Serie A side would have demanded for the Nigerian. So the focus was very much on Jesus and Arsenal wanted to get a deal done early. Arteta knew the importance of acting swiftly in the market. He was determined to take full advantage of having his first proper pre-season in charge of the team. Arsenal were due to travel to Germany in the first week in July for a training camp at Adidas headquarters in Herzogenaurach, a trip that would end with a friendly against FC Nürnberg. Arteta wanted Jesus signed in time to be part of the travelling squad.

Arsenal's summer plans were not solely focused on the City striker, however. They wanted a full-back, a right-winger and potentially another centre-back. Leeds winger Raphinha was on the list and they did make a move for him, but it soon became very clear that his heart was set on Barcelona so they backed off. Then, completely out of the blue, Fábio Vieira became the first signing of the summer.

It's very rare these days that a transfer goes through and catches pretty much everyone unaware, but this was one of those occasions. Arsenal moved very quickly for Vieira and managed to keep things completely under wraps until the deal was pretty much done. At £30 million, it was big money for a 22-year-old playmaker who had only just started to make an impact at Porto. Arteta and Edu believed, however, that he had the creative talent to come in and make an impact at Premier League level. Again, it was a signing that fitted the profile that Arsenal were now known for. Vieira was young, talented, versatile, and he was someone the club believed could be developed into a difference-maker in the final third.

Another player Arsenal were very keen on ahead of the new season was Ajax defender Lisandro Martinez. They made multiple bids for Martinez during the summer, the highest of which was around £40 million, but were unable to agree a fee. In the end the Argentine signed for Manchester United. Arsenal were looking at Martinez because he could play at left-back and centre-back. They liked how aggressive he was and how good he was on the ball. The way Arteta's team had evolved over the years meant that any defender who came in now had to be comfortable playing out from the back and moving into the midfield areas when Arsenal were in possession.

Arsenal were frustrated to miss out on Martinez, but they had no intention of paying the £56.7 million that

United eventually shelled out to get him away from Ajax. One of the key areas of Arsenal's improved transfer policy is that they now always have multiple back-up options. They don't go into the window focused on just one player. They have several irons in the fire, and if they are unable to get one, they swiftly move on to another. We saw that first-hand during this window, when they missed out on Martinez but quickly transitioned to Oleksandr Zinchenko.

Jesus had been signed by this point. After weeks of talks, a deal of £45 million had been agreed with City for the striker. Despite interest from Chelsea and Tottenham, Jesus only wanted Arsenal, so the transfer was finalised quickly and he was signed in time to start pre-season with the squad and head out to Germany for the summer training camp. It was a big signing for Arsenal, and Arteta was convinced his new striker could take the team to another level.

'The club has done a tremendous job to recruit a player of this stature,' he said. 'This is a position that's been on our radar for a long time now and we have managed to get a player that we all wanted, so I'm really happy.'

When Arteta, Edu and other key figures in Arsenal's recruitment network sat down to map out their plans to revamp their attack ahead of the summer, the vision was clear. Any incoming striker would have to cause minimum disruption to the system Arteta had worked hard to instil in his team over the past two seasons. They had to be a goal threat, of course, but they also had to lead from the front in terms of intensity and pressing. In Jesus, Arsenal felt they had signed someone who ticked all the necessary boxes. He was also viewed as a leader. He may have only been 25 years old, but he had won the Premier League title four times at City. That was vitally important to Arteta. He knew he needed to add a bit more experience to his young team.

The signing of Jesus created a real buzz around the club. He made a big impact behind the scenes very quickly. His new teammates were blown away by him in training. Not just by what he could do with the ball, but the way in which he approached each session. There was a real hunger about Jesus from the first day he walked through the door at Arsenal. Despite everything he had achieved at City, he'd always had to play second fiddle and he'd never really been able to shake off the image of being Sergio Agüero's understudy. That was one of the main reasons he was so determined to join Arsenal. He wanted to be the main man, the leader of Arteta's attack.

'In my life, I always liked projects,' he said. 'When Edu came to talk to me, I was so happy with the ideas of the club. The way they want to go, the things they want to do. Then I was pretty sure I would come to Arsenal. But after I talked to Mikel, I was 100 per cent sure. Because I trust in him, I trust in this big club and I trust in myself and the players as well.'

Jesus made an immediate impact at Arsenal, scoring twice on his debut, against Nürnberg. Arsenal were losing 2–0 when he came on at half-time. Within 90 seconds he had scored a wonderful goal to make it 2–1 and he added another soon after as Arteta's side went on to win 5–3. It was a dream debut – and a sign of things to come from the Brazilian that summer.

After returning from Germany, Arsenal flew out to the United States for their pre-season tour where they would play games against Everton, Orlando City and Chelsea. Players who had been given a bit of extra time off during the summer due to international commitments joined up with the squad ahead of the trip, including Bukayo Saka, Martin Ødegaard and, most notably, William Saliba. It had been three years now since Saliba had joined and he was still to make his competitive debut for the club. The longer that run went on, the more doubts there were surrounding his future.

Understandably, he and his representatives had been surprised by how things had gone since his move to Arsenal. They felt he had not been given a proper chance to impress and there was definitely a sense of resentment over how some things had been handled, especially the period when he was left to play with the under-23s during the first half of the 2020–21 season after a loan move to Saint Etienne had collapsed on deadline day. But Saliba now had a real opportunity to impress. He'd had a fabulous season on loan at Marseille during the previous campaign, one that saw him called up to the France national team and win the Ligue 1 young player of the season award.

Arteta wanted to use the summer to have a good look at him. He still had doubts about whether the young centre-back was ready, but these quickly disappeared when he started to watch him in training. Arteta took an interesting approach to integrating Saliba into the squad. He knew that the defender would probably be a bit suspicious about him, given how the past few years had unfolded. So Arteta deliberately opted not to talk to him during the first week they were together. He just wanted to watch him, to observe how he acted around the squad and how he trained. It didn't take him long to realise that Saliba was more than ready to make a big impact.

Saliba was thrown straight into the starting XI for the opening game of the tour, playing alongside Gabriel in the heart of the defence as Arsenal beat Everton 2–0. Jesus opened the scoring before setting up Saka for the second. It was the perfect start to the tour for Arsenal and they made it two wins from two when they beat Orlando City 3–1 a few days later thanks to goals from Gabriel Martinelli, Eddie Nketiah and Reiss Nelson.

Zinchenko was in the crowd watching the game, sitting alongside Edu and Stan and Josh Kroenke. Arsenal had agreed a £30 million deal with Manchester City just ahead of the match, and with City also in the States for some pre-season fixtures Zinchenko quickly got on a plane so he could link up with his new teammates.

'We're really happy to have him,' Arteta said. 'I know the player really well, he's an exceptional footballer and he is someone that is going to bring another competitive edge to that dressing room.'

With the capture of Zinchenko, Arsenal had now spent around £115 million in the window, adding to the £145 million they had spent the previous summer. In Zinchenko and Jesus they had added two proven winners, players who could come in and make an immediate difference, both on and off the pitch. Vieira was more of an unknown quantity, as was Marquinhos, the teenage Brazilian winger who had arrived from São Paulo for £3 million. United States keeper Matt Turner was the other addition, for around £7 million. Arsenal had signed five players before they had even returned from their trip across the Atlantic. It was the window Arteta wanted.

There was still plenty of time left until the transfer window shut, but Arsenal's focus was now on moving people on. There would be no further business done in terms of incomings. Ideally, another winger would have come in to provide cover for Saka on the right, but Arsenal felt there was no one available who they really wanted. So, just as they had in January when Aubameyang left, they decided to bide their time.

The club were happy with the business they had done and there was a real buzz around the squad. Jesus's impact behind the scenes had been transformational and Zinchenko also made an immediate impression. He was thrown straight into the starting XI for Arsenal's final game of the tour, against Chelsea, lining up at left-back. It was the first time Arsenal started a game with a back four of Zinchenko, Gabriel, Saliba and White, and it was a sign of things to come.

Arteta's side were sensational against Chelsea. Jesus scored yet again before goals from Ødegaard and Saka either side of half-time made it 3–0. A late header from Lokonga completed a 4–0 rout. It was a real statement performance from Arsenal. They looked miles ahead of Chelsea in terms of their preparations and the result put the seal on what had been a hugely successful tour.

There was a real sense of momentum building at Arsenal when they returned from the States. Club sources were delighted with how the trip had gone, labelling it an over-whelming success. It was the first normal pre-season tour Arteta had been involved in since he arrived at the club. With Covid measures finally scrapped, he had been able to work with his players without restrictions. The fact that the club had moved quickly to land their priority targets was a real boost, as it gave the new additions time to firmly adjust to their new surroundings ahead of the start of the Premier League season. Arteta wanted them with the group as quickly as possible, which is why Zinchenko was flown straight over to link up with the squad and why Vieira travelled even though he was injured with an ankle problem.

For Arteta the trip wasn't just about the games; it was about forging a real team spirit and bond between the players. He didn't want any cliques forming, so he made sure players switched tables every single meal time while they were away so that they would sit next to different teammates each time. And Arteta dedicated one night of the tour to a big squad barbecue. Every member of the travelling party, including all the club staff, were invited. Again, all the tables were mixed up and games were put on throughout the evening aimed at bringing the squad closer together. When they returned to England, sources at the club were all talking about how the squad felt as united as it had done in years. There was genuine optimism about how things were shaping up, and that only increased when Arsenal thumped Sevilla 6–0 in the Emirates Cup to bring the curtain down on an unbeaten pre-season campaign.

Arteta's side were 4–0 up inside 20 minutes and added two more after the interval. Jesus scored a hat-trick in his first ever Emirates appearance in an Arsenal shirt, while Saka with a brace and Nketiah were also on target. Arsenal played some fabulous football. The pressing from the forwards was incessant and the pace and movement of some of the attacking play was a real sign of what was to come. The victory meant Arsenal had won all five of their pre-season games, scoring 20 goals and conceding just four. When you compared that to the previous summer, when Arteta's side failed to win a single game, you could see just how better prepared they were for the start of the new league season, which was to get underway at Crystal Palace.

'We are really excited for the season,' Arteta said following the win against Sevilla. 'We know that Friday night is going to be a very different game, with a different context and atmosphere. We have to prepare really well for that.'

For the second successive season, Arsenal were involved in the Premier League curtain-raiser. Again, it was an away match in a London derby, and again, it was under the lights on a Friday night. But unlike at Brentford 12 months previously, Arteta's side were properly prepared and ready to go.

They travelled to Crystal Palace and claimed an excellent 2–0 victory to get their season up and running in style. They were exceptional for the opening 25 minutes. Palace just couldn't cope with their pace and intensity. The only negative was that they only had Martinelli's early header to show for their dominance. After that they had to withstand some pressure from the home side and they did just that, with Saliba exceptional on his Premier League debut. He and Gabriel were already showing signs of forming a formidable partnership at the back, and Zinchenko and White were impressing at full-back.

Saliba's form during the summer left many wondering what Arteta would do with Ben White. But with Takehiro Tomiyasu struggling with injury, the England international had been moved out to right-back and was showing he could do a fine job there.

The addition of Zinchenko had seen a real tactical shift from Arteta. The Ukrainian was starting at left-back but was moving into central midfield when Arsenal were in possession, getting on the ball and creating an overload in the central areas. Playing with an inverted full-back was something we'd seen from Guardiola at Manchester City, but this was the first time we'd really seen Arteta do it at Arsenal.

It was also clear that Xhaka was now being asked to operate in a far more advanced role than we'd really seen from him before. There had been signs of it towards the end of the previous season, but it was glaringly obvious now. Partey was operating on his own in front of the back four, with Xhaka playing alongside Ødegaard in a left-sided number eight position. It was a surprise to many people to see Xhaka that high up the pitch, but Arteta was convinced he could cause problems there. He wanted goals from those positions. He knew if his side were going to hit his target of scoring between 90 and 100 times during the season, his attacking midfielders had to contribute more. He held talks with Xhaka ahead of the season about the matter.

'I spoke to him and said, "I need to unlock something in your brain because you're so comfortable and confident playing in this area,"' Arteta would later reveal. 'I said, "Unless you unlock that I'm going to have to do something about it." He took it straight away. He came to pre-season fitter than ever, slimmer than ever, and he knew that if we wanted to take the team to a different level we had to change his role. He knew that was coming.'

Xhaka showcased those new attacking qualities when Arsenal made it back-to-back wins with a 4–2 success against Leicester at the Emirates. He scored one and set one up during another excellent display from Arteta's side. Jesus marked his competitive home debut with a first-half brace and Martinelli also scored. The game saw Saliba make his home league debut for Arsenal three years on from joining the club, and there was a remarkable moment in the second half when he scored an own goal that briefly made it 2–1. After a few seconds of stunned silence around the ground the Arsenal fans let out a roar of encouragement for Saliba, and then the next time he touched the ball the whole stadium stood and applauded as a show of support.

'The way they reacted was something I've never seen in football,' Arteta said afterwards. The crowd reaction meant a lot, not just to Saliba, but to the squad as whole. So many players would mention it to us during interviews down in the mixed zone after games. It was the moment they knew the crowd was really behind them, a real symbol of the unity that had now been created between the team and its supporters.

There was real excitement at how Arsenal had started the season. It wasn't just the victories, it was the manner of them: the football the team were playing and the intensity they were playing with. It was obvious, even at this early stage, that they had really gone up a level from the previous season. Zinchenko and Saliba had made a huge difference in terms of how the team was playing out from the back, and up front Jesus had made a transformational impact in the final third.

A lack of goals was what really held Arsenal back in 2021–22, whether it was during the opening months of the campaign when the misfiring Aubameyang was still there, or when Lacazette was leading the line from Christmas onwards. Lacazette managed just two goals from open play during the entire season, a figure Jesus matched in 12 first-half minutes against Leicester. But the impact Jesus had on this Arsenal team was not just about goals; it went far further than that.

For the first time in a long time Arteta's side had a presence inside the box. While Lacazette did plenty of good work from deep during his final year at the club and linked up well with runners going beyond him, he rarely got himself into positions that would trouble the opposition centre-back. In his final 20 Premier League starts for

Arsenal, the Frenchman had just 31 touches of the ball inside the penalty area. Jesus had 26 in his first two Arsenal appearances. His impact was remarkable and Arsenal now looked a totally different proposition going forward.

Off the pitch he had made a real difference as well. Arteta immediately made him part of the leadership group, alongside Xhaka, Holding and Ødegaard, who had now been named as club captain on a full-time basis following Lacazette's departure. Club sources would all talk glowingly of the way Jesus had conducted himself following his arrival. Understandably he had forged a close bond with the Brazilian contingent and had taken summer signing Marquinhos under his wing, but he and the other Portuguese speakers would all ensure they spoke in English as much as possible to avoid the potential for anyone to feel left out. Jesus had also made a point of telling his teammates that he felt the squad was capable of winning the league. It was a message both he and Zinchenko sent out to the squad almost as soon as they arrived.

A comfortable 3–0 win at Bournemouth made it nine points from nine for Arsenal and sent them to the top of the table. They then came from behind to beat Fulham 2–1, with Gabriel scoring a dramatic winner right at the end. That late winner sparked some great celebrations at the Emirates, although they did not go down well with everyone. Former Sky Sports anchor Richard Keys, who was now working at beIN SPORTS, was quick to have his say.

'Steady, it's Fulham,' he said. 'They're four games into the season. Look at the manager. Enjoy it, but I don't understand this. They've beaten Fulham. They've won nothing. They've over-celebrated this.'

The comments were ridiculous, although not surprising given who they came from. The celebrations weren't about the players or the fans getting ahead of themselves; they were just the celebrations of a club and fanbase that had been totally re-energised. It would have been easy for things to turn a bit nasty at Arsenal given the way the previous season had ended, but things had gone the complete other way. You'd seen that when Saliba scored his own goal against Leicester, and you saw it again when the stadium stood and urged their team on in the moments after Aleksandar Mitrović had given Fulham the lead early in the second half.

It was clear that the connection between the team and supporters that Arteta had long been craving for had been restored. Going to games at the Emirates was now a completely different experience. The streets outside the ground were packed three hours before kick-off and the atmosphere inside was on another level to what it had been. The division and the infighting that had become the norm at Arsenal under Wenger and Emery now felt like a long time ago. The reaction to going behind against

Fulham was the perfect example of that. There were no boos, no groans; it was just unwavering support and that's why there were such passionate celebrations at the end. It was obvious that something special was starting to build. Arteta knew it and so did the players.

'We went 1–0 down and they were still cheering for us,' said Saka. 'That didn't use to happen at the Emirates. The fans have really stepped up and supported us. We believe in each other more and we are performing at a high level right now.'

That high level continued as Arsenal claimed another home win next time out, beating Aston Villa 2–1 thanks to a Martinelli winner. The game against Villa came 24 hours before the end of the transfer window and Arsenal were now pushing to bring in a new midfielder before the deadline. Their target was Douglas Luiz, who scored the goal for Villa at the Emirates. They had been interested in the Brazilian for a while but had not been planning to make a move for him during the summer. A bad hamstring injury to Elneny, however, combined with a thigh problem for Partey, changed their thinking.

Talks with Villa executives over a move for Luiz actually took place during the game at the Emirates and a bid was made the following morning. The offer was rejected, however, and when a further two improved bids were also turned down, Arsenal accepted defeat. 'Villa wouldn't budge,' one source told me after the deadline had passed.

Arsenal's highest bid for Luiz totalled around £25 million. As much as they wanted him, they decided that they weren't going to go any higher for a player who had less than a year left on his deal and hadn't even been under serious consideration for a summer transfer prior to the injuries to Partey and Elneny. Partey was also expected to be back relatively quickly. The deadline passed without any further additions.

It had still been a good window for Arsenal. In Jesus and Zinchenko they had added real quality and experience, and while Vieira and Marquinhos were young, they were clearly talented. Saliba also felt like a new signing, even though he had been at the club for years.

With the distraction of the window now over, full focus could turn to the league and Arsenal had a huge game at Manchester United to prepare for. Arteta's side were travelling to Old Trafford sitting top of the table, having won their opening five league games for only the fourth time in the club's history. But as impressive a start as it was, it had still been brushed off by many, who pointed to the standard of the teams Arsenal had faced over the opening few weeks of the campaign. There were plenty who still doubted Arsenal, but a result at Old Trafford would change that – and the way they had been playing, you really fancied them to get one as well.

You could feel the belief around the squad. The winning run had generated real confidence among the players, not least because of the way in which they had been secured. Twice they had been pegged back by Leicester, and on each occasion they'd responded almost immediately with a goal themselves. They had fallen behind against Fulham, only to turn things around and snatch all three points late on. And then the game against Villa looked set to end in disappointment when Luiz struck in the final 20 minutes to make it 1–1. But again, within two minutes of the restart, Arsenal bounced back through Martinelli to secure all three points. Responding quickly to adversity had been a running theme of this team throughout the early stages of the season. It was a mindset we'd not seen much of from Arsenal in recent years. 'The game changer at the moment is the mentality,' Xhaka revealed ahead of the game at Old Trafford.

Transforming the mentality around Arsenal had been one of Arteta's primary focuses since he replaced Emery in 2019. When he arrived he walked into a club that was used to losing. That was something he'd worked tirelessly to try to change during his three years at the helm. Building a culture that was based around winning was essential, not just on a Saturday, but every single day at London Colney. At training Arteta divides the players up into teams and gets them to compete at everything. It doesn't matter what it is. It could be small-sided games, full-pitch matches, rondos (a piggy-in-the-middle type passing exercise) or shooting practice, Arteta has all the players competing and he collates the results. Those results are then put into tables so the players can see who wins and loses.

Unfortunately, that new mindset wasn't enough to avoid defeat at Old Trafford. There was a lot to like about Arsenal's performance, but they fell into United's trap and got picked off on the counter-attack as they were beaten 3–1. It was the first defeat of the season and one that left Arteta very frustrated. He knew his side were the better team on the day, but they showed a bit of immaturity which cost them. They were excellent early on and thought they had taken a deserved lead through Martinelli, but the goal was chalked off by VAR after Ødegaard was very harshly adjudged to have fouled Christian Eriksen in the build-up. United then went in front through Antony, but Arsenal levelled in the second half through Saka. At that point you really thought they would go on to make it six wins from six, but in pushing forward for a second goal they left themselves exposed at the back and Marcus Rashford struck twice on the break to earn the hosts all three points. There was a real sense of disappointment afterwards. 'The game was there for the taking,' said a frustrated Arteta.

As disappointing as the result was for Arsenal, there were plenty of positives to take. They had gone to Old Trafford and played the way they wanted to. This wasn't like the countless abject performances Arsenal had served up at United over the years. They had played well and on another day they could have won comfortably. So it was no surprise to see them respond well. A much-changed team went to FC Zürich and won to kickstart the Europa League group-stage campaign, and then a dominant performance at Brentford saw them cruise to a hugely impressive 3–0 win in west London. It was a win that sent Arteta's side into the first international break of the season sitting top of the table, one point clear of Manchester City and Spurs.

There was a moment at the end of that win at Brentford that epitomised the feel-good nature of Arsenal's start to the season. As the players made their way over to celebrate with the away fans, a Granit Xhaka chant started to ring around the ground. It had been sung during the win at Bournemouth a few weeks earlier, but this was different. It was sung over and over again. For most players, getting serenaded by your own fans would be nothing new. But in terms of his relationship with the Arsenal supporters, Xhaka is obviously no ordinary player. The previous season had seen him take great strides in fixing the issues of the past, but this had now turned into a redemption story that no one would have ever predicted.

'It's a very, very special day for me,' Xhaka admitted after the game in an emotional message that he sent out via Arsenal's Twitter account. After six eventful years at Arsenal, this was the season many felt Xhaka would finally be eased out of the starting XI, especially with the change of system introduced by Arteta in which he played in that more advanced midfield role. But instead, he had cemented his place in the team. A player who not so long ago had been viewed as a calamity waiting to happen was now pretty much undroppable.

'You see our supporters and the way they were singing to him. It makes him emotional,' Arteta said. 'I think he feels now that the love and respect goes both ways and I'm really pleased for him because, in my opinion, he fully deserves it.'

There was real hunger about what Arsenal were doing during the early stages of the season. The disappointment at losing out to Tottenham at the end of the previous campaign was something the players were clearly using to drive themselves on. Ramsdale opened up about it to a few of us after their next game.

'We all have the fire burning inside, because of what happened,' he told us. 'The day I returned to pre-season, I came back and the standard of training had increased. People are demanding more of each other, training is a lot more competitive and there is definitely a mood swing when you lose. There were always certain people who were upset when losing in training, but now it is a collective. The team spirit is really, really strong.'

Arsenal had two huge home games immediately after the international break, against Spurs and Liverpool. It was a massive week for the club and one that could hardly have gone better. Given everything that had happened against Tottenham just a few months earlier, Arteta's side went into that north London derby determined to put things right. They did just that, blowing their neighbours away 3–1. Xhaka scored again to continue his remarkable redemption story, with Partey and Jesus also on target.

Liverpool were then seen off 3–2 in a thrilling game. It was the first time Arsenal had beaten Jurgen Klopp's side since 2020 and it was another big statement of intent sent out to the rest of the Premier League. Liverpool pegged Arsenal back twice in the game, but a penalty from Saka finally decided a dramatic contest. The atmosphere was incredible. It had been all season, but the noise during those final minutes against Liverpool was unlike anything the Emirates had really generated before.

'I've never seen it like this,' Arteta admitted after the game. 'You cannot imagine how much it helps the players. It's one of the nicest things we've done since we have been together here. To unite everybody.'

The atmosphere at the Emirates had never been anything special since the move from Highbury in 2006. There had been some great nights, of course, but on the whole the stadium could be pretty quiet, and during the final years of the Wenger era and towards the end of Emery's short tenure it was notoriously fractious. But that had completely changed. It was something Arteta and the club had really worked on. The demographic in the ground had changed post-Covid. There was certainly a younger feel to the place and the club had put a lot of effort into connecting with the fanbase. They were more open and more willing to engage with fan groups.

The introduction of the Ashburton Army, who all sat together in the Clock End, had made a real difference. It was a group that was born out of a few young fans who got together before the pandemic to try to improve the atmosphere at home games. Football going behind closed doors put a stop to its momentum, but it had really taken off since fans had been allowed back into the stadium. After holding talks with the club, the Ashburton Army were initially given some space at the back of block 25, but they were moved to the front five rows for the start of the 2022–23 campaign and have become a key ingredient of the vibrant new atmosphere that has swept around the Emirates.

Inspired by the ultras culture common with teams across Europe, the group dress all in black for games and stage a march to the stadium before every match. It is independent of the club and there have been some issues, as was highlighted when they staged a protest over what they described as 'unwarranted levels of harassment from the authorities' during a game against Chelsea towards the end of the season. But on the whole they have played a major part in transforming the atmosphere at home games. With the Ashburton Army at one end of the stadium and the more established REDaction continuing to operate at the other, watching football at the Emirates is now a completely different experience to what it used to be.

'I think after so many years of having a bit of a toxic home atmosphere that many people have rediscovered their love for football a little bit,' Raymond Herlihy of REDaction explained. 'I think the fans are a bit different now as well, the average age has come down and we just want to have some fun. We've got some home-grown players we can really connect with and lots of great players from other parts of the world that really feel a part of it. We're also winning a lot of games. If you put all those things together, with the Ashburton Army developing and doing what they are doing, then a really strong feel-good factor comes from it. It's fun watching Arsenal again and the scramble for tickets shows that. The last few years we were struggling to give tickets away, now the demand is absolutely off the scale. People want to come into the ground and experience what is happening.'

Given the results it was no surprise that demand for tickets had gone through the roof. When Arsenal went to Leeds and won 1–0 thanks to a first-half Saka strike, they made it nine wins from their opening ten games. It was the club's best ever start to a Premier League season, and with Manchester City losing at Liverpool the same day it meant that Arteta's side were now four points clear at the top of the table.

There were so many reasons behind the record-breaking start. The fearlessness of youth was a big factor. It was clear that Arteta's young side were not afraid of anybody. It didn't matter who they were against, they would play the same way and would be on the front foot from the start. Early goals were becoming the norm. The high-tempo football was great to watch and opposition teams were struggling to deal with the pace, movement and incessant pressing of the frontline. Saka's winner at Elland Road was the 24th league goal Arsenal had scored during the opening ten games of the campaign, with nine of those coming from players aged 21 or under. Many felt Arsenal's youth could be their downfall, but for now it was proving to be the driving force behind their stunning early season form. They did endure a difficult week, however, when they were held to a 1–1 draw at Southampton and lost 2–0 at PSV in the Europa League, but a thumping 5–0 home success against Nottingham Forest put a swift end to suggestions that they were about to fall away. It was a win that sent them into their game at Chelsea with renewed belief.

Chelsea had endured a pretty miserable start to the season, one that had seen head coach Thomas Tuchel replaced by Graham Potter. But this was still a big test for Arsenal. Could they go to Stamford Bridge and win for a third successive season? They had already beaten Spurs and Liverpool at home, but the one away game they had played against one of the so-called 'big six' had ended in defeat at Old Trafford. So victory at Chelsea would send out a real message in terms of their potential title ambitions.

There was also the added narrative of Aubameyang to deal with. He had just returned to the Premier League after his spell with Barcelona and this would be the first time he'd come up against Arsenal since leaving the club. Obviously there was a lot of talk about the striker in the build-up to the game, especially after he recorded a promotional advert for BT Sport that featured him saying: 'Arsenal, nothing personal. I'm back, I'm blue, I'm ready. Let's go.'

Arteta did his best to avoid getting sucked into making any headlines, but the prospect of facing Aubameyang understandably reignited the debate over his departure. It was impossible not to look at the position Arsenal were now in and the way they were playing, however, and not come to the conclusion that Arteta had done the right thing. The decision to cut him loose was a big one, but it was one that had certainly benefited the team in the long term. Elneny spoke about it in the build-up to the game at Stamford Bridge and gave some telling insight into the impact of Arteta's handling of the situation.

'Everyone was scared,' he admitted. 'Everyone looked at themselves because [if] Mikel did that to the captain of the team, what is he going to do with another player? This showed that we can't play around. Everyone is scared because this happened to Aubameyang. If anyone makes a small mistake, they are going to have the same problem and no one needs that problem.'

The Arsenal squad was certainly in better shape than it had been for a long time. It wasn't about big-name individuals anymore, it was all about the team. 'This is the dressing room we have now,' Elneny added. 'Everyone loves each other and everyone works for each other. This is what actually makes our squad really strong, because we don't have egos in the team.'

Aubameyang's words in that pre-match promo video certainly came back to haunt him, as he endured a miserable afternoon against Arsenal. Arteta's side were exceptional at Stamford Bridge. They won 1–0 thanks to Gabriel's second-half goal, but the scoreline did not reflect their dominance. This was as one-sided a game as you could get. Arsenal bossed Chelsea from start to finish. If they were feeling any pressure after briefly being knocked off top spot by Manchester City's win against Fulham 24 hours earlier, they certainly didn't show it.

'What we did today was just phenomenal,' Arteta said afterwards. There were so many good performances on the day from Arsenal, but Saliba was incredible. He dominated Aubameyang, limiting him to just eight touches of the ball. The partnership he and Gabriel had formed in the heart of the defence since the start of the season was absolutely integral to the way Arsenal were performing. Any doubts that may have been hanging over Saliba's ability to cope with the demands of the Premier League had long since disappeared. His performance at Palace on the opening night had set the tone, and from then on he had gone from strength to strength. Both he and Gabriel had started all 13 league games so far and the pair had been the bedrock behind Arsenal's table-topping start to the campaign.

'There is a connection,' Arteta said about his two centre-backs. 'You can feel it. There is a chemistry. I think they make each other better with the qualities that they have and they have been really consistent in terms of their performance. The way William has established himself, the composure and leadership he has shown on the pitch has been really good. And he has done it in a really natural way, without any flashing lights, just being himself. He's very quiet and at the same time very confident.'

There was now just one league game remaining for Arsenal before the mid-season break for the World Cup. They went to Wolves knowing that victory at Molineux would guarantee they would be top when club football returned after Christmas. Arteta's side did exit the Carabao Cup prior to the game at Wolves, but very few tears were shed at that defeat by Brighton. The league was very much the priority now, although the defeat did highlight again a lack of squad depth.

Arsenal's success during the early stages of the season was built around a starting XI that rarely changed. Arteta had some injuries to deal with, such as one that kept Zinchenko sidelined for over a month, but on the whole he did not have to tinker too much with the team he put out in the Premier League. When he shifted things around, however, as he did against Brighton and also throughout the group-stage campaign in the Europa League, the dip in performance level was very noticeable. Arsenal did top their Europa League group and only lost once, away at PSV, but some of the performances were far from convincing. Summer signing Vieira was struggling for form after a bright start to his Arsenal career and players like Lokonga, Holding, Cédric, Elneny and Marquinhos were clearly nowhere near the standard of the players they were coming in to replace.

Vieira was an interesting one. Arsenal had spent big money to bring him in from Porto, but aside from a few flashes of quality – most notably when he started and scored in the win at Brentford – he had failed to make much of an impact. There were question marks over his slight frame when he arrived and whether he would be able to cope with the physical side of playing in the Premier League. Technically, he was gifted and he had shown he could make a difference in the final third when given some space and time on the ball, but so far he had been unable to really seize control of a game and that was a bit of a concern, although not to Arteta. 'Every new player needs time to adapt,' he said in defence of the new arrival. 'I'm not worried at all.'

Arteta's defence of Vieira was well timed, as the Portuguese playmaker went on to play a major role in Arsenal claiming yet another win as they signed off for the World Cup with a 2–0 success at Wolves. Coming off the bench early on to replace Xhaka, who was struggling with illness, Vieira produced a real moment of quality to set up Ødegaard for the goal which broke the deadlock early in the second half. Arsenal's skipper added another soon after to seal the victory. It was a huge win for Arsenal. The squad had sat together and watched Manchester City suffer a shock home defeat at the hands of Brentford earlier in the day, so they knew a victory would send them into the break with a five-point lead at the top of the table. Again, they showed no sign of feeling the pressure as they got the job done in convincing style. It was a win that capped a remarkable start to the season. They had played 14 league games and won 12 of them, losing just one and drawing the other. They sat five points clear of City, eight points above Spurs, 14 points ahead of United and fifteen in front of Liverpool. 'Nobody expected us to be where we are right now,' said Arteta. 'We are enjoying the moment.'

The break for the World Cup was frustrating for Arsenal. Understandably, they just wanted to keep going given the momentum they had built up. But it did give Arteta time to take stock. He gave the players who weren't going to be involved in Qatar some time off to relax before whisking them away to Dubai for a warm-weather training camp, which would also feature two games, against Lyon and AC Milan.

Ahead of the trip, it was announced that Edu – who had been technical director since 2019 – had been promoted to the role of sporting director. The timing of the announcement was no coincidence, with Edu having been attracting admiring glances from clubs across Europe. Arsenal were well aware of the interest in the Brazilian and moved quickly to ensure that nothing happened to rock the stability that had been built up at the Emirates over the previous couple of years.

No one quite knew what to expect when Edu returned to the club in 2019 as technical director. He had done good things with the Brazil national team, but his role was very different to what he would be doing at Arsenal. It was a bit of a gamble by the club, but one the owners and the board felt had paid off. That's why they were more than happy to reward him with a promotion. Edu had shown he was not afraid to be ruthless and that was something Arsenal had needed for a while. His preference to cancel contracts early certainly divided opinion among the fanbase, with so many big-name players having been let go on his watch without the club receiving any sort of transfer fee. But what Edu's approach did was trim a bloated and underperforming squad dramatically, getting rid of highly paid players who were not going to get any game time and freeing up space on the wage bill for young and hungry players to come in and replace them.

'When the player is 26-plus, with a big salary and he's not performing, he's killing you,' Edu had explained when talking to the media during Arsenal's pre-season tour in America. 'You don't have a valuation to sell the player, the player is comfortable – Arsenal, London, beautiful, everything is fantastic – and a good salary. How many players with that kind of characteristics did we have in the past? Eighty per cent of the squad. Try to avoid one more year with the problem in the dressing room. Take it out. Even if you have to pay, because that guy is sometimes also blocking someone.' It was a ruthless approach from Edu, and although it did attract some criticism, it's impossible to argue that the squad is not in a far better place because of it.

Edu and Arteta get on very well and have built up a very strong relationship since 2019. They have both worked tirelessly to reshape the squad and instil a new way of working at Arsenal. Crucially, both share the same vision about where they want the club to be in the future. Sometimes there can be friction between a manager and a sporting director, especially if they have differing views in terms of the direction in which they want to take a club or the way they want to operate in the transfer market. But that has not been the case at Arsenal. Arteta, Edu and academy manager Per Mertesacker have helped bring a real sense of alignment to the club during their time working together.

This was very apparent when Jack Wilshere was appointed as Arsenal's new under-18s head coach at the start of the season. Wilshere had spent some time at Arsenal the previous season, training with the first team and doing his coaching badges while helping out within the academy. When Arsenal's under-18s coach Dan Micciche left to go to Crawley Town, Wilshere was one of the names in the frame to replace him. Arteta was heavily involved in the recruitment process and interviewed the candidates alongside Edu and Mertesacker. Together they came to the decision to give Wilshere the job. They knew it was a bit of risk because of his inexperience and that he would need to be given a lot of support as he got used to the role, but they all felt it was the right decision to bring Wilshere back to the club. He was an Arsenal man and that was very important to the three of them.

Having that alignment from the youth teams right through to the senior side is seen as absolutely crucial at Arsenal and that's why it's been so important to have three men in charge who share the same ideas. Arteta and Mertesacker go way back. They both signed for the club on that crazy deadline day in 2011. They were teammates for five years. Mertesacker was vice-captain when Arteta was skipper and he then took on the armband himself when Arteta left in 2016. One of the last things Arteta did when he retired was to send a note to Ivan Gazidis, who was chief executive at the time, urging him to find a way to keep Mertesacker at the club. And then when Wenger left, Mertesacker returned the favour by pushing the powers that be to appoint Arteta as his successor. Obviously those appeals fell on deaf ears, as Emery got the job, but that's how close the pair are. When Arteta eventually arrived in 2019, Mertesacker was delighted, and the pair of them, alongside Edu, have put a lot of emphasis into connecting the club at all levels ever since.

Arteta takes a very keen interest in the academy and the young players coming through. That's why he was so heavily involved in the appointment of Wilshere to the U18s job. Ensuring there is a pathway through to the first team is seen as crucial to the way Arsenal operate, and aligning how all the teams play is an important part of the process. This is something Arteta grew up with while he was coming through at La Masia as a youngster. Barcelona have always had great success with young talent coming through and being able to naturally slot into the first team's way of playing when given an opportunity. At Arsenal, they want to be in a similar position, and youth coaches such as Wilshere are tasked with doing all they can to try and mirror how the senior side plays.

Wilshere takes inspiration from Arteta and the way he works. Those few months he spent training under him while he was back at the club really inspired him to push on with his badges and to make the transition from playing into coaching.

'There is no way, if you are around Mikel and you see him coach, that you wouldn't want to go and do your badges,' Wilshere told a group of us during an interview at London Colney. 'There is just no way. It is the way he coaches and the passion that he has with it. It's just inspiring. Just being around Mikel, watching him set up the team the way he does. I actually love it. Going over there the day before the game, watching the team and watching Mikel do it and then bring it to life. It's a good place to be. I love the way that he sees football. I love the way that the team plays.'

A number of Wilshere's players travelled with the first-team squad for the training camp in Dubai during the World Cup. Talents such as Amario Cozier-Duberry, Myles Lewis-Skelly, Lino Sousa and Ethan Nwaneri were all given the chance to impress. One of the main reasons Arsenal chose to go to Dubai was that it was close to Qatar, allowing players who were knocked out of the World Cup with their national teams to quickly link up with the squad ahead of the return of the Premier League.

The trip went well, with Arsenal picking up wins against Lyon and AC Milan. But the club were rocked when news filtered through that Jesus had suffered a nasty knee injury while playing for Brazil. The striker was swiftly ruled out of the remainder of the World Cup and, after returning to

England for further tests on his knee, his and Arsenal's worst fears were realised when scans revealed that he needed an operation and would be out for around three months. At the time it felt like a hammer blow. The fans understandably felt like the club's title chances had gone. While Jesus had gone on a long run without a goal in the build-up to the World Cup, he was still a huge influence on every game he played in and the only recognised back-up within the squad was Eddie Nketiah.

The young striker had proved he could make an impact towards the end of the previous season, but many doubted he would be able to fill the significant void left by Jesus for a three-month stretch. There was a lot of pressure on Nketiah as Arsenal returned to England and, with the World Cup over, prepared to face West Ham on Boxing Day.

Aside from Jesus, Arteta had everyone back who had travelled to Qatar. Saka, who had been sensational for England, returned in time and was thrown straight into the starting XI, along with Martinelli, Saliba, Partey, Xhaka and Ramsdale. Lots of questions were being asked of Arsenal ahead of the game. Could they pick up where they had left off before the break? How would they cope without Jesus? Would they struggle to regain their momentum?

They were questions that were answered in emphatic fashion. Trailing 1–0 at half-time, Arteta's side were at their thrilling best in the second half. Saka equalised, Martinelli added a second and then Nketiah gave the night the perfect finish when he spun his man and expertly fired a low shot into the bottom corner to seal a 3–1 win. It was like Arsenal had never been away, and the night was made even more special as it saw Wenger return to the club for the first time since he left in 2018.

Wenger's return was a closely guarded secret. We got wind of it down in the media room just before kick-off but agreed not to put anything out. The Sky cameras picked Wenger out early, so everyone watching at home knew he was in the directors' box. But he wasn't shown on the big screens inside the stadium until after Martinelli's goal went in during the second half. It was a really special moment as the fans realised he was there and a huge cheer swept around the ground. Getting Wenger back to the club was something Arteta had put a lot of work into. He knew a lot of bridges had to be built, but he was determined to make it happen and spent months pushing for it.

'It was a really special day,' Arteta said afterwards. 'His presence is something that has to be very attached to this football club. I've been involved in the process, but it's about him, the timing that he needed to make that step, and hopefully he's going to live here and be willing to spend more time with us because he's such an influence. For me personally – my career and the way I see the game – but as well for this football club.'

After beating West Ham, Arsenal brought the curtain down on 2022 with an excellent 4–2 success at Brighton on New Year's Eve. Nketiah was on target again as Arteta's side continued to shrug off the absence of Jesus. Ødegaard was exceptional, as he had been all season. The pass he produced to send Martinelli away for the fourth goal was out of this world. The win sent Arsenal into 2023 with a seven-point lead at the top of the table.

It was now transfer window time, and Arsenal went into January having already seen a £55 million bid rejected for Shakhtar Donetsk winger Mykhailo Mudryk. Jesus's injury meant Arsenal were looking to add another option to their attack and the exciting Ukrainian was seen as a player who could come in and fit Arsenal's system. At 21, he was within the age profile that Arsenal tend to look for and he could play in multiple positions across the frontline. There was an expectation at the start of the window that the deal would get done, even though Shakhtar had rejected Arsenal's opening offer out of hand. Mudryk was desperate to join and made no secret of the fact with some very public flirting on social media. An improved offer was made just before Arsenal were held to a frustrating 0–0 draw by Newcastle at the Emirates, but Shakhtar knocked it back again.

Sources at the Ukrainian side were always absolutely adamant that their star man would not be sold for anything less than £88 million, a figure way above what Arsenal were offering. Arsenal meanwhile were always privately insistent that they would not be bullied into overpaying, especially with Chelsea lurking in the background. As the month progressed it looked like a compromise was going to be reached, but then Chelsea pounced. They offered what Shakhtar had been asking for all along and the player ended up at Stamford Bridge.

It was a tough one for Arsenal to take and the fans were left frustrated at losing out on a player after such a public saga, but Arteta was philosophical in defeat. 'We want to improve our squad,' he said, 'and when I say we, I mean myself, the coaching staff, the staff, the players, the board and ownership. We are all in this together. But we will do the deals that we can do and that we believe are right for the football club.'

As frustrated as Arsenal were to miss out on Mudryk, there was no sense of panic. Edu, Arteta, Richard Garlick and the board had a plan that had served the club well in recent windows and they were never going to do something rash because they had lost out on a target. They had back-up options, just as they did when they turned to Zinchenko after missing out on Martinez at the start of the season. This time the back-up option was Brighton winger Leandro Trossard and a £25 million deal for the Belgian international was wrapped up very quickly. It immediately looked like a smart piece of business, especially for a team going for the title. Trossard was 28, so a bit older than the players Arsenal would usually go for, but he was proven in the Premier League so wouldn't need time to adjust. He could just come in and hit the ground running and he had shown during his time with Brighton that he could score goals.

'He can have an immediate impact on the team,' Arteta said. 'We have to think short-term, but also medium- and long-term. I think he gives all that.'

Arsenal had travelled to Tottenham and secured a fabulous 2–0 win a few days prior to Trossard's arrival. It was the first time since the 2013–14 season that they had secured a league double over their north London rivals and the first time since March 2014 that they had picked up three points at the home of their neighbours. The victory maintained their eight-point lead at the top of the table and sent them into their home game with Manchester United in buoyant fashion.

United were still the only team to have beaten Arsenal in the league that season and there was a determination within the squad to avenge that defeat. In a thrilling encounter, which Arsenal edged 3–2, Nketiah was the hero, scoring twice, including a last-minute winner. Trossard played his part on his debut, coming off the bench to play a major role in Nketiah's dramatic late strike which sparked chaotic scenes at the Emirates. 'Extraordinary,' Arteta said afterwards. 'It doesn't get much better than that.'

The victory, Arsenal's 16th of the season, took them to 50 points at the halfway stage of the campaign – a feat no Arsenal side had ever previously achieved. Even the Invincibles of 2003–04 hadn't managed that many, with Wenger's iconic team amassing 45 points from their opening 19 fixtures. That was the standard Arteta's young side were now setting.

I sat down with Takehiro Tomiyasu just after the United game and we spoke about the vast improvement Arsenal had made in the space of just 12 months. I asked what he put that improvement down to and he was adamant that it was the players simply having a better grasp of what Arteta was asking from them.

'We understand more [about] Mikel's football,' he told me. 'We've got depth, we've got some new players, but the biggest thing is we understand Mikel's football more. Last season we understood, but we couldn't express it. But this season we understand and we are showing how he wants us to play. This is the big difference. Mikel knows about football, he knows about football structure, everything. Our job is to just explain on the pitch what he says. I believe in him. He's just amazing, the best manager I've ever played with.'

Aside from the goalless draw with Newcastle at the start of the month, it had been a perfect return to football for Arsenal following the World Cup. But a bump in the road lay in wait. Having beaten Oxford United in the FA Cup third round earlier in the month, Arsenal were handed the toughest of fourth-round ties when they were drawn to face Manchester City at the Etihad. The Premier League's top two hadn't faced each other yet, so there was a lot of interest in the game, even though both sides were expected to make several changes. City won 1–0, but Arsenal played well and were a touch unfortunate not to go through. They were the better side in the first half and had some good chances, with Trossard particularly impressive. But they couldn't take advantage of some of the good areas they got themselves into and Nathan Aké's second-half goal proved decisive. It was disappointing for Arsenal, but with the first league game of the season against City fast approaching, there was a lot they could take from the performance.

Before that huge game against City, Arsenal had to travel to Everton and then host Brentford. They added Jorginho to the squad just before the trip to Goodison Park, bringing the midfielder in from Chelsea on deadline day. They had spent the final few days of the window pushing hard to sign Moisés Caicedo from Brighton, offering up to £70 million for the Ecuador international. But Brighton were adamant that Caicedo was not for sale, so Arsenal moved quickly for Jorginho to bolster their midfield options following a season-ending injury to Elneny. It wasn't the sexiest of signings, but it looked like another smart piece of business from Arsenal. Arteta had long been an admirer of the Italy international and had tried to sign him before.

This time he got his man and in doing so added real experience to a young squad ahead of the second half of the season.

'He is a midfield player with intelligence, deep leadership skills and a huge amount of Premier League and international experience,' Arteta said. 'Jorginho has won in his career, but he still has the hunger and huge willingness to contribute here.'

The Italian's debut did not go to plan. He was on the bench for the game at Everton but came on after half-time. A couple of minutes later, James Tarkowski scored a header from a corner to give the home side a 1–0 win. It was Arsenal's first league defeat since the 1–0 loss at Old Trafford back in September.

A controversial 1–1 home draw against Brentford followed. It was a really tight game which Arsenal looked to have edged when Trossard struck midway through the second half, but Ivan Toney nodded in an equaliser soon after to earn the visitors a point. At the time it looked like there was offside in the build-up to the goal, but after a long VAR check the goal was given. It would later turn out, however, that the Video Assistant Referee, Lee Mason, had forgotten to draw the lines to check if Christian Norgaard was offside when setting up Toney's equaliser. Had he done so, the goal would have been chalked off and the score would have remained 1–0. Arsenal were understandably furious. Referees chief Howard Webb called the club to apologise, but that did little to improve Arteta's mood.

'I will only be satisfied if they give me the two points back, which is not going to be the case,' he said. 'That wasn't a human error. That was a big, big, big not under-standing your job and that is not acceptable. Everybody makes errors and mistakes and we are part of that, me the first one. But that was something else. I wasn't having it, the club wasn't having it and I think it's clear, the conse-quences of what happened.'

It was easy to understand why Arsenal were so angry. When you are competing against a team like City for the title there is almost no room for error. So to have two points taken away because of such a monumental error was extremely difficult to accept. But it wasn't just about the two dropped points. The draw meant that Arsenal's run without a win had stretched to three games in all competitions, and with City to come next in the league that just increased the pressure.

It was a monumental game, arguably the biggest the Emirates had ever seen. Arsenal went into it three points clear at the top and with a chance to make a real statement. Arteta's side had overcome almost every obstacle that had been put in front of them during the season, but beating City was the one thing they still had to achieve. They had already been beaten by them in the cup and had lost all of the last ten league meetings between the sides, scoring just three goals and conceding 26. That was the challenge they had to try to overcome and their chances were not helped when Partey was ruled out on the day of the game due to injury. Jorginho came in for his first start and for 45 minutes Arsenal were excellent. An awful Tomiyasu error gifted Kevin De Bruyne the opening goal but Arsenal deservedly levelled before half-time through a Saka penalty. You really felt at this point that they would go on and win after the interval, as they had all the momentum behind them. But it just didn't happen. Guardiola made some tactical tweaks and City got on top as the game wore on. They just ground Arsenal down, and after Jack Grealish had restored their lead, Erling Haaland added a third to wrap things up.

It was a crushing defeat for Arsenal, one that saw City move above them in the table for the first time since November. Coming away from that game, it was tough not to think the title had gone. Even though Arsenal still had a game in hand, City now had their noses in front and that felt very significant. Arteta did his very best to pick his players up. 'Psychologically, there is a marathon still,' he said. But Arsenal had now gone four games without a win. The momentum they had built up all season had stalled at the worst possible time. And with two tricky away games, at Aston Villa and Leicester, to come, things were not going to get any easier.

One of Arteta's greatest strengths is the belief he has in himself and that is an attribute he has worked hard to drive into his players. He has pushed them to believe in themselves and what they do from the moment he returned to the club. One of the sportsmen Arteta admires the most outside of football is Rafael Nadal, and a large part of that admiration is down to Nadal's refusal to ever give up when he is on the tennis court. Nadal has fought back from seemingly impossible positions to win matches time and time again throughout his illustrious career, and Arteta – who once weighed up pursuing a tennis career himself before eventually choosing to play football – loves that type of mentality. He is always looking to improve and to find new ways to inspire and motivate his players.

Arteta spends a lot of time talking to coaches in other sports to find inspiration. He is part of a group of coaches that includes figures from the NFL, NBA and rugby, such as former England rugby head coach Eddie Jones, as well as Matt LaFleur of the Green Bay Packers, Mike Dunlap of the Milwaukee Bucks and NBA legend George Karl. They regularly get together on Zoom to discuss ways to take coaching forward. Jones and Arteta especially have built up a very good relationship. They first met when Arteta visited an England training camp to watch Jones put his squad through their paces, and they have remained close ever since. Arteta finds great value in sharing his experiences in football with coaches like Jones and using their experiences to help him improve and grow as a coach. He would have used all that experience to get his players up again after the City defeat in time to face Villa at the weekend. There was very little time to do much work on the training ground. Arsenal lost to City on the Wednesday night and the game at Villa Park was on Saturday lunch-time. So it was just about trying to lift the squad up again mentally after such a morale-sapping night. If Arsenal wanted to stay in the title race, they had to bounce back immediately.

A thrilling 4–2 win at Villa demonstrated that this side had the resilience to fight back and remain in the hunt. At half-time they were trailing 2–1 and could easily have just waved the white flag, but instead they did the opposite. They levelled through Zinchenko before snatching all three points in dramatic fashion with two goals right at the end. The first came in the 90th minute when Jorginho's stunning hit came back off the underside of the bar and deflected in off the back of Emi Martinez's head. Martinelli then raced away on a counter-attack a few minutes later to add a fourth and spark wild celebrations in the away end.

It was a remarkable win and exactly what was needed. You could see the belief flooding back into the faces of the Arsenal players as they celebrated in front of the away fans at full-time, and that belief only increased when City slipped up at Nottingham Forest a couple of hours later. Arsenal were suddenly back at the top of the league again with a game in hand.

Arsenal won their next two games, against Leicester and Everton, before Bournemouth arrived at the Emirates at the start of March. Everything pointed towards another comfortable Arsenal victory, but it was anything but. What followed was one of the most dramatic afternoons in the history of the Emirates Stadium. Arsenal were behind within ten seconds, Philip Billing firing Bournemouth ahead with the second-fastest goal in the history of the Premier League. The visitors then doubled their lead with half an hour remaining.

Arteta's side looked dead and buried. But, as they had done all season, they responded. Partey made it 2–1, then White equalised. With 20 minutes still remaining you felt certain that a winner was coming. But despite incessant pressure, Bournemouth held out. Finally, in the seventh and last minute of stoppage time, a corner was cleared to Reiss Nelson on the edge of the box. The substitute took the ball down perfectly, steadied himself and hit the most perfect left-footed half-volley into the far corner. Bedlam!

'I started to run, but I didn't really know what I was running to,' Arteta said afterwards, and 60,000 people inside the ground understood exactly what he meant. There have been several truly memorable moments since the move to the Emirates in 2006. I was there for Thierry Henry's homecoming against Leeds, Andrey Arshavin's winner against Barcelona and Danny Welbeck's header against Leicester. But I've never heard the ground louder or seen celebrations wilder than what followed Nelson's shot hitting the back of Bournemouth's net. The joy was unbridled and, given the context of the season and what Arsenal were going for, entirely justified.

'It's probably the loudest and the most emotional moment we have lived together,' Arteta said. 'The journey we have been on together and how the supporters and the team are together, it added to that moment. It was really special.'

Those scenes after Nelson's goal will live long in the memory of everyone who was inside the Emirates that day. It was one of those moments in football that genuinely took the breath away – when despair turned into elation in the blink of an eye. Arteta summed it up perfectly. 'When you go through moments like this, you have to enjoy it,' he said. 'Because there aren't a lot in football.'

The Europa League started up again after the Bournemouth game, with Arsenal travelling to Lisbon to take on Sporting CP in the first leg of their last-16 tie. They returned with what looked like a decent 2–2 draw ahead of the second leg at the Emirates.

Arteta's side went to Fulham before that and cruised to a 3–0 success notable for marking the return to action of Jesus after three months on the sidelines. The Brazilian came on as a second-half substitute to huge cheers from the away end. It was a massive boost for Arsenal to have him back, but they had coped very well without him. When he got the injury many felt Arsenal's title chances had gone. But they were five points clear at the top when he went to the World Cup and they were still five points clear now that he had returned. Everyone had stepped up in his absence. Nketiah had done an excellent job and scored some important goals, as had Saka, Martinelli and Ødegaard.

Arteta handed Jesus a start in the second leg of Arsenal's Europa League tie against Sporting. He played the first 45 minutes and Arsenal had a 1–0 lead at the interval. But that was the only real bright spot of what was an awful night for Arsenal. They ended up going out on penalties after Pedro Goncalves had scored a stunning equaliser for the Portuguese side. But going out of the competition was the least of Arsenal's worries. The big issue was that they lost Saliba and Tomiyasu to season-ending injuries in the space of a few minutes. Saliba had made himself an absolutely integral part of the side. He'd started every single league game prior to the injury and formed a formidable partnership with Gabriel. So losing him was a dreadful blow and to lose Tomiyasu at the same time just compounded the problem. Had the Japan international been available, Arteta would have been able to play him at right-back and move White inside to partner Gabriel. But that option was no longer available to him. They coped well initially, with Rob Holding coming in at centre-back. There were successive 4–1 wins against Crystal Palace and

Leeds either side of the final international break of the season. But then they went to Liverpool.

With a five-point lead at the top of the table and just nine games remaining, this was seen as a massive test. Having lost against City in February, Arsenal had won seven league games on the bounce. Should they go on and make it eight wins from eight at Liverpool, it would be the biggest sign yet that they were ready to finally end their long wait to be crowned champions. But Anfield had been a miserable destination for Arsenal in previous years. Since winning there 2–0 in 2012, they had picked up just two points from nine games, conceding a staggering 32 goals in the process.

'We really need to embrace the moment and go for it,' Arteta said. 'The team is full of enthusiasm and positivity and we know that we have a big challenge, but I see a big opportunity to go to Anfield and do something that we haven't done for many years. That's what is driving the team in the last few days.'

It was a huge occasion. Liverpool had not had the best of seasons but were still eyeing a Champions League spot, so both teams had something to play for. And for 40 minutes Arsenal were exceptional, racing into a 2–0 lead. But then Mo Salah pulled one back just before half-time and Anfield was alive again. After surviving almost incessant pressure after the interval, Arsenal eventually succumbed when Roberto Firmino equalised with just three minutes to go. It could actually have been worse for

Arsenal, but Salah missed a penalty near the start of the second half and Ramsdale made a couple of sensational saves late on to ensure Arteta's side at least went back to London with a point. A draw at Anfield is not the worst result, but what really stung was that Arsenal had got themselves into a position to win the game. Losing a two-goal lead and conceding the equaliser so late made it feel more like a defeat than a draw. What happened at West Ham a week later was far more catastrophic, however.

Arteta and his players knew the importance of responding well at the London Stadium. The season-defining game at Manchester City was now just ten days away, but before that Arsenal had to face West Ham and then Southampton. Six points from those matches felt essential and things started well in east London, just as they had at Anfield. Arsenal raced into a two-goal lead once again and were in complete cruise control. But they got sloppy just before half-time and were punished. A dreadful piece of play from Partey gifted West Ham possession and then a rash challenge from Gabriel gave them a penalty. Saïd Benrahma converted from the spot and all of a sudden it was 2–1.

There was now a real sense of déjà vu for Arsenal. For the second weekend in a row they had failed to kill a team off and now they were under pressure. They did have a glorious chance to restore their two-goal advantage just after half-time, when they were awarded a penalty of their own. But when Saka sent his spot kick miles wide, you knew what was coming. Sure enough, West Ham went on to equalise through Jarrod Bowen and Arsenal had dropped points again.

Usually, two draws away from home in the Premier League would not be considered a disaster, but when you are going head to head with City during a title run-in, that's exactly what it is. Suddenly all the talk was about Arsenal 'bottling it', which you could understand. But they certainly didn't appear to be feeling the pressure when they flew out of the blocks at Anfield and the London Stadium and raced into two-goals leads. Arteta's side were playing with the same freedom they had done all season. The difference was that they took their eye off the ball. It was almost too easy for them. Instead of going for the kill, they eased off. They got cocky and they paid the price.

Those two draws left them with no room for error when they faced bottom of the table Southampton at the Emirates. They simply had to win to give themselves some momentum to take up to the Etihad a few days later. But again, they fluffed their lines. Southampton scored within a minute after a disastrous Ramsdale mistake and from then it was a torturous night. Arsenal did manage to salvage a 3–3 draw having trailed 3–1 with just a few minutes remaining, but that did little to raise the mood. The title hadn't gone, but it suddenly felt a long way away.

After drawing against Forest, City had won six straight games. Guardiola's side were now five points behind

Arsenal with two games in hand. It wasn't quite winner takes all when the sides met at the Etihad, but it was certainly starting to feel like that because of what had gone on in the weeks leading up to the encounter. For Arsenal it felt like a must-win or, at the very least, a must-not-lose game. But given the form both teams took into the match you really did get the sense it was going to be a real struggle for Arteta's side.

The continued absence of Saliba was a real problem. Holding was doing all he could, but he just wasn't up to the same level of the young Frenchman. Saliba's injury had highlighted how important he was to the team, not just defensively but also going forward. When he was in the team Arsenal could hold a much higher line thanks to his recovery pace, and his ability on the ball allowed them to be far more controlled in possession. Without him they dropped much deeper, the players around him looked far more nervous and the ball was progressing forward far more slowly.

There was an expectation going into the City game that Arteta might try something a bit different. He'd done it previously when he'd come up against them. But on this occasion he stuck to the system that had served him well for the majority of the season and Holding once again got the nod at centre-back. There had been so much build-up ahead of the game, so much hype. Arsenal went into it knowing they had the chance to write their name into club folklore, but it was a step too far. They were completely overwhelmed by a City side who were utterly relentless on the night. It was 4–1, but it could have been much, much more. Arsenal were poor, but City were magnificent.

'The better team won the game,' Arteta admitted. 'They were probably at their best, especially in the first half, and we were nowhere near our level. When that happens, the gap becomes too big.'

Arsenal returned to London still sitting top of the table, but City were now just two points behind them with two games in hand. The momentum had firmly swung in their direction. Arsenal had five games remaining and even Arteta accepted that they had to win all five just to stand a chance. Even then, City would still have to slip up more than once.

It was now obvious that a third successive title was heading to the Etihad. It was a tough pill to swallow for Arsenal. Having led the way for so long, the disappointment of letting things slip right at the end was huge. But Arsenal didn't lose the title against City; Guardiola's side just cemented it. Arsenal lost the title in those three games leading up to the match at the Etihad. Their safety net had vanished, their momentum had been killed. City, meanwhile, had hit top gear. To beat City to the title you have to be pretty much perfect, as Liverpool had found out to their cost in previous years. Arsenal had been great, but they hadn't been perfect. The key thing now was not letting such a good season just fizzle out completely.

Arsenal actually qualified for the Champions League on the night they lost to City due to results elsewhere. At the start of the season that was very much the target. They had been trying since 2017 to get back among Europe's elite and they had finally done it with five games to spare. That showed how good a season they had enjoyed and Arteta wanted his players to remember that. He was also refusing to wave the white flag completely in the title race.

'We have achieved what was difficult to achieve and we can still achieve the Premier League,' he said, ahead of a meeting with Chelsea. 'A lot of things are still going to happen. What we have to do is forget about what happened and put things right.'

Arsenal were much better against Chelsea. They won 3–1 to finally end their four-match run without a win and they backed that up with a magnificent victory at Newcastle. That 2–0 success at St James' Park was right up there in terms of the best win of the season. It was a brutal game played amid an incredibly hostile atmosphere. Arsenal could easily have wilted, especially after what had happened at Newcastle at the end of the previous season, when they let their Champions League hopes slip away. But they stood up to the test and claimed a brilliant win that at least kept their title dreams alive for another week.

City were just marching on relentlessly, however. They had now won ten league games in a row. They then went to Goodison Park and claimed a 3–0 success that sucked the life out of Arsenal's faint hopes of catching them. With Everton fighting against relegation, it was a game everyone at Arsenal was looking towards as a potential banana skin for Guardiola's side, especially as it came off the back of them playing a demanding Champions League semi-final in Madrid a few days earlier.

Arsenal were hosting Brighton at the Emirates on the same day and you could really feel a sense of hope in the streets around the ground in the build-up to City's game at Everton. Arsenal even opened the stadium and its bars early so fans could go in and watch the game on the screens around the concourse. So when City just demolished Everton without even breaking a sweat, it was a real hammer blow. You could genuinely feel the hope drain out of everyone at the ground and that may have been a contributing factor to what happened on the pitch an hour or so later.

Brighton were excellent, but Arsenal were awful. As soon as they fell behind early in the second half they just looked like they had no fight left. In the end they lost 3–0 and that was that. Mathematically, City still hadn't won the title, but they were now just one game away. The press conference after that defeat against Brighton was the most dejected I've ever seen Arteta. He looked and sounded crushed.

'Today, we have to apologise to our people, especially for the performance in the second half,' he said. 'I hate the

feeling of letting people down when they are really expecting something. That's the biggest regret I have today. We
have to apologise for that.'

It was now inevitable that the title was heading to City,
and it was finally confirmed when Arsenal were beaten 1–0
at Nottingham Forest the following week. It was another
horrible performance from a team that looked like it had
completely run out of steam.

Arteta tried to shake things up. Centre-back Jakub
Kiwior, who had arrived in January, came in at left-back
and Partey – whose form had fallen off a cliff in the final
weeks of the season – was moved to right-back, with White
playing alongside Gabriel in the heart of the defence. The
changes made no difference. Arsenal saw a lot of the ball,
but after going behind in the first half they never really
looked like getting back on level terms. After such a good
season, it was a real shame for things to end with a bit of a
whimper. But while mathematically the title may have been
decided at the City Ground, Arsenal's race had been run a
long time before that.

The key thing now was to go out on a high. There was
one game left. It was at the Emirates and everyone just
wanted to have a bit of a party. Going up to the ground
that day you could feel there was a buzz around the place.
Everyone was obviously disappointed at how things had
ended up, but there was a sense that the fans just wanted
to celebrate what had still been a remarkable season. The

supporters and the players had shared so much during the past ten months that they deserved a bit of a send-off.

It was a great day. The sun was out, Arsenal were brilliant and the atmosphere was fantastic, as it had been all season. There had been lots of stories in the build-up to the game about it being Xhaka's last appearance ahead of a move to Germany in the summer. So it was very fitting that he scored the first two goals in a 5–0 win.

The scenes when he was substituted in the second half were pretty remarkable. As he left the pitch with chants of 'Granit Xhaka, we want you to stay' ringing around the Emirates, it was impossible not to think back to the flashpoint less than four years earlier when he was being jeered and booed down the tunnel after being replaced against Crystal Palace. He had come full circle and his redemption story was a symbol of the revolution that had taken place at Arsenal following Arteta's appointment in 2019. There was unity again at a once-divided club.

Arteta came out to speak to the crowd after the final whistle, but initially he was unable to say anything because the fans were singing his name over and over again. No one had left. Everyone was on their feet. You could see the emotion in his face and hear it in his words.

'I just want to say thank you,' he said. 'We have reconnected the soul of this football club and the soul of this football club is you guys. We know our destination is to bring success, joy and trophies to this club, but in the meantime enjoy the journey. I could not be more proud to do this journey with you, the staff and everyone at this club.'

The lap of appreciation that followed was like nothing the Emirates had seen before. It was packed an hour after the final whistle as the players made their way around the pitch. 'We just wanted to say thanks for an amazing season,' said Raymond Herlihy of the Arsenal supporters group REDaction. 'They made so many good memories. Yeah, we all started to believe we could win it, but it was great to end with a 5–0 so we could forget about the Brighton and the Forest games. People just wanted to say thanks for a season that was beyond our wildest expectations. To go from fifth to second with a 15-point swing and to show so much improvement and to win 26 league games in a season was unbelievable. Everybody wanted to be there and to say thanks, because they all deserved it.'

Arsenal finished with 84 points; only the Invincibles and the 2001–02 double team had ever finished with more in the Premier League era. They also scored 88 goals, the highest the club had ever scored in a 38-game season. They finished 17 points ahead of Liverpool, 24 points ahead of Spurs and 40 ahead of Chelsea. They had also ensured that Champions League football was coming back to the Emirates for the first time since 2017. Ultimately, they didn't have enough to topple the juggernaut that is Guardiola's Manchester City, but they pushed them all the way.

It was impossible not to look back at some crucial moments and wonder what would have happened had things turned out differently. Would the team have kept on winning had Arteta decided not to play Saliba against Sporting? What if Saka had scored that penalty at West Ham, or Liverpool had not scored that late equaliser at Anfield? There were so many what-if moments to look back on, and they will never go away. But the fact is that City – who went on to win the treble – were just too good in the end, and that was nothing for anyone at Arsenal to be ashamed of.

The big challenge they now faced was building on the progress they had made. There was little expectation that Arsenal were going to excel when they kicked off the 2022–23 season. What they'd subsequently done ensured that this would no longer be the case. It was going to be tough – such was the competitive nature of the Premier League – but they had given themselves a great chance of pushing on.

The club felt like it was in a great place again after years of discontent. The squad was now full of some of the best young talents in world football and the club had worked hard to secure their long-term futures. In years gone by, Arsenal would build an exciting squad and then the vultures would swoop and pick it apart. But those days had gone. Gabriel, Saka, Martinelli, Ramsdale and Saliba had all committed themselves to the project, and others would follow. And why wouldn't they? Who wouldn't want to be a part of the movement that was now taking place in north London? Players wanted to play for Arsenal now. Big names wanted to sign, and the ones that were already at the club wanted to stay and continue to experience what was happening.

Saka, Saliba and Martinelli were all players that every club in Europe would want. Arsenal would have found it incredibly difficult to keep hold of them in previous years, yet all three had signed new deals since the start of 2023. Top talent no longer believed they had to leave to achieve big things. Instead, they felt they could fulfill their ambitions at Arsenal. In Arteta they had a manager they wanted to play for, and the importance of that shouldn't be underestimated. Look at Saka and the player he had turned into. He wasn't a talented youngster anymore; here was a genuine world superstar who had performed on the biggest stage for both club and country. He could have played for anyone, yet he had committed himself to Arsenal. The same could be said for players like Martinelli and Saliba. The fact that these players were happy to stay was perhaps the biggest compliment you could pay Arteta, Edu and the club for the work they'd done to transform things in the past couple of years. All the ingredients were now there for Arsenal to kick on and become a major force once again, both domestically and abroad. The 2022–23 season had shown that Arsenal were ready to compete again with the best. The bar had been set, but now they needed to show they could leap just a little bit higher.

PART SIX

CONTROL

(2023–24)

The way the 2022–23 season ended really hurt Arteta. He was desperate to bring the Premier League title back to north London and he knew his side had allowed a golden opportunity to slip through their fingers. But it wasn't just the missed opportunity that made it so painful. Arteta also felt like he had let people down. He and his team had made so many believe that what had seemed impossible was actually possible. They had made millions of fans around the world believe that they were finally going to witness their side win the title again, only to miss out right at the end. It took a while for Arteta to get over that.

He went away and questioned himself in the weeks immediately following the end of the season. Going as far as asking himself whether he was still the right person to take the club forward. 'It took a big reflection, but the answer was yes,' he would later reveal when recalling what he admitted were 'tough times'.

When things get difficult, Arteta always looks to find strength through his family, whether that's with his wife and children, his parents back in Spain or his sister. He will also often fall back on the words of wisdom that his grandfather used to instil into him when he was growing up back in San Sebastian. I sat down with Arteta at the training ground not long after the title had slipped away and he told me about the relationship he shared with his grandfather. It was one he described as 'extraordinary'. 'We used to talk a lot,' Arteta said. 'One day he said to me, "When a door closes, a window opens, so focus on that window. The door is closed for a reason. But now the window is open and the opportunities are much bigger. It has happened for a reason. Don't try to find that reason right now – you will probably understand it in some time."'

It was those words that Arteta kept in his mind during the first few weeks of the summer. That's what he drew strength from. And deep down he knew that he didn't have much time to feel sorry for himself as there was still lots of work to be done. If the end of the season had taught him anything, it was that the gap between Manchester City and Arsenal was still significant. His squad had come a long way in a short space of time, but he was well aware that he had to continue to improve it if Arsenal's 2022–23 campaign wasn't just going to be a one-off.

The club had already put lots of work in behind the scenes when it came to the transfer market, with Declan

Rice the priority target. We'd heard from around January time that the West Ham captain was the man Arteta wanted in the heart of his midfield, and discussions had been going on for months to ensure the club was best placed to land the England international over the summer. Everyone knew Rice was going to be on the move, and West Ham had long accepted that. It was just a case of where he would end up and for how much. Arsenal were confident they could get him – and it had been made clear to them that he wanted to sign – but with Manchester City and Bayern Munich also in the running, the move was still far from a foregone conclusion.

West Ham were also adamant that they wouldn't lose their captain on the cheap, and that was a message they made clear when they rejected Arsenal's opening bid of around £80 million. Another, this time for £90 million, was then also knocked back before City made their interest official. When news of City's opening bid broke, there was understandably concern from the Arsenal fanbase that the club's big summer target would go elsewhere, but inside the club there was a feeling of calm. They remained confident that Rice only wanted to join them, and ultimately they were proved right. Arsenal upped their offer to a record-breaking £105 million and City immediately backed off. The deal was done soon after.

It's difficult to describe just how big a deal it was for Arsenal to sign a player of Rice's quality. The club were delighted to get him, even at such an eye-watering price. In my mind it was Arsenal's most significant transfer since the move that saw Sol Campbell arrive in 2001. Rice was a player at the very top of his game. He was one of the first names on the England team-sheet and had just led West Ham to a first major trophy in 43 years. Europe's top clubs wanted him, but he chose north London. Just a couple of years earlier a move like that would have been unthinkable – Arsenal just wouldn't have been able to win such a transfer battle for a player of Rice's stature. But the work that had gone on under Arteta, Edu and everyone else at the club had made it possible. It was a hugely exciting moment, one that showed that top players now wanted to sign for Arsenal and to be a part of what was happening there.

'I'm so excited,' Rice told the official club website when he joined. 'He [Arteta] speaks for himself. You see how he works and not only as a coach, but psychologically how good he is with players, how he improves players. He's a massive factor in the reason why I've come here. I know he's going to get the best out of me. I know I've got more levels to go up in my game, and I feel like he's the manager to take me to those next levels. I'm really excited to be working with him.'

Rice was the headline act of the summer for Arsenal, but they moved relatively quickly to sign Kai Havertz from Chelsea and Dutch defender Jurrien Timber from Ajax. Timber was an exciting addition, a talented defender who could play in a number of positions across the backline. But the addition of Havertz was one that caught almost everyone by surprise. No one would have gone into the summer window predicting Arsenal would have moved to bring the German across London. He may have scored the winning goal in the Champions League final for Chelsea, but on the whole his time at Stamford Bridge had been underwhelming. So there was genuine surprise when Arsenal spent around £65 million to bring him to the club. But Arteta felt he could unlock Havertz's undoubted potential.

With Xhaka being allowed to complete his £21 million move to Bayer Leverkusen, Arteta believed Havertz could come in to replace the influential Switzerland international and bring something different to that left-sided role in the heart of the Arsenal midfield. It was definitely a risky move, though. Replacing a player as influential as Xhaka with another who had never really played in that position certainly felt like a bit of a gamble from a man who had built his team so carefully over the past couple of years. 'Kai is a player of top quality,' Arteta said at the time. 'He has great versatility and is an intelligent player. He will bring a huge amount of extra strength to our midfield and variety to our play.'

Arteta's aim during the summer was to build a squad that was a bit more unpredictable. During the 2022–23 season, by and large he stuck to the same formation in every game and made the fewest changes to the starting XI of any team in the Premier League, averaging just one a game. If everyone was fit, it was pretty easy to predict how Arsenal would line up and what shape they'd be in. That wasn't necessarily a bad thing, as their impressive second-place finish proved, but it made things relatively easy for opposition managers and analysts when it came to planning for games against them.

'The idea is to be more unpredictable every year, to become more difficult for the opponents to stop and nullify what we want to do,' Arteta said after Havertz had scored one of Arsenal's goals in a 5–0 win against the MLS All-Stars during the club's pre-season trip to the United States in July. 'That's what we have now, especially at the back and in the midfield. The options we have, to open up the spaces ... we have many more options than we had last year.'

And he was right. In Havertz, Arsenal had signed a player that had clearly been earmarked for a specific midfield role, but he could also operate as a central striker, a number 10 or even out wide. Timber was viewed as a right-back following his arrival from Ajax, but was known to play as a central defender and also as a left-back, while Rice could play anywhere in the midfield three and could also fill in as a centre-back if needed. The addition of these three players certainly gave Arteta options he did not previously have, and it was why, as the new season approached, he felt happy with the business that had been done in terms of incomings.

While Xhaka was the most high-profile of the summer outgoings, there were plenty of other interesting exits. Folarin Balogun, who had enjoyed such a successful loan spell with Ligue 1 side Reims the previous season, returned to France but this time on a permanent basis, signing for Monaco in a deal which would eventually fetch £35 million. There were lots of Arsenal fans who wanted the club to give Balogun a chance in the first team, but realistically it was always a case of when he would be sold, rather than if. His contract was running down and he had no interest in signing a new one. Arsenal had to sell, and given he had just come off the back of a season when he'd scored 22 goals for Reims in all competitions, his value was never going to be higher.

Other notable departures included Kieran Tierney, who moved on loan to Real Sociedad for the season after an expected move to Newcastle failed to materialise; Sambi Lokonga, who joined Premier League new boys Luton Town on loan; and Nicolas Pépé, who was released on a free after the club agreed a deal with the winger to cancel his contract a year early.

Another player who left was goalkeeper Matt Turner, who moved to Nottingham Forest just a year after arriving from the United States. Arsenal had been expecting Turner to stay and continue as understudy to Aaron Ramsdale.

But the USA international made it known to the club that he was keen to leave due to his lack of playing time, and this started a chain of events that would lead to a new signing that caught everyone by surprise. Arsenal knew they would have to replace Turner if they were to let him go, but instead of moving for another reserve goalie, they shocked everyone by launching a bid to sign David Raya from Brentford. The Spaniard had earned himself a reputation as one of the league's best keepers during the previous couple of seasons, and Arteta had actually wanted to sign him before he signed Ramsdale. Brentford were not interested in doing a deal in 2022, however, but this time things were different. A deal was there to be done, due to Raya only having one year left on his contract in west London, so talks began between the two clubs.

When the news started to filter through that discussions were ongoing, it sparked plenty of reaction. Ramsdale had made a huge impact at Arsenal in the two years he had been at the club. He was immensely popular in the changing room and with the fans and seemed to be firmly established as the club's number 1. Yet suddenly, Raya looked set to come in and the fear was – certainly amongst the fanbase anyway – that his arrival right on the eve of the new season could disrupt things behind the scenes. But Arsenal and Arteta felt otherwise, and Raya was signed a couple of days before the first league fixture, with the club agreeing to loan him for a season, but with the option to sign him on a permanent basis in the summer of 2024.

There was so much debate over the move. Everyone was having their say. 'I absolutely do not get it,' Manchester United legend Peter Schmeichel told BBC Radio 5 Live. 'I cannot understand how a manager can come to the conclusion that it's a great thing to have competition for the number 1 shirt.' Arteta was having none of it, though. 'To have two excellent goalkeepers is great – there's nothing wrong with it,' he said in his first press conference after Raya was signed. 'We have two great left-wingers, two great strikers and great holding midfielders. We have Jorginho, Thomas [Partey] and Declan [Rice], and that is not a problem. We want to be better every single day – and to be better, the environment has to change and be better. I've seen that close up with my own eyes with the players that we have now, compared to the players we had two years ago. If we want to be better, we have to create that environment.'

Just before Raya's arrival, Arsenal had got the new season off to a good start when they won the Community Shield at Wembley. Ironically, Ramsdale was one of the heroes of that success, saving from Rodri in a penalty shootout as Arteta's side beat Manchester City 4–2 on spot kicks following a 1–1 draw in normal time. It felt like a big moment for Arsenal, especially with it coming so soon after City had hunted them down and taken the title. Arsenal's win ended a run of nine straight defeats against City in all competitions. It was a victory that felt far more significant than the actual prize of the trophy itself. 'For us it's a statement,' Ramsdale said during his post-match interview on ITV. 'It's a marker to know we can go and beat Man City in a big game when it matters. I'm not sure what it will be like this season, but that mental block is gone. We're ready to push on now.'

The Premier League season started a week later, and Arsenal got up and running with a 2–1 home success against Nottingham Forest. They followed that up with a 1–0 win at Crystal Palace before being held to a frustrating 2–2 draw by Fulham at the Emirates. An exciting 3–1 win against Manchester United came next, a game that featured a first Arsenal goal for Declan Rice, who struck in injury time to put Arteta's side 2–1 in front. Gabriel Jesus then added another moments later to make it three wins from four games for Arsenal, who went into the first international break unbeaten, but two points behind City, who still had a 100 per cent record. It had been a decent, if slightly unconvincing start. It was a different type of Arsenal. The exciting and at times chaotic football of the previous season had been replaced by a more measured and controlled approach. And make no mistake about it, that was by design. It was what Arteta wanted.

Over the summer he had spent a lot of time working out what he believed was needed for Arsenal to continue to compete with City. He was determined to build on the progress and not let standards slip again. For that to happen, he felt that his side needed more control and had to dominate higher up the pitch, to make it incredibly difficult for teams to get through them. The capture of Rice was integral to them being able to do that.

In terms of the system, there had been a bit of a shift from what we'd become accustomed to the previous season. Thomas Partey was playing at right-back, with Ben White moving inside and playing alongside William Saliba at centre-back. That meant Gabriel Magalhães had to make do with a place on the bench in the early weeks of the season. Publicly, Arteta was adamant that Gabriel's absence was tactical, but the fact that there was strong transfer interest from Saudi Arabia in the defender was definitely a major factor. The Brazilian was being offered huge amounts of money to leave England, and my understanding was that his head had definitely been turned a bit by the attention he was getting, which was understandable given the life-changing sums that players were being offered to move to the Saudi Pro League. It was no surprise to me, however, that once the transfer window closed and the prospect of a move was gone, he was brought back into the side.

One massive blow Arsenal suffered in those early stages of the season was the loss of Timber to a long-term injury. The new signing tore the cruciate ligament in his right knee on his league debut against Nottingham Forest, basically ruling him out for the season. It was a huge setback both for the player and for Arteta, as it left the Arsenal manager without a defender who could play in any of the positions across the backline, depriving him of a player who had looked set to play a key role in his new-look side.

Arsenal returned from the international break and claimed a good 1–0 away win at Everton, a game that saw David Raya preferred to Aaron Ramsdale in goal for the first time. Arteta had always maintained that he would choose his goalkeeper based on what he was seeing each week, but the expectation was always that Raya would come in at some point. The only real surprise was that it had happened so quickly. The feeling was that the change would probably take place after Ramsdale had made an error, but he had started the season well. Obviously, there was lots of focus on Arteta's decision and you could see it that he was annoyed at the constant line of questioning that came his way. 'It is the same rationale about why Fábio [Vieira] played or Eddie [Nketiah] ahead of Gabriel Jesus,' Arteta said after the win at Goodison Park. 'I haven't had a single question on why Gabriel Jesus didn't start. He has won more trophies than anybody else, including me, in that dressing room. I cannot have two players in each position and not play them. David has tremendous qualities, like Aaron has, and we have to use them.'

It was a bold move by Arteta, but one that had felt inevitable from the moment Raya had come in. Arteta wanted a goalkeeper who liked to play with the ball at his feet and would operate on the front foot. As good as Ramsdale had been since arriving at Arsenal, it was tough to argue that Raya was not better suited to what Arteta desired from his number 1. It felt like a ruthless move, but when it comes to improving and trying to take the team to the next level, Arteta is ruthless, unafraid to take difficult decisions if he thinks they will benefit the team.

The win at Everton took Arsenal into their first Champions League group stage clash of the new season. It had been six years since they had last featured in Europe's elite club competition, so it was a big moment for everyone connected to the club. There was a real sense of anticipation ahead of the home game with PSV Eindhoven and you could feel that the players really wanted to put on a show. And they certainly did that, thrashing a PSV side that had come into the match on a 26-game unbeaten run 4–0. Fittingly, it was Saka who scored Arsenal's first goal back in the Champions League. The academy product, who was really the poster boy of the revolution that had gone on at the club following Arteta's arrival, struck inside eight minutes and set the tone for what was a perfect night at the Emirates.

A 2–2 home draw with Spurs followed in the first north London derby of the season before Bournemouth were eased aside 4–0. Kai Havertz, who had endured a difficult start to the season following his move from Chelsea, scored his first goal for the club in that win on the south coast. It was a penalty, which his team-mates opted to allow him to take in the hope it would give him the boost he needed to really kick start his career. 'I'm delighted they made that decision,' Arteta said afterwards. 'To show that empathy to a player that has some question marks to resolve externally, they warmed me even more today. If there's a player who deserves that it's Kai, I'm so happy for him. Probably it will change everything. If he had any question marks about how we feel about him, about what he does, I think they are out.'

Manchester City were up next in the Premier League, a game Arsenal went into having been beaten 2–1 at Lens in the Champions League. It was not ideal preparation for such a huge fixture, nor was the fact that Saka suffered a hamstring injury during the game in France that saw him miss the City match. With Gabriel Martinelli only fit enough for a place on the bench due to his own hamstring issues, Arsenal had to rejig their attack, with Gabriel Jesus playing out wide and Eddie Nketiah playing through the centre. It was an incredibly tight game, one that Arsenal snatched 1–0 late on when Martinelli – who had come on at half-time – scored with a deflected effort. It was a massive win for Arsenal, one that saw them move above City in the table. The noise when Martinelli scored was incredible, and you could feel just how much that win meant to everyone inside the stadium that day. Beating

City on penalties in the Community Shield was obviously a big thing mentally for Arsenal, but this was different. It was the first league win for Arsenal over City in eight years and another big step forward for Arteta's young side, who limited City to just one shot on target throughout the game. 'A great feeling obviously,' Arteta said afterwards. 'We have beaten in my opinion the best team in the world, and we've done it in a great way.'

The win sent Arsenal into the second international break of the season second in the table, behind Spurs on goal difference. They were still unbeaten domestically, but despite the strong start, there was certainly a feeling among the fanbase that the team were not playing as well as they had the previous season. It was always going to be hard for Arsenal and Arteta to live up to what they did in 2022–23, because this time around expectation levels were far greater. No one had expected Arsenal to do what they'd done that season, but this time it was very different. Fans were geared up for a title challenge and anticipated more of the same in terms of the exciting football that they had grown accustomed to.

The football was quite different now, however. What had made Arsenal so exciting the previous year was the air of chaos that they sometimes brought with them to matches, but Arteta had spent the summer working out how to try to eradicate that from his team. His desire was for control over chaos, and you could see that with the players he had brought in and the way his team were playing. The results were still there, but there were some concerns from the fanbase over the lack of creativity and goal threat in their play at times. It did lead to criticism of the management, but that was something Arteta has come to expect during his short time holding the reins.

I spoke to him before the season began about all the criticism and abuse he and other managers face at times, and the stresses that are involved in doing such a demanding job. It was really interesting listening to him explain what keeps him coming back for more. 'Why do you do what you do? I think of the question every single day,' Arteta told me. 'Because some days you tend to forget it and the pressure is so high and the amount of things that you have to get done are so urgent all the time. It comes down to the passion that I feel about the game, the incredible opportunity that you have to transform people's lives and to share incredible experiences. That has to be the aim every single day, to enjoy those little moments. Winning or losing is going to dictate for how long you are going to be able to do it in the position you are as a manager. It's as simple as that. So in the little things you have to find enjoyment.'

In those dark times when Arteta finds himself questioning if it is all worth it, it doesn't take much for him to remind himself that it is. His players are what drive him on – that he's able to develop them, to give them the chance to improve and seize the opportunities that their talent has given them. 'You go into a dressing room full of different people and different characters,' he told me. 'I was looking at them the other day, just walking around, and I realised we had 19 different nationalities. The way they interact with each other, the way they talk to each other, the way they have banter with each other, the way they demand from each other, it's fascinating. They all have their own story, but they are all in London, at Colney, together seeking the same dream. It's extraordinary. It doesn't happen in many industries, and I must enjoy that.'

Arsenal returned from the international break with a 2–2 draw at Chelsea, a game that saw them come from two goals down to get a point. They then claimed a fine 2–1 win at Sevilla in the Champions League, before smashing Sheffield United 5–0. A 3–1 defeat at West Ham followed in the Carabao Cup, before they suffered their first league defeat of the season, losing 1–0 at Newcastle in highly controversial fashion.

Arteta was apoplectic after the game, launching into a furious tirade during a series of post-match interviews at the fact that Newcastle's winning goal had been allowed to stand. The goal survived three separate VAR checks, with Arsenal believing the ball had initially gone out of play before then appealing for a foul and an offside before it was eventually turned in by Antony Gordon. Despite the protests, the goal was not overruled – and it proved to be the winner. Arteta was furious. 'I feel embarrassed,' he said. 'I feel sick to be part of this. It's an absolute disgrace that this goal is allowed. There's too much at stake here, we put in so much effort and it's so difficult to compete at this level. It's an absolute disgrace. I've spent more than 20 years in this country, and this is nowhere near the level to describe this as the best league in the world. I am sorry.'

Arteta's reaction was a huge story, plastered all over the back pages the following morning, with many high-profile figures in the game criticising the Arsenal boss for what he had said. But Arsenal stood by him and even put out a statement defending his actions. 'Arsenal Football Club wholeheartedly supports Mikel Arteta's post-match comments after yet more unacceptable refereeing and VAR errors on Saturday evening,' the statement read. 'The Premier League is the best league in the world with the best players, coaches and supporters, all of whom deserve better. PGMOL [Professional Game Match Officials Limited] urgently needs to address the standard of officiating and focus on action which moves us all on from retrospective analysis, attempted explanations and apologies.' This did little to dampen the backlash – in fact it led to more. The FA went on to charge Arteta, alleging that his comments constituted misconduct, but the Arsenal boss was later cleared of the charge, with an independent regulatory commission finding that it was not proven. In the written reasons accompanying the decision, Arteta was described as an 'impressive witness' who successfully argued that his comments were focused on a wider frustration with the VAR process, rather than on the match officials themselves. I smiled to myself when the findings came through and immediately thought back to that comment Ødegaard had made during his interview with the Players' Tribune when he challenged anyone to 'come away from a meeting with Arteta and not believe everything he tells you'.

On the pitch, Arsenal responded well to the defeat at Newcastle, winning six games on the spin in all competitions. Their victories against Sevilla and Lens in the Champions League secured passage through to the knock-out stages as group winners with a game to spare, as accompanied by victories against Burnley, Brentford, Wolves and Luton in the Premier League. The 4–3 win at Luton at the start of December, sealed by a stoppage-time winner from Declan Rice, briefly moved Arteta's side five points clear at the top of the table. Things were going well, but a bump in the road was coming.

It started with a 1–0 defeat at Aston Villa. That was followed by a 1–1 draw at PSV Eindhoven in the final fixture of what had been a successful Champions League group stage campaign and a 2–0 home win against Brighton. The ensuing 1–1 draw at Liverpool meant that Arsenal would be top of the table at Christmas for the second year in a row. It was a decent performance at Anfield, but the draw meant the Gunners had picked up just one win in four games. There was a sense that a bit of fatigue was beginning to creep in, but no one really expected what happened next.

West Ham came to the Emirates and won 2–0 on 28 December, inflicting a first home defeat of the season on Arsenal. It was a game that saw the hosts dominate possession and fire in 30 shots on goal, but they failed to capitalise and were picked off by the visitors, who were only denied a 3–0 win when David Raya saved a late penalty. The concern after the game regarded Arsenal's lack of killer instinct in the final third, and that only increased when they travelled to Fulham on New Year's Eve and were beaten 2–1, despite taking an early lead through Bukayo Saka. It was an awful end to the year for the club, who suddenly found themselves five points off leaders Liverpool. And when Liverpool travelled to the Emirates and struck twice late on to win an FA Cup third-round tie just a few days later, Arsenal's season was suddenly in danger of collapse.

They had won just one game in seven in all competitions and had only scored five goals during that miserable run. The players looked devoid of ideas and out on their feet. Suddenly Arsenal were being written off and Arteta was again coming in for some fierce criticism. His decision to spend £65 million on Havertz in the summer rather than spending that money on a new forward remained a big talking point, one that was brought into sharp focus due to the club's struggles in front of goal. Havertz had started to improve as the season had gone on, he'd scored important goals against Brentford, Brighton and Luton, but he'd still not done enough to silence the long list of doubters that had questioned Arteta's decision to bring him in from Chelsea. For the first time in the season, it felt like the dark clouds of discontent were gathering over the Emirates. Fortunately for Arsenal and Arteta, they now had an opportunity to get away from it all thanks to the two-week mid-season break.

So the squad jetted off to Arteta's favourite training destination, Dubai. It was a break that would transform their season. There has been lots of talk about precisely what went on in Dubai that led to such a dramatic turnaround in terms of not just results, but performances. The truth is that nothing majorly different occurred. It was a tough training camp, as it always is when Arteta takes the squad to the UAE. They worked on things like set pieces, but it was nothing out of the ordinary, simply a chance for the squad to get away from the pressures of football and get out of the public eye. Arteta did allow the players to take their families with them, as he felt their presence would allow them to properly unwind away from the training pitch. They played golf, had meals out together and some of them even enjoyed trips to the zoo.

Blocking out the pressure of football is something Arteta has spent a lot of time working on. He once told me about a book he was reading called *Noise: A Flaw in Human Judgment*, about the psychology of decision-making when under pressure. 'I am finding it fascinating,' he said. 'It is about making decisions when it gets noisy, when there is pressure and lots of opinions around. I am always listening to podcasts and following different types of people. For me it's really important to take me out of my daily thinking and the tunnel vision that we sometimes have when we are in this environment.'

Reading and education have always been key to Arteta, so much so that he often sits down with university academics to learn from them in an attempt to continue growing as a leader. He is always looking to evolve his leadership style and believes learning from previous experiences – even bad ones – is key to that. 'Failures are part of any success that we are going to have in life,' he told me once. 'Unfortunately, there are many more failures than successes and that is necessary to enjoy the process and to enjoy the journey. I think where I was born has had a huge influence on me because the education that you get when you are in San Sebastian is in a certain way. The way my parents were raised, the relationship they had with my family and then all the coaches I have had through my career and the experiences I had as a professional footballer. The fact that I moved to different countries and experienced different cultures opened my mind in a way to develop certain skills. Being able to communicate with people in various languages is really important. In the end I think we are a consequence of our experiences. We are all different and unique because of that.'

Arsenal returned from Dubai looking a completely different side to the one that had faltered so badly before the mid-season break. They exploded into life, not just in terms of results, but in terms of their attacking output. They won eight league games in a row, scoring a staggering 33 goals in the process. Crystal Palace and Burnley were beaten 5–0, while West Ham and Sheffield United were thumped 6–0. There were also victories against Newcastle, Brentford, Nottingham Forest and, most importantly, Liverpool.

The Liverpool game was crucial. Arsenal went into it five points behind Jürgen Klopp's side, who were top of the table at the time. Defeat, and the gap would have stretched to eight points, a deficit that would have started to feel too big to close, even though the fixture fell in early February. It was a high-pressure game and Arsenal were excellent, winning 3–1 thanks to goals from Saka, Martinelli and Trossard. It was the game that saw Arteta move Havertz into the central striking role and the German was top drawer, even though he didn't manage to score himself. He offered Arsenal something a little bit different. His hold-up play was superb, as was his work rate, and the likes of Saka and Martinelli seemed to really benefit from having him as the focal point of the attack.

This was a really important moment in the season for Arsenal. Jesus's ongoing knee issue that could be traced all the way back to the injury he suffered at the World Cup in Qatar was clearly limiting his play. Availability-wise, he hadn't actually missed too much football, but despite some flashes of real quality, the Brazilian was looking a far cry from the player who had come in and 'changed Arsenal's world' with his performances at the start of the previous season. Nketiah had also failed to build on some promising early appearances at the start of the campaign, so Arteta needed to find something. And in moving Havertz up top he managed exactly that. It was a tactical shift that would transform Arsenal over the second half of the season.

The 2–1 win against Brentford on 9 March, which was sealed by a late Havertz header, was Arsenal's eighth in a row in the Premier League and it moved them top of the table for the first time since December. It also sent them into the second leg of their Champions League last 16 clash with Porto in confident mood. Their only blemish up to that point since returning from Dubai had come in the first leg in Portugal, when they had stumbled to a late 1–0 defeat, a loss that left them needing a win in London to make it through to the quarter-finals. It had been 14 years since Arsenal had reached the last eight of Europe's elite club competition, so the tension that night was under-standable. It went all the way to penalties, after Leandro Trossard's goal had sealed a 1–0 win, drawing them level on aggregate. David Raya was the hero in the shoot-out, saving twice to spark wild scenes of celebration at the Emirates on what was a highly emotional night. You could see and feel what it meant to everyone to get through and end Arsenal's long and painful run of last-16 Champions League defeats. And it was another big moment in terms of the evolution of the club under Arteta, another mental barrier that had been overcome.

The win sent Arsenal into the final international break of the season right in the mix in both the Premier League and the Champions League. You felt that they had a real chance of going on and winning one of the big two competitions, given the run that they were on and the momentum they had built up. In the league, it was a three-horse race. Arsenal sat top, above Liverpool on goal difference and one point above City, who they would play at the Etihad immediately after the international break. It was a huge game. Memories of Arsenal's mauling there towards the end of the previous season were still fresh in everyone's mind. But things were very different this time around. In 2022–23 Arsenal travelled to City missing some key players and on the back of three games without a win. City had all the momentum, and that showed as they demolished Arteta's side to all but seal the title. This time, however, Arsenal made the journey north full of belief, and that showed in the way they comfortably held City at bay and claimed a 0–0 draw. The game was far from a classic, but it demonstrated the improvement in Arteta's side. City barely laid a glove on them throughout the contest. Saliba and Gabriel were excellent at the heart of defence, with Jorginho and Declan Rice providing them with all the cover they needed from midfield. It was a proper team performance from Arsenal, from Havertz up front to Raya in goal, with everyone contributing both on and off the ball.

A lot of the talk around Arsenal following the trip to Dubai was about the incredible number of goals they had started scoring, but at the other end of the pitch they were also absolutely watertight. The clean sheet at the Etihad meant they had conceded just four goals in their last nine Premier League games, and they followed that up with two more shutouts in wins against Luton and Brighton as their title charge gathered pace. This was always Arteta's vision at the start of the season. He knew that his side had to be tougher to beat if they were going to seriously challenge City again. That's why the club pushed so hard to bring Rice in from West Ham. A few weeks after arriving, Rice gave an interview to Sky Sports in which he admitted he was already 'seeing football in a completely different way' under the guidance of Arteta. 'It's honestly crazy,' he said. 'You think you know football growing up and when you play, but when you meet managers like Mikel, you realise you don't really know anything. There are different styles and different ways of playing that I've never experienced before.'

It sounds stupid to label anyone who cost £105 million as a bargain, but Rice had shown during his debut season in north London that he was worth every penny that Arsenal had spent to sign him. 'Declan Rice, we got him half price,' was a chant you often heard from Arsenal fans throughout the season, and it was tough to argue with that assessment. His arrival had improved Arsenal immeasurably. Off the ball he was a machine, with his work rate and ability to win back possession so crucial in making Arsenal the best defensive team in the Premier League. But going forward he was also providing big moments, scoring important goals and providing a decent number of assists. As the run-in progressed and Arsenal's system shifted to Havertz playing as the central striker, Rice started to operate in a more advanced left 8 role alongside Martin Ødegaard, with either Jorginho or Thomas Partey playing as the holding midfielder in front of the back four. That tactical tweak gave Rice far more freedom to be able to show what he could do in the final third, and his ability to influence the game in that area caught plenty by surprise. He was now taking set pieces as well, with his exceptional delivery from corners proving to be a real weapon for Arteta's side.

For all of Arsenal's excellent attacking play throughout the season, their prowess from dead-ball situations was making a real difference. A lot of the work Arteta and his coaching staff do behind the scenes is based around fine margins. The attention to detail is so precise as they know how important that extra 1 or 2 per cent can be when it comes to deciding matches. That's why set pieces are seen as a crucial part of the game, with set-piece coach Nicolas Jover such a key figure in what Arsenal do. When you walk through the indoor training pitch at London Colney and look up at the wall, you see the message 'Win the games on set pieces' now printed in huge letters. It's a message that the players have clearly taken in.

Arsenal's 3–0 win at Brighton on 6 April, combined with Liverpool's 2–2 draw at Manchester United 24 hours later, ensured that Arteta's side were top of the table once again, with seven games remaining. They sat ahead of Liverpool on goal difference and one point ahead of City. It was the most exciting title race in years, with Arsenal going toe to toe with the two clubs that had taken standards to a new level in the Premier League over the course of the past decade. For Arsenal, the most exciting thing was they did not appear to be suffering from any sort of inferiority complex. They were playing with real personality and had a clear belief in what they were doing.

That's why they went into their Champions League quarter-final with Bayern Munich full of belief. The win against Porto in the round of 16 was a big moment for Arsenal, but this was taking things to another level. Bayern may have been lagging behind Bayer Leverkusen in the Bundesliga, but they were still one of the favourites for the

Champions League and were formidable opponents, with the likes of Harry Kane, Leroy Sané, Serge Gnabry and Jamal Musiala within their ranks. The first leg was at the Emirates and it was a huge occasion for the club, one that started perfectly when Saka scored early on. Ben White then missed a huge chance to double the lead before the game swung, with Gnabry and Kane scoring in quick succession. Leandro Trossard did equalise in the second half as the game finished 2–2, but it felt like a big missed opportunity for Arsenal ahead of the second leg in Munich.

Worse was to follow a few days later when Arteta's side slipped to a 2–0 home defeat at the hands of Aston Villa in the Premier League. It was Arsenal's first league defeat since they had been beaten at Fulham on New Year's Eve and it handed the title initiative to Manchester City, who now knew they would go on to be crowned champions for a fourth successive year should they win all of their remaining games of the season. Arteta tinkered with his system against Villa, bringing Gabriel Jesus back into the line-up and starting him as the central striker, with Havertz dropping back into the attacking midfield role we had seen him struggle in during the early months of the campaign. It was a decision that saw Arteta heavily criticised after the game, but it was difficult to find fault with Arsenal for the way they performed in the first half. They were excellent but just couldn't score, with Trossard wasting a glorious chance to break the deadlock when he shot straight at Emi

Martinez from point-blank range after he had been picked out by Jesus. Had that gone in, you felt certain that Arsenal would have gone on to win the game, such was their level of dominance. But it didn't and the game changed completely after the interval. Arsenal lost their way and Villa started to dominate, with late goals from Leon Bailey and Ollie Watkins giving them the win.

It felt like a hammer blow to Arsenal's title chances, especially as Liverpool had lost at home to Crystal Palace earlier in the afternoon. There was still a long way to go, but City were now in control of their own destiny, and given their quality and experience in coming through title run-ins, it seemed almost inevitable that they wouldn't let their advantage slip. Arsenal's back-to-back defeats against West Ham and Fulham at the end of 2023 meant that they had to be pretty much perfect throughout 2024 to win the title. Up to this point they had been, but this one slip-up against Villa meant the title was now out of their hands, despite all of the good things they had done since the turn of the year. 'We knew this moment could come,' Arteta said after the defeat. 'Now it's about reacting and keep believing and doing what we can. Now is the moment to stand up as a leader, as a character to make yourself count, because when you win and win and win and win for four months it's very simple to do it. The moment is now.'

Arsenal had to try and shake off their disappointment quickly, as they now travelled to Munich for the second leg of their Champions League quarter-final. Arteta was in a confident mood, even after the 2–2 draw in London in the first leg, but it always felt like it was going to be a tough task for his side. Bayern may not have had the best season domestically, but they were still formidable opponents – especially at home. It had been a long time since Arsenal, as a club, had been in this sort of position in the Champions League, while for the vast majority of the players it was a completely new experience. Bayern, meanwhile, were seasoned campaigners, and that showed as they edged a tight game 1–0 thanks to Joshua Kimmich's second-half header. It was a really disappointing loss for Arsenal and it did feel like a missed opportunity. The tie was there to be won in the first leg, but they didn't take their chance. 'It was a tie of very small margins,' Arteta said afterwards. 'In the first leg, we conceded two very poor goals and that had a big effect in the tie. We haven't played in the competition for seven years and we haven't been in this position [the quarter-finals] for 14 years. We have to learn it, when you look historically, all the clubs to get to certain stages, it took them seven, eight, some of them ten years to do it.'

The fall-out from the defeat was pretty brutal, especially as it came on the back of the loss against Villa. Suddenly, all the talk was about Arsenal 'bottling' it again, with plenty pointing to what happened in 2022–23 when they let the season unravel after they had got themselves into such a commanding position. Arteta was adamant that things were now different, however, and that his team would respond. They now knew exactly what was in front of them. They had six league games remaining, including difficult matches against Chelsea, Spurs and Manchester United. They had to win all six and hope that City slipped up once. Should that happen, then Arsenal would be champions.

I remember travelling to the game at Wolves on the Saturday evening after the midweek trip to Munich. I had arrived back from Germany on Thursday and still felt physically drained as I walked into Molineux, so I could only imagine what the players were feeling. So many were expecting Arsenal to slip up again that night, and I have to admit I had a bad feeling about what was going to happen. You could really sense in the build-up to the game that the knives were being sharpened, with plenty ready to write off Arsenal's chances. Arteta knew this could be the defining point of the season so he sat his players down ahead of the game and gave the squad a real rallying cry, drumming into them the importance of not allowing the season to just slip away following a couple of poor results. He asked everyone to step up, to give it one last big push through to the end of the season, and the team responded really well, claiming what was a fine 2–0 success given the circumstances. 'The boys were unbelievable,' Arteta said at full-time. 'It's a joy to work with them.'

It was a big win for Arsenal, one that moved them a single point above City, albeit having played an extra game.

Defeat at Molineux would have been all but impossible to recover from, given what had happened against Villa and Bayern, but now Arsenal had a spring in their step again and they took that into their game with Chelsea, who they demolished 5–0 at the Emirates. Havertz scored two against his former club that night and added another a few days later during a frenetic 3–2 win at Spurs in the north London derby. Arsenal led 3–0 at half-time, before two late goals from the hosts made for a nervy ending. It was another huge win that briefly saw Arsenal stretch their lead over City to four points, but Guardiola's team closed that gap to one when they beat Nottingham Forest 2–0 at the City Ground a couple of hours later. And they still had that all-important game in hand. At this point it felt like whatever Arsenal did, City would match them. It was a bit demoralising for the fans, who were left disappointed again a week later when Arsenal's fine 3–0 win against Bournemouth was immediately followed by a thumping 5–1 victory for City against Wolves.

Liverpool had started to fall adrift of the top two by this point. Jürgen Klopp's side had been unable to keep up with the incredible pace that was being set, with a defeat at Everton and draw at West Ham all but condemning them to a third-place finish in Klopp's final season. There were now just two games remaining for Arsenal, a tough-looking trip to Manchester United before the season finale at home to Everton. City still had three, the first of which was at Fulham, 24 hours before Arsenal's game at Old Trafford.

In the build-up to the game in Manchester, Arteta wanted to try and ease any tension within the camp, so families were invited into the training ground. Everyone got together. The players, their partners, their children and the staff all just had a day enjoying each other's company. This is something Arteta absolutely believes in. He wants everyone to feel connected, as he believes that is the only way a group will ever be truly successful. One way he has tried to demonstrate the principle to his players is with an olive tree that he has planted at the training ground. He uses the tree as a metaphor for the club and how everyone needs to work together for it to flourish. The fruit symbolises the first team and is obviously the showpiece of the tree, but without the branches, the roots and everything else that goes into supporting it, it would die. The tree now sits outside Arteta's office and everyone is responsible for it. It's another example of the little things he has introduced to try to bring the group closer together. Another, perhaps the most popular of them all, is the introduction of Win, a chocolate Labrador who is now based at the training ground. The players love her and regularly take turns taking her home for a weekend. 'I carefully chose the dog,' Arteta once explained to us in a press conference. 'She is one of us. She is going to be on this journey with us together. It's something that changes your mood. She gives you all the love and suddenly you feel the energy of the place. It's just beautiful and to me those things are very important.'

Following that training-ground family day, all eyes turned to Craven Cottage, with Arsenal fans once again hoping for a slip-up from Manchester City. But it was business as usual for the champions, who cruised to a 4–0 win to pile the pressure on Arsenal. Arteta's side travelled to Old Trafford – a ground where they had won just once in the league since 2006 – knowing they simply had to win, with any other result giving City the chance to wrap up the title at Spurs two days later. It was an incredibly tense affair. Arteta's side were far from their best, but after Leandro Trossard had struck yet another big goal in a big game, that watertight defence again ensured they returned to London with maximum points. The celebrations at the end told their own story. Whatever happened between City and Spurs later in the week, Arsenal now knew that for the first time in 25 years they would go into the final day of the season with the chance to win the Premier League title. The win at Old Trafford was also Arsenal's 27th victory of the season in the league, a number the club had never hit before in a 38-game campaign. 'That's not progress, that's history,' Arteta was quick to point out after the game. 'We really wanted to knock that door and open that box of dreams to live the last day of the season in front of our people with the opportunity to win the Premier League. That's something we're now going to live together, and I'm so pleased we're going to do it with these players and staff.'

Arsenal now had a week to wait for the big season's finale against Everton, but before that there was the small matter of City's midweek trip to Spurs. Everything about that night was strange. Tottenham went into it still with an outside chance of beating Aston Villa to the fourth and final Champions League spot. But to do that they had to win, a result that would leave Arsenal – their most bitter rivals – on the verge of their first title since 2004. Even a draw would have handed Arteta's side the advantage going into the final day. There were lots of Tottenham fans who actually wanted their side to get beaten and plenty even gave up their tickets as they didn't want to watch. It was such a strange situation. You had Arsenal fans wanting Spurs to win and Spurs fans wanting their side to lose.

With City's final game of the season at home to West Ham, it always felt like the Tottenham match was going to be the decisive moment in the title race, and that's ultimately how it proved. City weren't great and were clearly nervous. And while the atmosphere was, as expected, very flat, Spurs actually played pretty well. City eventually took the lead just after half-time through Erling Haaland, but the big moment of the night arrived on 86 minutes when Brennan Johnson robbed Manuel Akanji of possession on the halfway line and sent Son Heung-min clean through on goal. This was it. The season for Arsenal and Manchester

City was on the line at this very moment. Time seemed to stand still as Son bore down on Stefan Ortega, City's reserve goalkeeper who had just come on to replace the injured Ederson. Guardiola collapsed to the floor on the sidelines, while Arteta – he would later reveal – was sitting in his front room with his children, screaming at the TV as the shot was about to be taken. A disbelieving hush swept around the Tottenham Hotspur Stadium as Son pulled his leg back to shoot. Was the Spurs captain really about to all but hand Arsenal the title? No, he wasn't, because he shot tamely at Ortega, who saved his effort with his outstretched foot. For a couple of seconds, Arsenal could almost see the title, but it was snatched away in the blink of an eye. City would then compound the misery by going down the pitch and adding a second goal a couple of minutes later through a Haaland penalty. An unprecedented fourth title in a row had not been won yet, but Guardiola's side were now top and in charge of their own destiny going into the final day of the season. A win against West Ham and City were Premier League champions; any other result, and Arsenal would take the title, should they beat Everton. It was as simple as that.

To be honest, there was always an air of inevitability about what was going to happen, even if Arteta did try and talk up Arsenal's chances in the build-up to the game. 'It's one of the biggest weeks for many of us,' he said. 'Certainly, now is the most important moment. I'm really excited and obviously I'm very optimistic as well with the possible outcome.' He was right, this was a big moment for Arsenal. It was the first time since 1999 that they were going into the final day of the season with a chance of being crowned champions. The Premier League trophy was going to be at the Emirates. When Martin Ødegaard woke up on the morning of the Everton game he knew that he had a chance of lifting that trophy at the end of the day and ending Arsenal's long 20-year wait to win the title. There were millions of Arsenal fans around the world who had never experienced something like that before and the occasion was spectacular. The scenes around the Emirates that day were incredible. There were 60,000 in the stadium, but tens of thousands more were packed into pubs around Islington hoping for a miracle that would have sparked off the mother of all north London street parties.

But there was to be no miracle. Phil Foden scored within 90 seconds to give City the lead against West Ham, and in the end they cruised to a relatively stress-free 3–1 win. Arsenal did what they had to do, with Kai Havertz's late goal earning them a 2–1 victory on the day, but it wasn't enough. City had won the title again, with Arsenal finishing as runners-up – again. The difference was two points. That's how close Arsenal came. It was one result, one goal even. The sense of disappointment was palpable. Everyone who had packed into the Emirates knew how close their team had come to beating the City juggernaut. 'Since

December we've been on an incredible journey,' an emotional Arteta said in his post-match press conference. 'Every performance has been at the highest level we have seen and it still wasn't enough. Today is mixed emotions, first of all to be really proud of those players, the staff, they have done an incredible job, they have pushed every limit, every margin that we could find to try to win this Premier League and unfortunately it was a bit short. We could not deliver the big prize that we wanted. They [City] took it away from us.'

Arsenal ended the season with 89 points. Only the Invincibles in 2003–04 have ever amassed more during a 38-game season for the club. That's the standard Arteta and his side set. They won 28 out of 38 league games, a new club record in the Premier League era. They scored 91 league goals – again, more than they have ever scored in a Premier League campaign. And they had the best defence in the Premier League, only conceding 29 goals. Their final goal difference of +62 was their best since 1935. After the turn of the year they had dropped just five points, amassing 49 from a possible 54. Eighteen games, 16 wins, one draw and one defeat. Firty-four goals scored, nine conceded. Arteta's side were also unbeaten against the so-called 'big six' throughout the whole season, picking up 22 points from a possible 30 in the games against City, United, Liverpool, Spurs and Chelsea. The numbers were staggering, yet it still wasn't enough.

In almost any other era Arsenal would have been champions with weeks to spare, and they would have been worthy winners. But this isn't a normal era; this is the Manchester City era. Guardiola's side have now won four Premier Leagues on the spin and six in the past seven years. Getting past them is today's ultimate challenge in football. Liverpool managed it once, but couldn't repeat it. And the exhausting nature of trying to compete with City has led to Jürgen Klopp waving an emotional farewell to the club he has led so impressively since 2015. So that's the task Arteta and Arsenal face, and it's the biggest question in football. How do you beat this City side under Guardiola? Many see it as impossible, but Arteta doesn't agree. 'We will win it,' he vowed, following the Everton game. 'When? I don't know. If we keep knocking, it will happen.'

And there is genuine belief at Arsenal that it will happen. It was obviously massively disappointing to miss out on the title for the second successive season, given how the team had performed and the standards they had set, especially since the start of 2024. But there was also an immense sense of pride at what they had achieved. There was no backlash from the fanbase or anything like that. No one left the stadium straight after the full-time whistle against Everton. For the second year on the spin the ground remained packed for the players' lap of appreciation. The connection that exists between the club and the supporters is as strong as it has even been. 'All this is happening because you started believing,' Arteta told the crowd as he stood, microphone in hand, on the halfway line. 'You started to be patient, you started to understand what we were trying to do. Now it's time to have a break, think, reflect and keep pushing. Don't be satisfied, because we want much more than that – and we're going to get it.'

These words were met by a huge cheer. Not just because it was what all the Arsenal fans inside the stadium wanted to hear. It was what they believed. And that's what Arteta has done since he walked back through the doors at Arsenal in 2019. He has restored belief and rebuilt a club that looked a million miles away from being able to compete with the very best. There is a hunger now at Arsenal, a desire to not just compete with the very best, but to be the very best. And that's what they are going to try to do. They will go again in the summer, they will add to the squad and they will push even harder to get past Manchester City. The journey that Arsenal are on is not about being second best, it's about being the best. 'I want to be clear that no one at the club will stand still,' Josh Kroenke pledged on the weekend of the Everton game. 'We're all working behind the scenes to move us forward – always forward – again.'

The title may have escaped Arsenal in 2023–24, just as it did 12 months earlier, but the trajectory the club is now on is there for everyone to see. The job is far from done and there is still a long way to go. But the desire from everyone to go one better and reach the summit is stronger than it has ever been. Arteta made that clear as he stood on the pitch and addressed the fans in the immediate aftermath of the Everton game. 'Don't be satisfied,' was the order. He's certainly not, and he won't be until the Premier League trophy is finally back in north London.

ACKNOWLEDGEMENTS

Thanks to my wife for putting up with me. Having a football reporter as a husband when you have two young kids can be hard enough to cope with, let alone when they decide to write a book on top of it all. So thank you, Michelle, for everything you do. To Amy and Luke, thanks for just being you. For bringing perspective to this mad world and making me laugh every single day. Dad, thank you for taking me to Highbury for that first time on 21 January 1989 and starting a love affair with the club that will continue until my final day in this crazy world. Thanks for paying for all those season tickets over the years and for giving me the chance to sit and enjoy watching Dennis, Thierry, Bobby, Wrighty, Freddie, Tony and all those legends every other week. Absolutely none of this would have ever been possible without the unconditional support you and Mum gave me, and I appreciate it more than you will ever know. Mum, I wish you were here to see this book come out. I know you would have been so proud. All those times you pushed (ordered) me to go to those shorthand lessons certainly paid off. Graham and James, thanks for your support and guidance. Having a little brother who was so much better than you at football must have been hard to deal with, but you handled it well. A huge thank you to Joel and everyone at HarperCollins for giving me the opportunity to write this book and fulfil what has been a childhood ambition. I couldn't have done this without the guidance (and patience) of Joel and I'll always be grateful of that. Thank you to the guys at GOAL who were happy for me to take this project on while I was there and thanks to every single person who contributed to this book and gave me their time to help put it all together. That same appreciation goes to the journalists in the Arsenal pack who have made following this crazy club during the past few seasons so much fun. The European trips, the Covid times, the countless hours spent standing around in mixed zones up and down the country. It's been a blast! And finally, thank you to all the Arsenal fans who engage with me every day and who make my job so much fun to do. I hope you enjoy this book and that the next few years bring us all plenty of reasons to smile.